TWAYNE'S WORLD AUTHORS SERIES

A Survey of the World's Literature

FRANCE

Maxwell A. Smith, Guerry Professor of French, Emeritus
The University of Chattanooga
Former Visiting Professor in Modern Languages
The Florida State University

EDITOR

Charles-Augustin Sainte-Beuve

TWAS 453

Charles-Augustin Sainte-Beuve

CHARLES-AUGUSTIN SAINTE-BEUVE

By RICHARD M. CHADBOURNE

University of Calgary

TWAYNE PUBLISHERS

A DIVISION OF G. K. HALL & CO., BOSTON

175701

Library of Congress Cataloging in Publication Data

Chadbourne, Richard McClain.
  Charles-Augustin Sainte-Beuve.

  (Twayne's world authors series ; TWAS 453 : France)
  Bibliography: p. 183–87.
  Includes index.
  1.   Sainte-Beuve, Charles Augustin, 1804–1869 —
Criticism and interpretation.
PQ2391.Z5C48   848'.7'09   77-25321
ISBN 0-8057-6290-6

To
Henri Peyre
''un homme qui sait lire et qui
apprend à lire aux autres'' —
with gratitude and affection

Contents

About the Author

Richard Chadbourne, a native of Providence, Rhode Island, received his B.A. from Brown University and his M.A. and Ph.D. from Yale University. He taught at Fordham University and the University of Colorado before assuming his present post as professor of French at the University of Calgary, where he has also served as head of the Department of Romance Studies. He has been visiting professor at Notre Dame University and the University of California, Los Angeles. In 1962–1963 he was awarded an American Council of Learned Societies postdoctoral fellowship and in 1966 was named Chevalier in L'Ordre des Palmes Académiques by the French government in recognition of his teaching. He has published two books on Ernest Renan, the first of which received the MLA-Crofts-Cornell Prize in 1956 and the second of which appeared in 1968 in the Twayne's World Authors Series (No. 34). He is also the author of numerous articles on other nineteenth century French writers, including Sainte-Beuve.

Preface

Charles-Augustin Sainte-Beuve is one of the few authors in any language to have achieved major stature on the basis of his criticism alone. This in itself is impressive testimony to his powers as a writer. In our own time his achievement as a *literary* critic (my reason for italicizing the adjective will soon become clear) has been radically questioned. His dependence on the biographical approach to literature, an approach now rejected by many as misleading; the somewhat narrow criteria that he used in his esthetic judgments; his failure to recognize the genius of certain contemporaries whom posterity has raised to the highest rank — these, among other alleged weaknesses, have cast serious doubts on his reliability as an interpreter of literature. Yet it is not clear who would replace him as France's greatest literary critic. Boileau? Baudelaire? Valéry? Sartre? For all the undoubted accomplishments of the Formalists, New Critics, Structuralists, and others, have they yet produced a critic of his stature? How many of them, like Sainte-Beuve, can be read with pleasure? How many, indeed, are readable at all, except by those who have managed to crack their code?

If Sainte-Beuve's staying power remains strong, it is chiefly, as I hope to demonstrate afresh in this book, because he was much more than a literary critic. "To read Sainte-Beuve," observed Irving Babbitt, "is to enlarge one's knowledge, not merely of literature but also of life."[1] For him literary criticism was always the pretext for an exploration of human nature, including his own nature, which went far beyond literary criticism in the usual sense. It is very significant that his professed masters were none of them primarily literary critics: they were the poet Horace, the essayist and moralist Montaigne, and the philosopher Pierre Bayle.

Early in his career he was himself a poet, and although he failed in his ambition to be remembered above all as a poet, he succeeded in writing, along with much clumsy verse, some very original, occasionally excellent, and highly influential poems. He was also the author of a flawed but no less original and influential novel. His poetry and fiction were not, as many believe, curious hors d'oeuvre, experiments leading nowhere. Not only did they open up new paths for other, and greater, French poets and novelists, they were also vital parts of his work as a whole, organically related to his development and character as a critic. In order to establish these points, as well as to show the intrinsic merits of the works in question, I have given them considerable space in this study.

As for his criticism, to read it as it deserves to be read and as I have read it in preparation for writing this book — that is, not in isolated fragments, but from cover to cover in the fifty-odd volumes that comprise it — is to discover how the unsuccessful artist survived and, what is more, prospered in the critic, to create a world of his own. It is a world peopled not with fictional characters but with other writers, other talents of many kinds; a microcosm of human life whose affinities link it less to literary criticism in the traditional sense than to *Les Caractères* of La Bruyère, the Memoirs of Saint-Simon, Balzac's *Comédie Humaine,* or the novels of Proust.

The view that Sainte-Beuve's real originality and greatness lie in his elevation of criticism to a creative art is by no means new. No book length study that I know of, however, has ventured as does the present one to take this as its central theme. My intention has been to argue for the recognition of Sainte-Beuve as a creator in his own right, paradoxical though it may seem to make such a claim for a critic. Therefore I have paid no less attention in this study to his artistry as a writer than to his opinions as a critic. But besides offering what may be a fresh perspective to those who already know Sainte-Beuve well, I hope that the book will serve as a useful guide for novices in their approach to his vast and complex work. May it even persuade a few students that the reading of Proust's *Contre Sainte-Beuve* is no adequate substitute for the reading of Sainte-Beuve!

Wherever possible I have furnished references for quotations from Sainte-Beuve and from frequently cited critics of his work in the text itself, following an initial full reference in a footnote. The translations are my own unless otherwise stated.

RICHARD M. CHADBOURNE

University of Calgary

Chronology

1804   Charles-Augustin Sainte-Beuve born in Boulogne-sur-Mer, December 23. His father, a tax superintendent, had died on October 4.

1818   Comes to Paris to complete his studies. Enters Institution Landry, a private school. Also takes courses at Collège Charlemagne.

1821   Enrolls at Collège Bourbon (now Lycée Condorcet). Takes courses on the side at the Athénée.

1823   Enrolls as medical student. Completes *baccalauréat ès lettres.*

1824   Completes *baccalauréat ès sciences.* First article for *Le Globe.*

1827   Begins friendship with Victor and Adèle Hugo. Abandons medical studies.

1828   Publishes *Tableau historique et critique de la poésie française et du théâtre français au XVI^esiècle.* Makes brief trip to England.

1829   Publishes *Vie, poésies et pensées de Joseph Delorme.* Begins writing for *La Revue de Paris.*

1830   Publishes *Les Consolations.*

1831   Frequents circle of Saint-Simonians. Visits Lamennais and his group at Juilly. First article for *La Revue des deux mondes.*

1832   Adèle Hugo becomes his mistress. First article for *Le National.* Publishes *Critiques et portraits littéraires.*

1833   Begins visits to Madame Récamier's salon at L'Abbaye-aux-Bois.

1834   Ends friendship with Victor Hugo. Publishes *Volupté.*

1837   Ends liaison with Adèle Hugo. Publishes *Pensées d'Août.* Begins course on Port-Royal at Académie de Lausanne, Switzerland.

1838   Completes course at Lausanne and returns to Paris.

1839   Travels in Italy and Switzerland. Publishes expanded five volume edition of *Critiques et portraits.*

1840 Publishes *Port-Royal,* vol. 1. Appointed *conservateur* at the Bibliothèque Mazarine.

1842 Publishes *Port-Royal,* vol. 2.

1843 Writes anonymous articles for *La Revue Suisse,* which will be published posthumously as *Chroniques parisiennes.* Has *Livre d'amour* printed privately in limited number of copies.

1844 Elected to French Academy. Publishes *Portraits de femmes* and *Portraits littéraires,* vols. 1 and 2.

1845 Received at French Academy in welcoming speech by Victor Hugo.

1846 Publishes *Portraits contemporains* in three volume edition.

1848 Publishes *Port-Royal,* vol. 3. Resigns from Bibliothèque Mazarine and accepts post at University of Liège, Belgium, to give a course on French literature and a course on Chateaubriand.

1849 Returns to Paris. Begins publishing series of articles in *Le Constitutionnel* which will be known as *Causeries du Lundi.*

1850 Mother dies, November 17.

1851 Moves into house at 11 Rue du Montparnasse, where he will live until his death. Publishes first of fifteen volumes of *Causeries du Lundi.*

1852 Continues *Lundis* in *Le Moniteur.*

1854 Appointed professor of Latin poetry at Collège de France.

1855 Course at Collège de France interrupted by student protests. Offers resignation, which is not accepted. Does not complete course but remains *titulaire* of post.

1857 Publishes *Etude sur Virgile* based on aforementioned course. Appointed *maître de conférences* at the Ecole Normale Supérieure.

1859 Completes publication of *Port-Royal* with volumes 4 and 5.

1860 Publishes *Chateaubriand et son groupe littéraire sous l'Empire* based on course at Liège.

1861 Completes teaching at Ecole Normale. Resumes collaboration with *Le Constitutionnel* with series of articles that will form the *Nouveaux Lundis.*

1862 Begins attending dinners with other writers at Restaurant Magny.

1863 Publishes (more or less complete) *Poésies* and first of thirteen volumes of *Nouveaux Lundis.*

1865   Named sénateur by Napoléon III. Publishes series of articles on Proudhon for *La Revue contemporaine.*

1866   Operated on for stone obstructing bladder. Health deteriorates sharply.

1867   Leaves *Le Constitutionnel* for *Le Moniteur.* Attacks clericalism; defends Renan, freedom of education, freedom of thought, in senate speeches.

1868   Leaves *Le Moniteur.*

1869   First article for *Le Temps.* Prepares expanded five volume edition of *Portraits contemporains* which will be published from 1869 to 1871. Dies October 13. Interred with civil ceremony in Montparnasse Cemetery.

CHAPTER 1

The Young Critic

I N the last months of his life, in 1869, Sainte-Beuve, though exhausted from a painful illness, was occupied with his secretary in putting his literary affairs in order, a task which included selecting for publication some of his earliest essays that had never been collected in book form. He called his activity "saving what he could of his baggage" for the journey into posterity. Lucid until the end, under no illusion as to the "glory" that might be his, he hoped nevertheless to be remembered as "an honorable witness" to his time. Expressing himself in the nautical imagery he so loved (he had left his native Boulogne-sur-Mer long, long ago but even in Paris had become a kind of literary mariner), he observed that to reach posterity safely "one has all precautions to take: one cannot too much act as a ship (*faire navire*), and keep one's course straight, to pass, without foundering, the perilous straits."[1]

His earliest writings had appeared in the form of articles for *Le Globe,* a daily paper of which he had been an apprentice staff member beginning with its founding in 1824 by the socialist Pierre Leroux and by his own former teacher, Paul-François Dubois. Together with essays published in another daily, *Le National,* and in two reviews, *La Revue de Paris* and *La Revue des deux mondes,* they form a substantial body of criticism covering roughly ten years, from 1824 to 1835. It was not until after his death that they were collected in book form under the title of *Premiers Lundis* (a title not of his own choosing), first by his secretary Jules Troubat in 1874 and then, in a more complete version, by the eminent *Beuvien* Maxime Leroy.[2]

The "young Sainte-Beuve" sounds as strange as the "young Boileau" or the "young Doctor Johnson," so accustomed are we to

thinking of these critics as having sprung into being full-blown, like
Athena from the head of Zeus. Yet even the magisterial patriarch of
the *Lundis* had once been young. What kind of mind and vision do
his early essays reveal? To what extent is the mature writer foreshadowed in them? In the first half of this chapter I shall focus on
the *Premiers Lundis;* in the second half, on his first book, *Tableau
historique et critique de la poésie française et du théâtre français au
XVIᵉ siècle* (1828), a work based largely on articles that had pre-
viously appeared in *Le Globe.* In between, I shall pause for a flashback on his intellectual origins and formation, which will also serve
as spiritual portrait of the youthful Sainte-Beuve.

I *Gropings and Beginnings*

"Mes tâtonnements et mes commencements," he called these
first efforts in *Le Globe.*[3] They are anything but amateurish, however. The young critic was called upon to handle an extraordinary
variety of subject matter, though little of it in any depth. The
results testify to how well his already wide-ranging curiosity fitted
in with the ambition of a journal whose very title had been chosen
to convey the idea of "encyclopedic investigation" (*Oeuvres* I,
387). His "premier souvenir littéraire," as he called it (*NL* V, 312),
looking back many years later, was a brief article (his first signed
one: "S.-B.") on the geography of Greece, a country much in the
news in 1824 because of its war of independence against the Turks.
But he also deals with Egyptian mythology, French memoirs, the
history of the French Revolution, tropical landscape in poetry, the
influence of climate on northern and southern populations, travel
books on England and Scotland, and the current state of English
literature, among other subjects. Whatever else this medley seems
to prepare us for, it is hardly for a critic limited in range or
restricted to literary criticism in any narrow sense.

Literary matters such as poetry, fiction, and other works of the
imagination do indeed concern him greatly. An aspiring poet himself, with a strong literary as well as scientific background, he is
constantly attentive to questions of form and style, seeking to
define the specific literary merit, to describe the "diction" or
"manner" of the author under consideration, whatever his type of
writing, for style "is a matter of importance in every kind of composition" (*Oeuvres* I, 83). His first major piece of literary criticism

was a remarkably well-balanced review of Victor Hugo's *Odes et Ballades* (*Le Globe,* January 1827) containing reflections on the nature of the poetic imagination. This pioneer essay on Hugo is important in at least two other respects: its claim that Hugo "revealed himself entirely" in his first volume of *Odes* (*Oeuvres* I, 194) is an early instance of the key importance that Sainte-Beuve attached to a writer's first published work, believing it somehow to contain *en germe* the essence of what he would become; and second, it clearly establishes the classical, or more exactly the neoclassical, bias of his own esthetics. The second point is especially noteworthy: before he ever met Hugo, became his friend, and then broke with him, and before he embarked on his temporary attachment to the Romantic movement, he posited certain canons of taste, sobriety, and perfection to which much of Romantic art, almost by definition, could hardly conform.

But literary matters share the spotlight with two other areas of major interest to him: one is history, and the other is that whole study of human character and behavior that we would today call "psychology" but which he called, according to French usage, *la morale,* the domain of *le moraliste.*

Sainte-Beuve singled out retrospectively as having special merit his articles on two historians of the French Revolution, Thiers and Mignet ("Ma biographie"), both of whom will return again and again as subjects of his mature collections of essays. Apropos of them he expresses his views on causality in history (rigid "laws" are not to be found and one must make allowance for the "unpredictable") and on the kind of freedom man possesses, a qualified, conditioned freedom (man is "part will and part fate"). In an essay on Thomas Jefferson for *Le National,* whose editor-in-chief, Armand Carrel, was a fervent *républicain* and admirer of American democracy, he develops the theme of comparative revolutions (English, 1688, and French, 1830; French, 1789 and 1830; American, 1776, and French, 1789). While showing respect for the great men of history, such as Jefferson, he introduces what will become one of the most characteristic themes of his later criticism: opposition to the apotheosis of great men and defense of the importance and the right to be heard of lesser figures. He refused to believe, for example, that Monsieur Roland was merely the mediocre husband of a great woman: "M. Roland, sans être un homme de génie, était un esprit rare et un plus rare caractère" (*Oeuvres* I, 548). There are a number of such anticipatory flashes of the mature Sainte-Beuve who, precisely because he was unwilling to "sacrifier le moyen au grand," has few rivals in the art of recreating secondary characters and revealing the significant historical roles that they often played.

From the outset he also proves himself to be a moralist, that is, both a curious, detached student of human manners (*mores*) and a critic willing to make distinctions, to raise issues, even to hazard judgments, of good and evil. His avid interest in memoirs, which first manifests itself in an essay of 1824 on Mademoiselle Rose Bertin, dressmaker to Marie-Antoinette (*Premiers Lundis*) and which will continue unabated until his last days, is to be explained largely by what they revealed to him about human conduct in private as distinct from public life, au naturel — the "dignity in misfortune" of Marie-Antoinette, the complexity of the character of Camille Desmoulins. Two further features of the apprentice moralist's approach that point ahead to the master are his emphasis on the exemplary nature of some lives and his distrust of abstractions. "Exemplary" in this context does not necessarily mean great: he is interested in the character whether great or small who perfectly illustrates a certain type. But more often than not it means a type of virtue or heroism. From the beginning his criticism is marked by a strong Plutarchian strain. The author of the *Lives of the Noble Greeks and Romans* would have understood his Jefferson, symbol of political integrity, or his "Four Sergeants of La Rochelle," a tribute to the fortitude of the four young soldiers executed in 1822 for conspiracy to overthrow Louis XVIII. (Troubat, reading aloud the description of the bravest of these, Bories, to Sainte-Beuve in his last year as they prepared his early papers for publication, was too moved to be able to finish, and the master himself "had to stifle his tears" [*Oeuvres* I, 1099]). Sainte-Beuve's intention was not to deny nobility of character (which he has been accused of doing) but to anchor our belief in it more firmly in reality; a central theme of his writing, from his schoolboy's notebooks to the last of the *Lundis,* is the effort to distinguish between true and false greatness.

But whatever the sources he draws upon — published works, letters, memoirs, or oral tradition — in order to portray his characters, and whether these are merely curious specimens or heroic examples worthy of emulation, the critic must not content himself with analyzing them. He must restore them to life in his reader's imagination, which means that he must become something of an artist himself, with the artist's skill in avoiding abstraction. Young Sainte-Beuve's critique of the Romantic philosopher Théodore Jouffroy (*Premiers Lundis*) is especially significant from this point of view. Had Jouffroy, he argues, heeded his "nature d'artiste" more and his "rationalisme" less, he would have acquired a firmer grasp on reality. In attempting to analyze human nature solely in terms of the individual "rational" self, independently of its relations to other selves and to nature, Jouffroy was making "mystical abstractions" out of "living men." Above all, he and his fellow *psychologistes,* as they were called, were robbing human beings of their "réalité physiologique"; in their contempt for "la matière" they were perpetrating, whether knowingly or not, the traditional Christian bias (as Sainte-Beuve considered it) in favor of the soul against the body (*Oeuvres* I, 407–428).

The significance of these remarks is worth stressing. In them we see emerging a view of human nature whose importance for the future "naturalist of souls" and exponent of "la critique dite naturelle ou physiologique" (*NL* IX, 69) cannot be exaggerated; a view defining man in terms of a complex network of interrelationships between individual and species, ego and society, mind and body, reason and nature.

But no less significant is the budding concept of the critic as artist, as "peintre," in other words as "creator" in his own right. This idea is developed in a very early essay (*Le Globe,* December 1824) on a fellow critic, Ferdinand Denis, whom Sainte-Beuve advises in future works to "efface himself" more from his criticism, so that his "characters" may act and speak more freely. "Do not intervene between them and us," he exhorts this author, "imitate Walter Scott and Cooper; disappear from view in order the better to paint" (*Oeuvres* I, 67). What is most curious here is that he is asking a *critic* (the author of a study of the Portuguese poet Camoëns) to learn greater objectivity from the examples of two novelists. He goes on to warn Denis, however, that by casting his life of Camoëns in the form of fictionlike narratives (*récits*) he has robbed it of truthfulness; with his knowledge of the subject, "he should have dared to do without these contrivances of the novelist and to seek out the interest of his subject in its simple reality" (I, 70). It is not only with admiration, it is with the ambition to emulate, *but in his own manner,* that young Sainte-Beuve elsewhere in the *Premiers Lundis* writes of Walter Scott and other geniuses of his "family" — Shakespeare and Molière — who could "depict all varieties of human passion and circumstance ... forgetting themselves and transforming themselves into a multitude of characters living, speaking, and acting in countless pathetic or amusing ways" (I, 466). Yet however much the critic may learn from these imaginative writers, creative artists in the accepted sense, the living reality he portrays (and here he differs fundamentally from them) must be based on documentary knowledge, or at least on reliable oral tradition, and must be shaped according to his own rules of art.

Here one can see taking shape in Sainte-Beuve's mind, at the age of twenty, the extraordinary challenge to his own powers that will lead eventually to his *Portraits, Port-Royal,* and *Lundis:* his wager with himself that the "simple réalité" of the critic-artist could be made to prove as interesting to readers as the fictions invented by novelists.

The variety of forms taken by these early essays — to turn to the art which characterizes them — is almost as broad as the variety of subject matters. They range from brief notices on individual books to ambitious attempts, made over the space of two or three issues of the periodical in question, to assess an author's genius (Diderot, Walter Scott) or to survey whole literary or social movements. The approach is already remarkably flexible and the composition allows, within a structure shaped usually by one or two dominant themes, for the free play of "impressions" and for a certain degree of "laisser-aller naturel" (I, 82). But the style is not yet equal to the wealth of ideas. Though seldom obscure, its proneness to huge sentences that pile up clause after clause makes for oppressive reading. Sainte-Beuve had been a good pupil — too good a pupil, perhaps — in rhetoric, and never overcame a certain propensity to the oratorical.[4] Only intermittently do the concision and sobriety, or the sharpness of wit, that he was later to master make their appearance. The predominantly grave tone (the very words *sérieux, sévère, austère, grave* recur frequently) adds to the impression of heaviness. To some extent this oratorical style reflects a France of the 1820s and 1830s in whose memory the rhetorical feats of the Revolution were still fresh and that had seen rhetoric put to renewed use by the Saint-Simonian and other reform movements; the France of Romanticism, immersed in oratory, lyricism, and imagery.

The extensive use of imagery is indeed another feature of Sainte-Beuve's early manner. All prose writers, including critics, feel the need to enliven their style occasionally with a comparison or metaphor. Sainte-Beuve goes far beyond this to a procedure that resembles thinking in images. He borrows these from many fields but tends to favor images related to sculpture and architecture, travel and movement generally, and landscape, especially aquatic landscape. He often mixes several kinds in a single sentence or paragraph. A striking example, from an essay on the Polish writer Adam Mickiewicz, is the elaborate and not entirely coherent sequence of images contrasting the journalist-critic (himself at this point) with the critic of established works of art; it is also the first of many variations we shall find in Sainte-Beuve's work on the theme of "la condition critique." In this passage the critic as journalist, in the endless variety of day-to-day judgments he is obliged to make, is first compared to a traveler constantly on the move, a gypsy, the Wandering Jew, or to an actor playing a different role each night. Then the two kinds of criticism are compared to rivers: the more leisurely species circulates at the base of the great monuments of art, each of which is like a "majestic, immobile rock," "surrounds them, bathes and reflects them in its waters, easily transporting from one to another the reader intent on knowing them," while the journalistic kind must resign itself to the constant diversion or interruption of its flow as it passes through a much less majestic, in fact a somewhat industrialized, landscape (*Oeuvres* I, 537).[5]

II *A Critic's Credentials*

The *Premiers Lundis* are a very uneven though still remarkable achievement for a man in his twenties. The *Tableau de la poésie française,* published when he was not quite twenty-four, is even more impressive. Sainte-Beuve needed little time to prove that he possessed a many-faceted gift for criticism. What were the main components of this gift and by virtue of what background had he acquired them? Before turning to the *Tableau,* let us sketch the makeup — or what he would undoubtedly have called *l'organisation* — of the writer on the threshold of his first major work. Without once again detailing his formative years, an already well-explored subject,[6] it is possible to single out some of the principal elements that went into the shaping of his critical intelligence and to trace them to their source.

The primordial source, on his own authority, was the influence of his father, Charles-François de Sainte-Beuve, who died before his son was born. (How touchingly appropriate that the future historian and biographer should have begun, even as a child, to reconstruct his father's memory by drawing on oral testimony and pondering the literary notes, the marginal annotations in books, that he had left behind!) It was to him that his son attributed his "taste for reading and for education" and the "pronounced literary vocation which accompanied a dreamy disposition almost from childhood."[7] While it was his mother who, in his words, transmitted to him his "firmness and critical decisiveness," (*CL* XVI, 40), he owed to his father "a lively sensitivity." The elder Sainte-Beuve was, in other words, something of a poet, given to musing as well as to note taking.

The tendencies received by him from his father — the love of books, especially of the ancient classics (the "Muse des Latins" above all); sensitivity; and musing — were confirmed by his subsequent education, reading, and experience as a young man. His competence in the classics, in rhetoric, and in history — in brief, the "humanities" — was strengthened by his training at the Institution Blériot in Boulogne and later, in Paris, at the Pension Landry, the Collège Charlemagne, and the Collège Bourbon. At sixteen, while still enrolled at the Pension Landry, the reading of Lamartine's *Méditations* came to him as "the shock of a revelation," a "new sun" warming him with its rays, and awakened his vocation as a poet (*NL* XIII, 26–27).

Among the critic's credentials, this *sensibilité* is worth insisting upon for several reasons. The most obvious is, or should be, that it is hardly a handicap for a critic to be able to feel deeply, especially if he has intelligence and judgment into the bargain. Sainte-Beuve himself, at least, considered keen sensitivity to be not an obstacle but an aid to lucid perception. In describing the piercing glance that the young Balzac cast on the Napoleonic Empire, he quotes "someone of the same age" (the ruse is a characteristic way of disguising his own thought: he means himself) as saying: "Even as a child I was able to penetrate things with such feeling that it was like a sharp blade cutting into my heart" (*CL* II, 444). His extreme sensitivity often took the form of a disposition to sadness, and this in turn, while leaving him with too little "cheerfulness to live off of the present" and not enough "hope to carry him into the future" (as he remarked in a letter of 1826),[8] may also have sharpened his talent as a historian by increasing his interest in the past.

Such a gloomy attitude toward present and future would seem to have promised little in young Sainte-Beuve by way of concern for social reform. However, "attacks of melancholy and of disgust with everything," as he called them (*B* I, 68), did not in fact prove incompatible in his complex makeup with social conscience. The tears of "human charity" which he learned that his father had been capable of shedding no less over the misfortunes of a poor peasant than over the sorrows of Virgil's Dido,[9] had their counterpart in his own sense of fraternity with the oppressed, as demonstrated in his poetic alter ego, Joseph Delorme, or in his association with such humanitarian movements as Saint-Simonianism and Mennaisianism.

This portrait of the young critic would be incomplete without mention of three further aspects of his formation: his religious feeling, his discovery of the philosophy of the Idéologues, and his study of medicine. Sainte-Beuve seems to have had a moderately Catholic upbringing. At the age of fifteen, beginning with his first year in Paris (1818–1819), he claims to have undergone an "intellectual emancipation" from religion, followed by "ten years of free thought" (*CL* XVI, 38–39). This period gave way in turn, toward 1830, to a temporary drift back toward Christianity, a "mystical" phase that he considered more poetic than truly religious. I shall return to this phase later and discuss the works inspired by it. Suffice it to point out here that the atmosphere in which Sainte-Beuve grew up was far from irreligious and that his *sensibilité* included an understanding of the religious point of view.

A chief factor in his freeing himself from dependence on religion was his discovery of the philosophy of the Idéologues, a school of thought that sought to provide a moral and social code based on the scientific explanation of human nature and that emphasized observation, analysis, empiricism, and induction as the most promising ways to truth. Sainte-Beuve's early notebooks are full of references to Locke and Francis Bacon, from whom the Idéologues derived many of their views.[10] He was born too late, of course, to have known the French ancestors of the school, Condillac, Condorcet, and Helvétius. However, his fellow Boulonnais, Daunou,

who became his friend and mentor, had been a disciple of Condorcet and thus transmitted to him, as though by apostolic succession,
the authentic tradition of the Idéologues. (A further example, incidentally, of the importance attached to oral tradition as a source of
biographical and historical knowledge by Sainte-Beuve, who had
first been obliged to use this approach in establishing intellectual
continuity with his own father.) Daunou, then in his sixties, had
also been an intimate of the Société d'Auteuil, a group of the faithful accustomed to gathering at the home of the widow of Helvétius
in what was then a village outside the gates of Paris.

But Sainte-Beuve in addition knew personally the chief Idéo-
logue himself, Destutt de Tracy, the author of *Eléments d'idéologie*
(1801–1815) from which the movement took its name. Sainte-Beuve
was permitted while still at the Pension Landry to take evening
classes at the Athénée, a kind of university extension school; and it
was there, about 1822, while pursuing a knowledge of physiology,
chemistry, and natural history, that he was introduced to "M. de
Tracy," then almost seventy. It appears to have been this venerable
figure who encouraged him in the study of medicine, to which he
devoted himself for four years (1823–1827) at the Ecole de Méde-
cine. His abandonment of this field as a career was due less to any
lack of qualifications than to practical reasons. Since he needed to
begin supporting himself as soon as possible, it seemed easier to
make a name for himself, to "percer," in literature than in medicine (*NL* XIII, 8). But there seems also to have been on his part
some distaste for the idea of practicing medicine. What remains
important, in any case, is that the future physiologist and anatomist of literature, who considered his whole work to be a long "cours
de physiologie morale,"[11] had actually been trained in physiology
and anatomy; the future "naturalist of minds" (*PM* 50) had been
also a naturalist in the scientific sense.

This flashback on the young critic's background can now be
summed up. Taking as his starting point the love of books and of
study inherited from his father, he had eagerly sought to absorb as
many kinds of knowledge and experience as lay open to him. A
highly precocious student of rhetoric and history; a brilliant
Latinist and budding Hellenist (his main purpose in coming to Paris
had been to be able to pursue his study of Greek); a fervent anno-
tator of books, something indeed of a born scholar; a lover of modern as well as ancient poetry; a poet himself, given to musing and

melancholy though interested in social thought and social reforms; gifted with a keen sensitivity, yet tough-minded enough to undertake the study of medicine and at least once (as a *roupiou,* the slang term for a medical student) to assist in a surgical operation; not without feeling for religion, though "emancipated" in reason and convinced, like the Idéologues, that man's physical side had never been given its due in the explanation of his nature — few critics have brought to their task such a wide variety of interests and competencies. The reader may almost have been led, by my emphasis on the many-sided faculties of Sainte-Beuve, to expect too much of his first book. Though on the whole brilliant, it has, as we shall see, curious limitations, as though its author, by concentrating on perfecting certain aspects of his talent, chose, for reasons of his own and for the moment at least, to sacrifice others.

III   *"Mon début en littérature"*

Sainte-Beuve was becoming more and more detached from his medical studies and increasingly absorbed in journalism and poetry when he learned in August 1826 that the French Academy had proposed as subject for its *prix d'éloquence* for 1827 a treatise on the history of the French language and literature from the beginning of the sixteenth century to the year 1610. Encouraged to compete by Daunou, he ended up — not unhappily — withdrawing as a candidate but turning the academic exercise into an opportunity to pursue his own inquiry into the origins, traditions, nature, and future of French poetry. The mixed intentions behind the book may explain its somewhat hybrid nature: it is both literary history and polemics, erudite (at times to the point of dryness) and provocative, a mixture of objective survey and practical inquiry on the part of a practicing poet interested in defining his own place in the stream of tradition.

Unlike the *Premiers Lundis,* the *Tableau* is a book composed by Sainte-Beuve himself. As such, it clearly foreshadows the way in which he will habitually conceive and assemble his books. First, it originated characteristically as *une oeuvre de circonstance,* the response to a specific request to express himself. It grew out of the French Academy's competition as the *Portraits* and *Lundis* will arise from the opportunity to write for various periodicals, and his books on Port-Royal and Chateaubriand from invitations to lecture first at the Academy of Lausanne and then at the University of Liège. His was an exceptional gift for adapting to the conditions imposed upon him as journalist or lecturer without sacrificing the elaboration of his own thought or denying his own literary personality. His "restless mind," observed Maurice Barrès, who especially admired the young Sainte-Beuve, "accepts ideas from chance, at the same time that it pursues a systematic work of its own."[12] Furthermore, like all his books, the *Tableau* is made up of texts that had appeared beforehand, in this case in periodical form; and yet it manages, like the others, to avoid the usual formlessness of such collections and to achieve some measure of unity and coherence.

Still another characteristic feature of the *Tableau* is that it became the object of revised and enlarged editions. Most writers welcome the chance to bring their work up to date or otherwise perfect it by way of revised editions. But few have had Sainte-Beuve's zeal for "correcting" his writings, that is, correcting factual errors when these occurred and, above all, adding notes and appendices. Annotating his own books as tirelessly as those of others, pursuing the truth across edition after edition, he pushed his scruples to the point where he appears to have conceived of a book as a flux that must never be allowed to solidify.

One of the main differences between the *Premiers Lundis* and Sainte-Beuve's other works is that he was no longer present to annotate it. Henry James showed fine insight into this aspect of Sainte-Beuve's practice when he expressed regret, in his review of the *Premiers Lundis* (the Troubat edition), for the "absence of the familiar footnotes, generally more characteristic and pointed than the text itself."[13] It is in the *Tableau* that this fascinating interplay between text and notes first begins.

The *Tableau,* like a palimpsest, consists of several layers of text: the original articles on the subject as published in *Le Globe* (July 1827–April 1828); the *editio princeps* of July 1828 based on these articles and adding selections from the poetry of Ronsard; the revised edition of 1843, further enlarged by the addition of footnotes and of "Portraits" (that is, verbal portraits) of the main poets discussed; and finally the so-called "definitive edition" of 1876 published posthumously by Troubat and based on the text of 1843.[14] But one finds the same zeal for revision at work in Sainte-Beuve's other books. These successive texts obviously offer a precious record of how his thought evolved on a number of questions. With the *Tableau* there is more consistency between the various versions than might appear at first sight, but one may clearly observe his original sympathies for the aims of the Romantic poets turning into disillusionment with their achievements.

The *Tableau de la poésie française au XVIe siècle,* as the work is usually called, is actually the title of only the first of the three sections into which it is divided. The other two deal respectively with the theater and the novel of the period. The author obviously set out to meet the challenge set by the academy to survey a whole century of literature. In the concluding section, however, he replaced the ambitious terms *tableau* and *histoire* with the more essaylike "On the Sixteenth Century Novel and Rabelais," as though he were abandoning the academic tour de force. These pages are in fact almost entirely limited to Rabelais, whose role as a physician-*littérateur* struck a personal chord in the erstwhile medical student. Poetry is the true subject of the book. Not only is the first section, on lyric poetry, the longest, comprising slightly over half the entire text, but the second concerns dramatic poetry, and even the third is linked to the other two by virtue of the author's concept of the novel as a "branch" of poetry. He cites as authority for this notion Walter Scott's affirmation that "a good novelist is more or less a poet even though he may never have written a line of verse."[15] It is the creator of Gargantua and Pantagruel, not Ronsard or Du Bellay, whom he considers the greatest poet as well as the greatest novelist of his time, "a farcical Homer" (*Tableau* II, 11), "our Shakespeare in the comic vein" (II, 20).

Sainte-Beuve intended his study primarily as an "introduction to the history of French classical poetry" (I, 3). Using a roughly chronological method of organizing his material, he traces five successive generations of poets, from the oldest ("survivors from the fifteenth century") to the "reforming generation of Malherbe" in the early seventeenth (II, 32). Within this chronological framework he proceeds first by sketching the lives and then by summarizing the works of the principal poets, quoting copiously, since most of the authors were little known to readers of his time.

The center of his focus is Ronsard and the Pléiade school. He departs frequently from the chronological sequence to compare the Pléiade with their ancient classical and medieval forebears as well as with their successors in the seventeenth century and their disciples among his own contemporaries, the young Romantics. The eighteenth century poet André Chénier is seen as the most important link between the Pléiade and the Romantics. (Sainte-Beuve's tendency to seek out networks of relationships may already be observed in the *Premiers Lundis* and will remain characteristic of his criticism; the high frequency of such words as *rapport, rapprocher* and *rapprochement, rattacher, analogie* is a marked lexical feature of all his works.) The Pléiade thus becomes the pretext for broad reflections on the national traits of French poetry itself, its limitations and possibilities, much as Port-Royal and Jansenism will later serve as the focal point for a study of French Classical literature, and Chateaubriand for a study of writers of the First Empire and a reassessment of Romanticism.

To what extent is the *Tableau* an attack on Classical poetics and an apology for the "new poetic school" and its recently discovered sixteenth century ancestors? In his Preface of 1828 the author does admit having lost no opportunity to establish the relevance of his history to the current debate as to the merits of Romantic versus Classical poetry. He showed greater appreciation for the Pléiade poets than most historians before him. He expressed a number of grievances against strict Classical versification and praised Hugo, Vigny, and their colleagues for "shaking off the yoke of the last two centuries" and daring to seek emancipation, in sixteenth century models, from the "narrow, symmetrical mold of Malherbe and Boileau" (*Tableau* II, 40). It was largely Sainte-Beuve himself who discovered these new ancestors for them. His fellow literary historian, Jean-Jacques Ampère, likened the *Tableau* to an "heraldic tree" of Romantic poets (quoted in *B* I, 74).

A manifesto, however, the work certainly is not, especially when compared with Hugo's *Préface de Cromwell,* which had appeared several months before (December 1827); at the most one might call it a qualified apology. For Sainte-Beuve in fact viewed the Pléiade movement as essentially a "first and abortive phase of French Classical poetry," "an early springtime too soon cut short," to be admired more for its "flower" than for its "harvest" (*Tableau* I, 2–3). Its lack of fulfillment he attributed to a combination of factors: failure to preserve continuity with medieval traditions; the confused state of the French language in the sixteenth century; the invention of a "learned language," an "élite language" for poetry cutting it off from its popular roots; servile imitation of ancient

Greek and Roman as well as modern Italian forms; and finally, the fact (at least he considered it a fact) that the Pléiade itself, though founded by "men of wit and talent" was without " a single man of genius" (I, 178–179).

Two metaphorical passages, both found in the original edition, sum up this severe view of Ronsard and his school. In the first, their "invasion of antiquity" is compared to a "rash avant-garde attack" resulting in a "literary disaster" from the ruins of which it took Malherbe to salvage something worth repairing (I, 285). In the second, the Renaissance, with its joining of medieval traditions and a rediscovered classical antiquity, is compared to a landscape where two great rivers meet; the works of Dante, Ariosto, and Tasso in Italy and of Spenser, Shakespeare, and Milton in England rise at the confluence of the two streams like magic palaces on enchanted islands; in France, on the other hand, all was "foam, muddy waters, and a passing uproar," until Malherbe (seen once again as a kind of engineer in literary reclamation) set up dikes and guided the waters back into their proper channel (II, 36–37).

Little wonder that Sainte-Beuve considered sixteenth century poetry to be a "frail legacy" for the Romantic poets to draw upon, at best a source of guidance in matters of verse technique (II, 39). As for the Romantics themselves, in the fourteen year interval between the first and second editions of the *Tableau* he became progressively disillusioned with their achievements. Concerning the dramatic genre, a passage in the 1828 edition supporting Romantic reforms in that field receives a footnote in 1843 suggesting tartly that freedom to experiment was not enough to produce great theater when genius for theater was lacking (I, 432). (A good example, this, of the "interplay between text and notes" to which I referred earlier.) His disappointment in Romantic lyric poetry was hardly less acute. The original Conclusion ends with a roll call of poets whose works he viewed as so many "preludes" to a new era in poetry: Lamartine, Béranger, Victor Hugo, Madame Tastu, Vigny (all except the second and the fourth have since been recognized as poets of the first stature). But his tone in announcing the dawn of this glorious age is curiously apologetic. "Enthusiastic praise of one's contemporaries is cause for annoyance or amusement, and resembles a form of illusion or flattery" (II, 44). Already circumspect in this epilogue of 1828, he frankly admits in the Preface of 1842 that his high hopes have been deceived, for by then he has discovered still another affinity between the Romantic poets and their Pléiade ancestors: their common destiny as premature springtimes, promising more than they accomplished.

IV   *A Spark of Genius*

As a lad of sixteen Sainte-Beuve had written in his scholastic notebook: "There is nothing more terrible for the soul gifted with a lively imagination, perhaps even touched with a spark of genius, than the age that separates childhood from truth, by which I mean adolescence and a good part of youth." He went on to describe his own "jealous restlessness at the sight of sublime works," his "noble tears of envy and emulation," which he compared to those shed by Themistocles at the sight of Miltiades' trophies, or by Caesar, on hearing the name of Alexander. "Such," he concluded, "is the travail of genius about to bring forth its own marvels."[16] Let it be noted, incidentally, especially by Sainte-Beuve's detractors, that his first recorded movement of envy was inspired not by the success of some rival but, according to a venerable humanistic tradition, by great achievements that he felt within himself the potential to emulate. But while most adolescent *étincelles de génie* are imagined, his was real.

In the verbose oratorical style of so many of his early essays, with their flowery and trite imagery and their overburdened syntax, one has trouble detecting the future inventor of the portrait and the *causerie,* the avowed enemy of rhetoricians, the stylist who will recommend "writing in so far as possible as one speaks, and not speaking too much as one writes" (*PM,* 207). Only rarely, as in the essay on the memoirs of Madame de Genlis (*Le Globe,* April–May 1825), singled out by Henry James for its "incisive irony," do we find what might be called a *causerie en herbe.* "The grasp may here and there lack firmness," observed James of these early essays as a whole, "but the hand is already the hand of a master."[17] With all their flaws, Sainte-Beuve was right to tell a young admirer named Zola many years later that almost from the first his essays revealed "the mark of the critic" (*B* XVI, 93). The defects of style cannot obscure the promise of genius revealed in the ease with which the young writer moves among subjects as divergent as Madame de Genlis and Thiers, Jefferson and Casanova, Jouffroy and Anacreon; in the skill with which he adjusts his tone to each new subject; and in the range of questions — biographical, historical, political and social, artistic, philosophical — that he is capable of discussing intelligently.

The *Tableau,* his "début en littérature" (I, 1), is even more clearly the work of a young master. Although generally well received by critics in his time, it has been the object of surprisingly little critical scrutiny in our own. Sainte-Beuve, usually his own best critic, recognized certain of its weaknesses, including his spotty knowledge of medieval poetry (I, 1) and the flaw in perspective that allowed Ronsard to overshadow unduly other major poets, a defect that the Portraits of the second edition were designed to correct (II, 166). The most serious limitations of the book, however, concern its overall view of sixteenth century French poetry and its judgments of individual poets. By approaching this poetry less for itself than as a means of "lighting up from behind" the literary age of Louis XIV (I, 33), by viewing it as an abortive attempt at classical poetry, he does it much less than full justice. The comparison of François Villon's achievement to a pearl hidden under a manure pile seems patronizing. The satirical Mathurin Régnier is probably overrated, while the hermetic Maurice Scève, and the Ecole de Lyon generally, are underrated, in fact almost ignored.

However, it is his treatment of Ronsard, now generally recognized as one of the greatest French poets, that is most debatable. For the critic who is supposed to have "rehabilitated" Ronsard and who insisted that this defiance of *les classiques* in 1828 had been an even "bolder" gesture than his defense of the anarchist Proudhon forty years later (*B* XVII, 326, 341), his praise of this poet seems lukewarm, his understanding of him surprisingly limited. There is no doubt that by seeking to establish the facts of Ronsard's life, by writing appreciatively of his work, and by presenting generous selections from it, Sainte-Beuve made a pioneer contribution to the long overdue upward reestimate of his stature. The fact remains that he underestimated both the genius of Ronsard and the breadth of his poetic powers. Raymond Lebègue cites his pages on Ronsard to illustrate how his own conception and practice of poetry influenced his critical judgments; the richly diversified work of Ronsard is reduced in his hands to that of an Anacreontic poet, best at praising love and wine, "a superior form of Béranger." Another distinguished *seizièmiste,* V.-L. Saulnier, is much closer than Sainte-Beuve to the true estimate of Ronsard when he calls him "one of the three or four greatest French poets."[18] (Saulnier does not mention his other choices; one can imagine Sainte-Beuve's horror if he had known that they might also have included Hugo and Baudelaire!)

Despite these shortcomings, Sainte-Beuve's first book is a brilliant one. He did not, as was long believed, rediscover French Renaissance poetry singlehandedly,[19] but his originality remains impressive enough, and it was his contribution that made the strongest impact. Although he had not yet fully developed his method as a critic, the "instinct for accuracy" (*Tableau* I, 1) that will become one of his trademarks is already clearly in evidence. A contemporary reviewer commended him for not dismissing accuracy as something pedantic (Henri Patin, quoted in *B* I, 73-74). This "goût de l'exactitude" meant not only getting his facts straight, no mean achievement; it also meant faithfulness — of a kind reminiscent of his master Montaigne, and which only Ernest Renan among his contemporaries will equal or surpass — in recording the shifting and evolving phases of his own thought. A bachelor who was to remain, sometimes to his bitter regret, unmarried and (so far as we know) childless, he lavished on the various editions of his works, beginning with his first-born child, the *Tableau,* all the care of a loving father for his children.

But the wealth of erudition and of perceptive comment, the sureness of grasp upon such an imposing mass of materials, to which the original edition of the *Tableau* already testifies, are extraordinary for an author of twenty-three. The style, furthermore, is much more concise than in his earlier prose manner; oratory has all but disappeared, and a new, relaxed, more "conversational" tone has been introduced. The poet's fondness for imagery persists, and the images are seldom very original; but they are used with greater discrimination than in the *Premiers Lundis,* tending (like the military and the aquatic landscape metaphors we cited earlier) to occur at important junctures in the development of his thought and to reinforce it.

How does this first book fit in with Sainte-Beuve's ambition of a few years before, as described earlier in this chapter, to become a *critique moraliste,* a *critique peintre,* rivaling imaginative writers by recreating characters and situations as vivid and engaging as those of fiction?

From this point of view, especially if one comes to the *Tableau* after the *Premiers Lundis,* as we have done, it appears to betray a certain narrowing of sights on Sainte-Beuve's part, as though he were deliberately sacrificing breadth and artistry in order to achieve a more limited objective, namely, to establish his credentials as something more than a journalist, to make his name as a scholarly historian of French poetry. One is surprised, nevertheless, that the erstwhile student of philosophy who wrote the *Tableau* has almost nothing to say in it about the relations of sixteenth century poetry to the great philosophical and religious movements of the Renaissance and Reformation, the student of history almost nothing to say of historical background. How far we are still from the rich texture of that other tableau, that immense fresco devoted to seventeenth century France, *Port-Royal!*

It might be argued, of course, that the Jansenist reform movement possessed, to begin with, inherently dramatic qualities lacking in a history of sixteenth century poetry. But even in the *Tableau* it is clear that Sainte-Beuve had by no means abandoned his broader literary ambition, that he was still on the track of a subject matter distinct from, though related to, the analysis of a poet's work: the whole domain of what he calls the poet's "destinée littéraire." The phrase occurs in a passage comparing Ronsard with Voltaire, as two writers who enjoyed unrivaled fame during their lifetimes. To appreciate the comparison he recommends that we "forget for a moment the works of Ronsard ... and imagine the spectacle of his astonishing literary destiny." To do so, he adds, is to discover a "drama that is both heroic and absurd, with its own morality, its own interest, even its own kind of emotion" (*Tableau* I, 110). What arouses his curiosity is not merely the works of Ronsard but the whole drama of his life and mind.

This passage was quoted by Maurice Bémol, in his suggestive *rapprochement* of Sainte-Beuve and Paul Valéry, to show that each of these poet-critics undertook a kind of survey, combining both "theoretical explanation and poetic representation," of the various ways in which the human mind expresses itself, and that Sainte-Beuve's approach to criticism foreshadowed Valéry's concept of it as the amassing of materials for a "'Comédie Intellectuelle,'[20] conceived on analogy with Balzac's 'Comédie Humaine.'" What Bémol failed to observe, however (it was less essential to his argument than it is to mine), is that neither Ronsard nor the other writers depicted in the *Tableau* come to life with much vividness. There is in fact more of an *art de peindre* (physical descriptions, gestures, conversations, anecdotes, dramatic scenes) displayed in the *Premiers Lundis,* though in embryonic form, than in the *Tableau,* at least in the 1828 edition. The passage quoted by Bémol describes an intention on the author's part rather than a type of criticism which he has already achieved. That Sainte-Beuve appears to have been aware of the missing dimension may be inferred from his Conclusion, where he apologizes to the reader for having resorted to what he calls "these rather dry though more or less accurate classifications" (that is, of his poets by generation) and begs him to furnish from his own imagination "the color and life without which there is no understanding of the past" (II, 33). He appeals to the reader, in other words, to supply those very qualities which in future critical works he will provide with unfailing abundance!

In 1828 Sainte-Beuve stood at a crossroads. He had proven his worth as a critic, but was far from certain that criticism should be his life's calling. Promising flashes of that genius which was to make of him the creator of his own "human comedy," with criticism as his instrument, illumine the pages of his early works. But he could hardly perceive as yet that this was the road he would eventually take. What young man, especially one who belonged to the Romantic generation, among the most ambitious and gifted that ever lived, would settle for criticism as a career when he nourished the hope that he might become a great poet?

CHAPTER 2

Unrequited Love: Poetry

I N a letter to an unidentified correspondent (it bears no date, but Bonnerot believes it was probably written in 1824), Sainte-Beuve confessed having composed poems for the past two years in an attempt to "define the vague fits of sadness" to which he was subject (*B* I, 56). It was not, however, until his momentous meeting with Hugo in 1827, and the beginning of their friendship and exchange of views on poetry, that he acquired enough confidence in himself to think of preparing his first book of verse. The result was the publication two years later of his *Vie, poésies et pensées de Joseph Delorme*. Although still to this day the best known of his poetic works, it was merely the first in a series of four major verse collections that he brought out between the ages of twenty-five and thirty-nine, the others being *Les Consolations* (1830), *Pensées d'Août* (1837), and, in a limited private printing, *Livre d'amour* (1843).

Before attempting to characterize each of these books, I should like to describe the general features that they share in common, so far as content is concerned. I shall return to their stylistic features later.

I *The Poetic Work as a Whole*

What links all four books together is that they are so many fragments of the poet's spiritual autobiography in his late twenties and early thirties, so many chapters of an intimate journal in verse form. The apparently haphazard way in which the poems were arranged was probably as much a matter of plan as of accident. Thomas Hardy, in one of his prefaces, wrote that much of his poetry "comprises a series of feelings and fancies written down in

widely differing moods and circumstances, and at various dates."
Yet he was not alarmed that this might produce on the reader the
effect of "little cohesion of thought or harmony of colouring,"
because, as he argued, "unadjusted impressions have their value,
and the road to a true philosophy of life seems to lie in humbly
recording diverse readings of its phenomena as they are forced
upon us by chance and change."[1] Sainte-Beuve would, I think,
have subscribed to this view. He in fact introduces his *Pensées
d'Août* with a very similar concept, in the form of an epigraph
from Goethe, who, in his *Conversations with Eckermann,* urged
poets to render "all the little subjects that present themselves"
from day to day and who described his own poems as "poems of
circumstance issuing from everyday reality and finding in it their
basis and support."[2]

The recurrence of certain stylistic traits and of certain preferred
poetic genres (elegiac, pastoral, narrative, epistolary) contributes
much to the unity of the four books, as does the "art poétique"
(basically unchanged from first to last) that guided the poet in
writing them. But the most powerful unifying force is the spiritual
drama underlying them. The poet, consumed with a sense of frustrated ambition and of impending failure, feels himself old before
his time, though in calendar years he is still a young man. In the
physical effects that accompany his spiritual illness — wrinkling
and yellowing of the skin, arching shoulders, thinning hair — there
is even the hint of some psychosomatic process at work. Has he
ever been young? Is he capable of being young? Lamenting in himself what Senancour's fictional hero, Obermann, a kindred soul,
called "le malheur de ne pouvoir être jeune" (epigraph of "Le
Dernier voeu"), he nevertheless seeks a way out of his despair, a
source of renewal and hope, turning at various times to love,
friendship, religion, to poetry itself, but never without some disillusionment. Tempted by "a great longing for the unknown" ("un
grand désir de choses inconnues" ["Le Calme"]), drawn to the
terrifying exploration of the "soul's abysses" ("L'Enfant
rêveur"), yet fearful of shipwreck on the high seas, he returns again
and again to the dream of a safe harbor, of the calm lake reflecting
his image. Fascinated by the strange beauty of the city (often a
paradoxical beauty in ugliness) and by the hidden dramas of its
inhabitants' lives, he turns from them frequently to the pastoral
motif: the secluded valley, the frugal cottage, an obscure life of

study shared with "a beloved spouse" and a few friends ("Bonheur champêtre").

These tensions, with their alternating moods of despair and consolation, are aggravated still further by the conflict between his desire to believe once again as a Christian and his love of the play of a mind inclined to skepticism and unwilling to fix limits to its curiosity. On the one hand, he longs for a resting place, for attachment to some person, to some conviction that might bring him stability; on the other, he delights in savoring various forms of belief without adopting any, in remaining unattached, "mobile," or, as André Gide would have said, *disponible*.

II Joseph Delorme

This first collection differs from its successors in two important respects: the fictional disguise by which the poems are presented not as Sainte-Beuve's own but as those of an imaginary poet, and the unusual tripartite form of a prose biography followed first by poems and then by prose "thoughts" supposedly selected from the poet's works.

Sainte-Beuve observed in retrospect that although Delorme's biography was not exactly the same as his own, he represented a "faithful enough moral image" of himself at the time (*NL* XIII, 29). Like his creator, Delorme, born in Picardy, an only child orphaned of his father and raised by his mother and a paternal aunt, had come to Paris as an adolescent to complete his studies, had developed an immense curiosity for science and philosophy, had lost his religious faith under the influence of eighteenth century rationalism, had studied medicine, and was given to roaming the *boulevards extérieurs* of Paris as evening fell, to writing poetry into the late hours of the night, and to dreaming of a virtuous and attractive young woman who might be his life's companion. So far the disguise is almost transparent. But Delorme is to some extent a hidden Sainte-Beuve, the depths of whose anguish were little known to his friends at the time, since discretion prevented his "displaying his ulcer" (*Poésies* I, 19).

The main difference between fact and fiction in this case, however, is that Sainte-Beuve projected into the life of his hero (or anti-hero, as it would appear today) an intensified vision of the sufferings that he had experienced, giving these a much more fatalistic, tragic quality than they had in his own existence. He had been poor, but never to the point of extreme poverty — a miserable sixth floor garret in wintertime. He was timid, but never quite so lacking in self-confidence nor quite so convinced that he was being victimized or exploited by others. The darkened coloring of Delorme's fate probably owes more to literary examples — Dr. Johnson, born poor and ugly; the persecuted misfit Jean-Jacques Rousseau; the English poets Chatterton and Kirke White, prototypes of the *poète maudit* — than to Sainte-Beuve's own experience. Thwarted in his attempts to survive honorably, Delorme eventually rejects life, and in a kind of prolonged suicide assisted by a fatal illness (none other than the poetic disease of tuberculosis, which had also carried off "le malheureux Kirke White" [*Poésies* I, 10–11]), dies while still only twenty-eight. His creator, on the other hand, outlived him by almost half a century. Delorme's solution to the anguish of what he felt to be the emptiness of his life was death; Amaury's (I refer to the hero of *Volupté*) will be the Catholic priesthood; Sainte-Beuve's, a vocation as critic.

The invention of a semifictional mask for the expression of intimate feelings was a Romantic tradition already well established by the examples of works admired by Delorme–Sainte-Beuve, such as Goethe's *Werther,* Chateaubriand's *René,* Senancour's *Obermann* (quoted in one of the two epigraphs introducing the life of Delorme), and Constant's *Adolphe.* In this last work, in fact, one finds not only the thinly veiled autobiography but also the story-telling device, dear to eighteenth century novelists and very similar to the one used in *Joseph Delorme,* of the manuscript brought to light by a sympathetic editor. But there is another, less solemn, side of Romanticism with which Sainte-Beuve shows affinity in his strategy of concealment: the love of mystification, of anonymity and pseudonymity, exemplified so well by Mérimée and Stendhal. Although *Joseph Delorme* is hardly a literary hoax of the order of Mérimée's *Théâtre de Clara Gazul* (1825) or *La Guzla* (1827), nor was it ever intended as such, the lengths to which Sainte-Beuve goes, especially in his notes and commentaries, to sustain the illusion that Delorme really existed testify to a sense of humor not unlike Mérimée's or Stendhal's.

Sainte-Beuve's need for *dédoublement,* for taking a critical perspective upon himself as well as upon others, was very keen. The creation of an alter ego permitted him to establish this dialogue

with himself. His role as "editor" allowed him to interpret
Delorme, to show how he differed from him, even to judge him
critically. At one point in the *Life,* for example, he quotes as an
illustration of "our poor friend's proneness to exaggerate"
(*Poésies* I, 13) a long passage from Delorme's journal, the emotional style of which contrasts with his own more detached prose.

The idea of casting his work in tripartite form Sainte-Beuve
probably derived from Robert Southey's edition of *The Poetical
Works and Remains of Henry Kirke White* (1806),[3] adding the
original twist of attributing his own verse to a "fictional" character. In a letter to the publisher Ladvocat he insisted, quite correctly,
on the relative novelty of a verse collection that also included critical reflections and a kind of brief novel ("de la prose et du
Roman" [*B* I, 108]). The imagination that "invented" Delorme
was obviously not very high powered; but there is at least some
effort at creating suspense, some semblance of a "plot," as we follow Delorme through the *péripéties* of his abandonment of poetry
for a more "useful" profession, his return to poetry when his medical career is thwarted, and his final effort to rouse himself from
despair by courting a childhood friend who ends up marrying a
rival.

Critics who have followed Sainte-Beuve's lead by referring to the
Life as a "roman" and who have even seen in it a kind of sketch of
Volupté are thus not too wide of the mark (see Antoine, pp.
xliii–xliv). Antoine goes further and suggests that this triptych is a
kind of prophetic symbol of the three parts into which Sainte-
Beuve's literary production as a whole will fall: fiction, poetry, and
criticism.

What may be more original than the form of *Joseph Delorme,*
however, is the choice of protagonist and of the milieu in which he
moves. When this unhappy poet complains of possessing vital ener-
gies deprived of a suitable outlet ("ses facultés sans expansion"
Poésies I, 11]), or of being cursed by fate, he reminds us of René.
But René, like his creator, was a nobleman. Joseph Delorme,
whose name is deliberately bourgeois, may be a "noble character"
(I, 13) — morally noble, that is — but he is condemned nevertheless
to middle class status. He is thus closer to Werther than to René.
Guizot, quoted by Sainte-Beuve, compared him to a Werther
turned partisan of the French Revolution and medical student, "un
Werther jacobin et carabin" (I, 299), and the author himself spoke

of him as "un Werther ou un René des faubourgs" (*CL* X, 82). He is poorer and of lower social status than any Romantic hero who had yet appeared.

Guizot's instinct was sound when he detected in Delorme an enemy of the established order of 1829, the Bourbon monarchy on the eve of the Revolution of 1830. The scarcity of direct political statements or references in the work should not deceive us as to its implied political meaning. Delorme's sympathy with the poor of Paris, his own poverty (even more than his humble social condition), and his distrust of the powerful make him a symbol of failed revolutionary ambitions and of the "liquidation" of revolutionary optimism among his generation — a new kind of Romantic hero, closer to Julien Sorel, whom he anticipates, than to Werther or René.[4] One's very reluctance to call him a "hero" is proof that he is of a different Romantic family than René, Dumas père's Antony, or Hugo's Hernani or Olympio. No grand gestures or noble stances for him, but a seedy, unhandsome appearance; no "illustrious misfortunes" but "a long trail of revulsions and ennuis" (*Poésies* I, 3), lacking in color and bordering on the ordinary.

The setting in which his dull, everyday melancholy and his poor pleasures unfold is also highly unusual in Romantic lyric poetry: the urban landscape of a modern city, in this case the *quartier Montrouge,* in 1829 at the extreme limit of Paris beyond Montparnasse where Sainte-Beuve lived. His "biographer" describes it as follows:

> The long black walls, boring to look at, a sinister belt enclosing the vast cemetery that we call a great city; the hedges with gaps in them revealing, through their openings, the wretched greenery of kitchen gardens; the sad monotonous alleys; the elms gray with dust [*ces ormes gris de poussière:* the name of this tree echoes his very name], and beneath them, an old woman crouching with children at the edge of a ditch; a disabled veteran returning late with drunken step to his barracks; sometimes, across the road, the bursts of joyful laughter from a workingman's wedding party — all this sufficed, during a week, to make up our friend's meager consolations. (I, 11–12)

Several of the best poems have as their *décor* a comparable urban landscape, among them the most famous piece of the collection, described by Sainte-Beuve as the "most important" (I, 301), "Les Rayons jaunes," an elegy set not in a country churchyard but in a faubourg of Paris. One has only to recall René posturing on the summit of Etna, Lamartine seated atop his mountain commanding the valleys, or Hugo communing with the sea in order to savor the originality of Delorme's visits at nightfall to the outer boulevards of Paris, along which he seems not so much to walk as to prowl (*rôder* is one of his favorite verbs), almost to creep.

III Les Consolations

All was not gloom in Delorme's life. In addition to his nightly stroll along the boulevard he had other small joys. Despite his "wholly inward life" (I, 20) he was not unsociable; he had literary friends in the Romantic group known as the Cénacle, he conversed and even flirted with women at dances (the *contredanse* or *scène du bal* is the scene of several poems). Poetry itself provided him with even stronger solace. Joachim Merlant observed that Delorme–Sainte-Beuve was an incurably "literary soul," a "craftsman shaping his own image," a "virtuoso," who enjoyed the pursuit of his true self and whose mind, alert in the midst of the worst sorrow, kept real despair at a distance so long as he was writing.[5]

The motif of "consolations," which in *Joseph Delorme* is subordinated to the portrayal of "une certaine naïveté souffrante et douloureuse" (*Poésies* I, 301), becomes the dominant theme of *Les Consolations*.

In the first of the two epigraphs introducing *Joseph Delorme* (the second, from Senancour, I referred to earlier), Sainte-Beuve suggests a comparison of his poet to Saint Augustine before his conversion, as described in the *Confessions:* "Sic ego eram illo tempore, et flebam amarissime et requiescam in amaritudine" ("So I was at the time, and I grieved most bitterly and found my repose in bitterness"). In the end it was Delorme's very lack of hope that became his chief consolation. In a marvelous image foreshadowing Verlaine, Sainte-Beuve compares this refuge in despair to "the sea bird whose wing is broken by the storm [and which] allows itself for a time to be cradled on the brink of the wave that will finally engulf it" (I, 18). But the Sainte-Beuve of *Les Consolations* who succeeds to "that deceased self I call Joseph Delorme" (I, 208) is hardly comparable to Saint Augustine fully converted. He possesses not faith but the desire for faith:

Pour arriver à toi, c'est assez de vouloir.
Je voudrais bien, Seigneur; je veux; pourquoi ne puis-je?

("To reach thee an act of will suffices. I would wish it thus, Lord. I will; why am I not able?" ["A M. Viguier"]).

Sainte-Beuve described the phase of his development during which he wrote *Les Consolations* as "the happiest moment of my youth" (*Poésies* II, 109), "six heavenly months of my life" (II, 127). The far from hostile reception given to *Joseph Delorme* made it appear for the moment at least that he might achieve his ambition to succeed as a poet. Above all, his friendship with the young couple, Victor and Adèle Hugo, promised both renewal of his poetic inspiration and spiritual renewal, perhaps even a way back to the Christian faith.

The passage quoted from Petrarch's *De vita solitaria* as one of the epigraphs of the book shows clearly his intention to draw on a venerable tradition for his concept of the spiritual value of friendship. The major theme of *Les Consolations* is friendship as an instrument of salvation. No less than twenty of the twenty-nine poems bear titles addressing them to friends, but the dominant friendship is by far that of Victor Hugo, to whom the book is dedicated. This relationship is distinct but inseparable from his friendship with Adèle, a form of *amitié* that slowly develops into *amour.* One need not wait for the *Livre d'amour:* the transformation may be observed taking place between the lines by any attentive reader (Hugo, though, seems not to have detected it).

The preface addressed to Hugo, in reality a ten page essay on friendship, is, in its exaggerated language and worshipful tone, an extraordinary document, very uncharacteristic of Sainte-Beuve. It is difficult to believe that such a naive expression of faith in "L'Ami" could have come from the critic who, only a few years before, had published his clear-eyed assessment of Hugo in *Le Globe.* But that was before he had met Hugo. Of all Sainte-Beuve's experiments in lending himself momentarily to various forms of doctrine — Romanticism, Saint-Simonianism, Lamennaisianism, Protestantism — only in succumbing to his fascination for Hugo and his world did he admit that he had suspended his will and judgment, and then only for a moment, "as though under a magic spell" (*PM* 48).

"This little book," he pointed out to Hugo, "is the faithful image of my soul, for in it a struggle is still taking place between doubts and good intentions" (*Poésies* II, 13–14). It is essentially the record of a failed religious conversion. The poet gives reason after reason for wishing to renounce the world but does not convince us that he has eradicated worldliness from his own heart. Of all the obstacles in the path of his return to God, the most serious, ironically enough, was probably his very concept of Hugo's friendship as a means of salvation. His "friend" becomes a being so much better, purer, happier than himself that one wonders why he needed God when he already had Victor Hugo. How lucky for him that he eventually discovered that Hugo's world had not even been "the grotto of a demigod" but instead "a Cyclops' cave" ("J'étais dans l'antre du Cyclope, et je me croyais dans la grotte d'un demi-dieu").[6]

Adèle Hugo was a different matter.

IV *A Book of Love*

Les Consolations was followed, in order of publication, by *Pensées d'Août.* However, in the preface to the latter work (1837) Sainte-Beuve alludes to a mysterious third volume of verse that he has already completed, of which he is especially fond, but which "discretion" ("la pudeur") will not allow him to publish "for a very long time" (*Poésies* II, 132). This missing link was *Livre d'amour,* inspired by his love affair with Adèle Hugo, which lasted approximately from 1830 to the winter of 1836–1837 and which stimulated two other imaginative works of his to be discussed in the following chapter: the novel *Volupté* (1834) and the short story "Madame de Pontivy" (1837). A limited anonymous edition of *Livre d'amour* in fact appeared six years after *Pensées d'Août,* in 1843, and over half the poems also figure in the 1863 edition of his *Poésies.* But it was only in 1906, long after the deaths of the three leading characters in this drama, that Troubat published the first true edition of the work.

No book of Sainte-Beuve's has aroused such controversy or has been so maligned. His enemies, who fancied themselves to be the defenders of Madame Hugo's honor, attacked it as a villainous account of how he had betrayed his best friend, avenging himself for Hugo's superiority over him and boasting of his conquest of a reluctant (so they liked to believe) mistress — if indeed he had not lied to begin with about her infidelity. Vanity undoubtedly played some part in Sainte-Beuve's decision to make these poems for Adèle public — the vanity of letting the world know that he had been the successful rival of Hugo in love if not in poetry. But his indiscretion has been greatly exaggerated. Gustave Michaut reminds us that it is a time-honored custom for poets to publicize their adulterous love affairs, and adds that the deceived husband himself had produced his own *Livre d'amour* only a few years before in *Chants du crépuscule* (1835), in which he had gone so far as to address love poems to both wife and mistress (the unnamed but easily detectable Juliette Drouet) in a single volume.[7] Furthermore, there is no evidence that Adèle objected to the publication of any of Sainte-Beuve's poems, or that she was anything but a willing partner in their affair.

In the heat of this quarrel over the right of *Livre d'amour* to exist, its nature as a work of poetry has been all but completely lost sight of. Although far from a neglected masterpiece (none of Sainte-Beuve's verse collections falls into that category), it contains some of his finest poems and has the advantage over its more shapeless companions of being better constructed. It reads, in fact, almost like a novel in verse form. (There are curious allusions in the author's footnotes to the lovers' project of a "roman par lettres" based on their relationship.) A kind of "plot" enables us to follow, across the forty-five poems, the genesis, growth, fulfillment, and decline of their passion, from their first attraction to each other —

> J'allais sortir alors, mais tu me dis: *Restez!*
> Et, sous tes doigts pleuvant, la chevelure immense
> Exhalait jusqu'à moi des senteurs de semence

("I was about to leave when you told me to remain, and your flowing hair as you undid it gave off a scent as though of seed" [*Livre d'Amour* VIII]) — to the acknowledgment in the final sonnet of the reason (at least as he saw it) for their eventual separation: "Je voulais la nuance, et j'ai gâté l'ardeur" ("I sacrificed ardent passion to my need for subtlety of feeling").

As in a novel there are also characters, settings, and atmosphere, both physical and psychological. Basically it is a *roman à deux,* with the husband ("Lui") as a threatening presence in the background. The cast of characters is small not only because the atmosphere is intimate (Troubat compared these poems to a form of "chamber music" [p. 15]), but also because the lovers had almost no intermediaries. The "action" could be summed up as their effort to find suitable places where they might be alone. These in turn become the characteristic *décors* of the poems: churches and cemeteries, obscure hotels, country lanes, and, at least once,(*Livre d'Amour,* XXX), a horse-drawn cab on the Champs-Elysées — the famous *fiacre* whose possibilities for lovemaking Sainte-Beuve exploited long before Flaubert made use of them in *Madame Bovary.*

The psychological atmosphere is one of frustrations, separations, long periods of waiting, attempts to communicate through glances and gestures in the presence of others. None of this is new to literature of course: poets and novelists have traditionally thrived on such handicaps. Where Sainte-Beuve is original is in the unromantic, bourgeois setting of some of the pieces, as for example in Poem XXXII, contrasting the idyllic rural trysting places of so much love poetry with the old hotel in a shabby section of Paris where he received his "Châtelaine."

A veil of sadness, of shadow, hangs over the work. The pleasures and joys of love, though real, are short-lived. The reader has been prepared beforehand for this melancholy view by the first poem of *Les Consolations,* "A Madame V.H.," with its epigraph from the eighteenth century playwright Jean-François Ducis ("Our happiness is but a form of misfortune more or less consoled") and its opening lines, "Oh! que la vie est longue aux longs jours de l'été, / Et que le temps y pèse à mon coeur attristé!" ("Oh, how long life is on long summer days, and how heavily time weighs on my saddened heart!") — lines which find an echo in such phrases of *Livre d'amour* as "notre courte joie / Et notre longue attente" (XXIII). Born to a mother already widowed, "discouraged from the cradle onward" and "poorly endowed with the faculty of hope" (as he wrote to Adèle in a letter probably of 1836 [*B* II, 114]), Sainte-Beuve seemed almost predestined to render just this strange nuance in his love poetry.

Yet despite the relative joylessness of a love that André Maurois described as having been "like dusk even from the moment it dawned" ("dès son aube, crépusculaire"),[8] several forces are at work in *Livre d'amour* that give the concept of love affirmed therein a surprisingly positive quality. One is the association of love with religion. Part of Adèle's attraction for Sainte-Beuve was her Christian faith, which he counted upon to support him in his own

spiritual quest. The lovers hoped to redeem their adulterous relationship by prayers for the dead and by alms giving; in the midst of
adultery they clung to an ideal of innocence and purity — a para-
dox that Baudelaire, if not Claudel, would have understood. Like
that other "book of love," *Volupté,* this one can be understood
only on the larger background of Sainte-Beuve's search for a dur-
able faith. Love is also associated with the intellectual, quasi-
scholarly pursuit which the poet calls "étude" ("notre amour, ma
seule et vive étude" [*Livre d'amour* IX]). Here it is the studious and
learned Petrarch who, having served to bless the concept of friendship in *Les Consolations,* is called upon to render a similar service
to love (XXXIII). Frequent allusions to classical mythology and to
the examples of lovers consecrated by classical and postclassical
tradition (Tibullus and Delia, Petrarch and Laura) add further to
the ennobling effect, as does the attempt to poeticize the lovers'
experience by sifting it through the filter of imagination and
memory.

These various forms of the ennobling of reality, similar to the
ones that he used in *Volupté,* testify to Sainte-Beuve's determination to extract some beauty, some spiritual meaning from the raw
material of a love affair that must at times have appeared to him
anything but noble. In this effort to shape his experience into a
meaningful fiction or myth, his intention was that of a true poet.
The resulting work, unfortunately, is not free from the notorious
defects of the rest of his verse, so often flat, laborious, and clumsy
in execution.[9]

V   *The Late Summer of Life*

Because of its great variety of "petits sujets" and "poésies de
circonstance," to quote the epigraph from Goethe that Sainte-
Beuve uses to describe his *Pensées d'Août,* this last volume of
entirely new verse which he published during his lifetime is thematically less unified than the others and consequently more difficult to
sum up briefly. Judging from the title, from the original Preface,
and from the first poem, also called "Pensées d'Août," he wished
to express a certain "moral season of the soul" (*Poésies* II, 131) by
establishing an analogy between the month of August, lying just
beyond the midpoint of the calendar year, and the late summer of
his own life when youthful ardor was beginning to give way to a

more disillusioned though perhaps wiser view of things — "l'âge où mon soleil, / Où mon été décline, à la saison pareil" ("Pensées d'Août"). He was not a bad prophet: thirty-three when he published this work (1837), he was in fact to live until the age of sixty-five.

Ever since *Joseph Delorme* his ambition had been "not to repeat himself" in successive volumes, to offer "something new and distinct" in each. The poet of *Pensées d'Août,* as he describes him, was "more disinterested, calmer, less given to personal confessions" than his predecessor and could therefore turn his attention to developing two types of verse that were more or less impersonal in nature: the "domestic and moral tale" ("le récit domestique et moral") and criticism in letter form ("l'épître à demi-critique") (II, 133).

It is obvious that each of these genres clearly overlaps with the biographical and critical prose essays of the *Portraits* and with the course on Port-Royal that he was producing during the same period. His Muse, never very robust, appears to be well into her decline. The verse of *Pensées d'Août* resembles more than ever prose in disguise, a fact that critics recognized by giving it the poorest reviews received by any of his books. The poet in him, on the other hand, far from disappearing, was taking refuge in his prose.

There are occasional light-hearted poems in this collection, such as the charming "Sonnet à Madame P." with its self-portrait of the poet as a straw-hatted villager strolling near Précy-sur-Oise, "heureux, loin de Paris." The dominant tone, however, is grave. Reminiscing with Franz Liszt in Rome about their younger and presumably happier years, the poet observes, in Pascalian manner, that even happiness contains a void within it reminding man of his "nothingness" — "Je ne sais quel vide / Qui dans le bonheur même avertit du néant" ("La Villa Adriana"). Many variations occur on the theme of death, for example, the autumn "death" of leafy trees on a Jura hillside as the evergreens look sadly on ("De Ballaigues à Orbe, Jura"), the death of Sainte-Beuve's friendship with Hugo finally recognized as they are obliged to share the same cab on returning from Gabrielle Dorval's funeral ("En revenant du convoi de Gabrielle") — a very different *fiacre* scene this time from *Livre d'amour!,* or the death of the poet himself, to be survived by the man, as described in a poem by Musset included in the collection, with its famous line "Un poète mort jeune, à qui l'homme survit" ("A Sainte-Beuve").

But melancholy, often bordering on despair, is only half the story in *Pensées d'Août;* the other half is that characteristic resilience of spirit with which Sainte-Beuve refused to surrender to despair and continued to seek ways to bypass it. Some of these proved less satisfactory than others. Nature consoled and even appeared to rejuvenate him for a while, especially in the landscape poems inspired by his visit to Lausanne to give his course on Port-Royal; but he confessed that nature meant little to him in itself, without the company of friends ("Réponse"). Friendship he still valued highly, but when he treats this theme it is less to celebrate his friends than to compare himself to them unfavorably and to seek strength in their example for overcoming his (supposed) weaknesses. The most persistent of his illusions led him into a final attempt at love — final, that is, at least so far as his recording it in poetic form is concerned. This time it was indeed an attempt at marriage: his unsuccessful courtship of Frédérique Pelletier (1840), the subject of the pathetic "Un dernier rêve," a kind of short story in verse and prose that serves as an epilogue to *Pensées d'Août* in the 1863 edition of his *Poésies.*

In the end it was his emerging vocation as a critic that seemed to offer him the least illusory form of hope for the future, the least unreliable means of filling the void within him and conferring order and purpose on his existence. Even while expressing envy of the calm, purposeful life of his childhood friend Eustache Barbe (who had become a priest) and comparing it plaintively with his own endless driftings, he seemed not unhappy with his fate as a critic, or with the "metamorphoses" that he underwent as he increased his knowledge of so many different subjects: "C'est mon mal et ma peine, et mon charme aussi bien" ("A l'Abbé Eustache Barbe"). For the Christian, prayer and sacrifice were the means of "restoring the dead to life again in ourselves," as Pascal wrote in his essay on the death of his father, quoted in the epigraph to "Monsieur Jean, Maître d'école." But could not the biographer-historian, even though an unbeliever, achieve a similar goal through the force of his learning and imagination? Could not a great work of criticism conceived in this generous manner provide him with his own mainstay against the oblivion of death?

VI *A Modern* Art poétique

As a poet-critic Sainte-Beuve, not surprisingly, was a very conscious theorist of poetry. His views, developed mainly in the *pensées* of Joseph Delorme, in several prefaces, and in the manifesto type poem, "A M. Villemain" (*Pensées d'Août*), belonged to what he called "l'Art poétique moderne" (*Poésies* II, 234) of the new Romantic school. But within this general movement they represented a kind of rival poetics which, especially in its questioning of certain conventional notions of lyrical poetry, was to have much more impact on succeeding generations of poets than on his associates in the Cénacle. It was a poetics that insisted above all on two concepts, originality and modernity, both of which, as Antoine has observed, were paradoxical in a poet so given to quoting, imitating, even translating other poets, so respectful of tradition and so willing to revive and adapt ancient poetic forms such as the elegiac, the pastoral, the epistolary.

That Sainte-Beuve was acutely aware of his need to stake out his own territory as a poet is very easy to understand. Lamartine, Vigny, and Hugo had already published highly successful and individualized major verse collections when *Joseph Delorme* appeared. He discovered that his originality lay in recognizing his limitations and exploiting a vein that others might consider minor, if not somewhat strange. He even incorporated into his poems this very theme of the latecomer's problem in defining his domain. In the best illustration of this, "A M. Villemain," a long poem built around a central horticultural image, he compares himself to Virgil's farmer in the *Georgics,* reduced to making the best of "a few acres of abandoned countryside"; evoking in rapid succession the revered precursor, André Chénier; Lamartine, "knowing little except his own soul"; the "powerful Hugo"; and Vigny, "withdrawn inside his ivory tower" (like the characterization of Lamartine, this was to become famous), he then goes on to describe the "narrow space" left for him to cultivate, an unpromising little garden confined within melancholy walls and producing flowers of whose names he was not even sure.

The key to both originality and modernity in Sainte-Beuve's poetics was his concept of the "analytical elegy" ("l'élégie d'analyse" [*Pensée* XIX]). It was natural that the man who described himself as prone to "sterile regrets, vague expectant

desires, moods of melancholy and languor following upon pleasures'' (*PM* 237) should turn to the poetic genre associated more
than any other with sadness and reverie. ''My imagination is elegiac,'' he observed, ''and my ideal, the picture drawn by Tibullus:
Quam juvat immites'' (*PM* 242) — a reference to the great Roman
poet's description of himself by the hearth on a stormy winter's
night, holding his mistress in his arms, content not to risk gale and
shipwreck in pursuit of fortune and to ''savor fully'' the ''narrow
range'' of the fire that warms them.[10]

Drawing to some extent on the examples of Chénier and Lamartine as elegists, Sainte-Beuve proposed modernizing the French
elegy even further by introducing into it stronger components both
of intimacy and of everyday reality. His imagination had also been
stimulated by the intimate poems in humble settings of the
''Lakistes,'' the English Lake Poets, but he admitted having recognized them intuitively as ''older brothers'' rather than having
known their work from close study (*NL* IV, 455).[11] In any case he
felt that he could surpass them in extracting poetry from nature and
the soul observed at close range, ''humbly and in bourgeois manner
[*bourgeoisement*] ... calling by their real names the things of private life ... and attempting to relieve the prosaic quality [*le
prosaïsme*] of such domestic details by the description [*la peinture*]
of human feelings and natural objects'' (*Pensée* XIX). Returning to
this concept in his dedicatory preface to *Les Consolations,* he
wisely eschewed as beyond his powers Hugo's prophetic aspirations, his ''familiar conversations with the Infinite,'' and claimed,
as the hallmark of his own poetry, ''the choice of certain subjects
taken from private life ... a domestic incident, a conversation, a
stroll, a piece of reading.'' His goal, he informed Hugo, was
nothing less than to raise this ''very commonplace reality'' to ''a
higher power of poetry'' (*Poésies* II, 13–14).

Opening up the elegy, and lyric poetry generally, to ''la réalité la
plus vulgaire'' meant not only choosing unconventional subjects
but also ''nommant les choses de la vie privée par leur nom,'' and
daring to use in verse the rhythms of everyday prose speech. Every
reformer of poetry — and Sainte-Beuve was as much a reformer as
Du Bellay and Malherbe had been before him or as Rimbaud and
André Breton would be after him — is really in search of a new language that alone can express a new thought, a new mode of feeling.
This meant for Sainte-Beuve using ''lower class words [*de basse*

bourgeoisie], for some reason excluded from the language of poetry" (I, 25). Thus in "La Plaine" (*Joseph Delorme*) — a serious lyric poem, it must be emphasized, and not a satire, where such words were traditionally acceptable — a shepherd boy, holding a loaf of wholemeal bread (*pain bis*), watches an old woman gleaning in the beetfield (*au champ de betterave*), while in the distance we hear a cart (*la charrette*) creaking along under its load of stinking manure (*le fumier infect*). There are enough objectionable words in these few lines to make the hair — or *perruque* — of any Classical partisan of "noble style" bristle with horror.

Revitalizing the language of poetry meant taking syntactic as well as lexical liberties with accepted practice. The colloquial syntax of many poems is well suited to their nature as "causeries," as for example in "Italie," which begins as though in the middle of a conversation: "Et pourtant le bonheur m'aurait été facile!" ("And yet it would have been so easy for me to be happy!"). The interrogative phrase interjected in the course of a sentence — "Mais dans la plaine, quoi? des jachères pierreuses" ("La Plaine"); "Bien des fois, n'est-ce pas? l'enthousiasme amer" ("A David statuaire") — foreshadows the *syntaxe familière* of Verlaine. The noble alexandrine itself is made to serve the purpose of this *prosaïsme voulu,* for Sainte-Beuve, like most of his Romantic colleagues, exacted as the price of remaining within a more or less regular prosody the right to take great liberties with this traditional meter, using it, so to speak, to subvert and humble, if not to democratize, itself. In his hands it becomes what Antoine calls "le vers prosé," an alexandrine without marked rhythm or pause, as in the line "Surtout j'aime ces deux dernières barcarolles," from the highly innovative "Causerie au bal," historically significant as Sainte-Beuve's first "élégie intime" or "causerie domestique" (Antoine, pp. 178–179).

But the problem remained of preventing this "commonplace reality" from becoming merely flat and banal, of transmuting it into true poetry. Here occurs, in Sainte-Beuve's *art poétique,* what might be called Delorme's equation: the more commonplace the material, the stricter the poetic form. "It is exactly in proportion as poetry approaches more closely to real life and lowly things," he cautioned, "that it must check itself with greater rigor," and seek safeguards "against the prosaic and the trivial" (*Pensée* VII). One major safeguard lay in the very use of regular rhymed verse, however numerous the liberties taken with it, for had he been more radical, Sainte-Beuve might have advocated *le vers libre* or *le poème en prose*. Instead, he reaffirmed the need to rhyme, in a virtuoso piece, "A la rime," reviving a difficult six line stanza form rarely used since Ronsard. He also renewed the sonnet, a highly disciplined form neglected (as he pointed out) by the other Romantics, those "swans and eagles" who might have broken their wings attempting to enter its cage, while poets like himself, "birds of less elevated flight and less wide expanse of wing," were at home there (*NL* III, 344).

There were many other means of redeeming the prosaic, advocated in theory though not always successfully practiced by Sainte-Beuve. By juxtaposing modern colloquial speech with archaic or neoclassical "noble" terms, he achieves a mixture of classicism and modernity that anticipates Baudelaire. No scene was too lowly for him not to attempt to ennoble it by alluding to the ancient classical poets. Imagery of course plays an essential role in the desired transfiguration of the commonplace. When an image serves as the outward sign of an inner reality, especially when it is repeated often enough to be associated with that reality — the child-dreamer who disturbs the calm surface of the waters to reveal terrifying depths beneath; the blighted tree; *les rayons jaunes* — it becomes a symbol. The poet is he who gives concrete form to this "inward other world"; it is the poet who has been gifted with "the key to symbols and the understanding of figures" (*Pensée* XX).

This gift in turn is part of the poet's power as a painter in words. Delorme, as we noted earlier, was a *paysagiste* of a new kind, specializing in "small-scale landscapes" (*Poésies* I, 25) — above all, those urban landscapes viewed from his favorite perspective of the *quartier Montrouge*. Many years later Sainte-Beuve claimed that the paintings of Théodore Rousseau and Corot which he saw in the Salon of 1857 had been anticipated in spirit thirty years earlier by his ill-fated poet (*PM* 259); and in a letter to Théophile Gautier of 1859 he called Delorme the "Potterley of poetry," after an obscure young French "peintre-coloriste" (*B* XI, 307). The extensive use of color, the search for *le pittoresque,* characteristic of some of his Romantic colleagues, were not to his taste, however. Instead he favored a technique of allusiveness that both harked back to the Classical *je ne sais quoi* and pointed ahead to the suggestiveness of the Symbolists (*Pensée* XX). "Indefinite, unexplained, vague words" that "hint at the thought" ("qui laissent deviner la pensée"), he argued, can often be more effective in poetry than precise ones that state it explicitly (*Pensée* XV). Sainte-Beuve had no intention, as he explained in a letter to Hugo, of setting up a "school of intimate literature" opposed to that of visually descriptive poetry, "la poésie visible" (*B* I, 380). But there is no doubt that he was less interested in describing objects, scenes, or landscapes as ends in themselves than in establishing their relationship — their *correspondance,* as Baudelaire would put it — with the invisible world. This emphasis was in keeping with his role as an elegiac poet concerned above all with rendering "the inward truth of feeling" (*Poésies* II, 132).

VII   *The Rediscovery of a Poet*

Joseph Delorme was the object of a mixed critical reception when it first appeared, as we learn from consulting the appendix of critical judgments that Sainte-Beuve added to the 1863 *Poésies* (he used a similar procedure with the revised editions of *Volupté* and *Port-Royal*). Even a friendly critic such as Magnin, in *Le Globe,* though recognizing a poetic talent "full of frankness, vigor, and truth," was uneasy about the harshness and strangeness ("bizarrerie") of so much of the verse (I, 292). As Antoine observed with the benefit of historical perspective, a work so at odds with the rest of Romantic poetry, sacrificing to none of the current fashions, "neither Philhellenic nor Oriental nor Byronic nor Biblical in inspiration, as in Lamartine, Hugo or Vigny" (pp. lxi–lxii), must have seemed too eccentric to be entirely credible. *Les Consolations* fared better; in fact, it alone among Sainte-Beuve's verse collections enjoyed something approaching a real success, perhaps, as Antoine suggests, because (ironically enough) it was less innovative than the others and made more concessions to the continuing public taste for Lamartine. The *Pensées d'Août* met with disaster. Typical was the critic in *Le National* quoted by Bonnerot, who pleaded with the author not to give up writing verse, since he appeared to have a "poet's soul," but simply to refrain from publishing it (*B* II, 342–343).

Yet Sainte-Beuve had faith in all three — in all four, to be exact — of his works of poetry. "I await my judge," he confided to his notebook, "in the belief that I have not yet been judged as a poet." He clung to his dream of a modest "poetic glory," not unlike that enjoyed by Theocritus or Catullus among the ancients, or Goldsmith or Cowper among the moderns (*PM* 262). Without suggesting that his real stature as a poet approaches any of these or, even less, that he is a *grand poète méconnu,* one must recognize that his faith was justified: posterity has indeed shown more esteem than most of his contemporaries for his achievement as a poet.

His influence as a poet upon other poets, as distinct from the rediscovery of his work by critics and the public, a much slower process, began almost with *Joseph Delorme,* which, according to Antoine, launched two fashions in poetry: "la poésie intime" and "la Muse phtisique" or "tubercular Muse" (p. ci). Both Hugo and Lamartine learned much about "la poésie intime" from their less gifted fellow poet, the first in *Feuilles d'automne* (1831) and the second in *Jocelyn* (1836). As the century progressed the younger poets developed almost a kind of underground cult for "l'oncle Beuve," as Gautier affectionately called him. Théodore de Banville dedicated his *Odelettes* (1856) to him in such laudatory terms that Champfleury was provoked to quip that Sainte-Beuve had become "the god of poetry," that *Volupté* had assumed "biblical proportions," and that suddenly "a Sainte-Beuve camp" had been formed (quoted in Antoine, p. cxxii).

Among these younger poets proud to trace their ancestry to Sainte-Beuve were two whose fame would eventually far outstrip his own: Baudelaire and Verlaine. The first remained all his life "an incorrigible admirer of Sainte-Beuve the poet and novelist" (Antoine, p. cxi). In a touching bit of testimony confirming the sincerity and durability of his cult for Sainte-Beuve, Troubat relates how Baudelaire, whom he visited in a nursing home only six months before his death, showed him "everything he loved: the poems of Sainte-Beuve, the works of Edgar Poe in English; a little book on Goya; and, in the garden of the home, a large exotic plant" (Antoine, p. cxi). A deep affinity existed between the two poets which Albert Thibaudet has summarized as consisting of at least four basic elements: an inner feeling for Christianity; critical intelligence; understanding for the secret life of a great capital, in this case Paris; and the desire to make prose an ally of verse.[12] Verlaine's reasons for esteeming Sainte-Beuve the poet were similar to Baudelaire's, with special emphasis on the poeticizing of conversational syntax. In a letter of 1865 to Sainte-Beuve he ranked *Joseph Delorme,* "for its melancholy intensity and power of expression, infinitely above Lamartinian and other kinds of jeremiads [*lamentations*]" (*B* XIV, 448). While pleased to learn this, Sainte-Beuve rose to the defense of Lamartine, reminding his young admirer what a powerful revelation the *Méditations* had been to *his* generation of poets, thirty-five years earlier, on the dreary neo-Classical scene.

The rediscovery of Sainte-Beuve's poetry by the critics took much longer, largely because his own success as a critic over-shadowed the rest of his production. In 1861 Charles Asselineau, the friend and first biographer of Baudelaire, pointed the way to the needed reassessment by reminding his contemporaries that Sainte-Beuve was "at once poet, novelist, and critic," and by sug-gesting that the "real" Sainte-Beuve might in fact be the poet, "the first-born, Joseph Delorme," whom they had lost sight of because the critic's voice had prevailed for so long over the poet's (*B* XII, 126). But rehabilitation began in earnest only after Sainte-Beuve's death. Anatole France in an essay of 1879 argued that Sainte-Beuve was a poet to reckon with despite his flaws. Ten years later Charles Morice observed that *Joseph Delorme,* jeered at for its eccentricity in the 1830s, was finally ready to be understood in the 1880s, and Paul Bourget, in 1904, went so far as to claim that Sainte-Beuve was "un grand poète," though of a single season only. His reputa-tion received a significant boost between 1910 and 1930 when André Barre and René Lalou showed in how many ways he had been a precursor of the Symbolists, and John Charpentier how "modern" were his use of analysis within the lyric poem and his freedom from the theatrical gestures that often marred the "con-fessional" poetry of the other Romantics.[13]

From this chapter in literary history, which I have sketched in broadest outline, one might be tempted to draw a moral unflatter-ing to Sainte-Beuve: that his influence was in inverse proportion to his merits as a poet. Ferdinand Brunetière indeed cited his case as proof that the poets "who found a school are those more produc-tive of ideas than of masterpieces, and full of excellent intentions that they are unable to carry out successfully." "The incomplete artist is choice game for more powerful animals," quipped Jacques Vier, citing a long list of poets who "redid" some aspect or other of Sainte-Beuve's poetry. He was certainly "l'artiste incomplet" and probably wrote more bad poetry than any other poet still worth reading. A catalogue of his faults would have to include his fre-quent lack of ear (few of his lines are musical and some are down-right cacophonous), his abuse of neoclassical rhetoric ("Too many *luths, lyres, harpes,* and *Jéhovahs,*" complained Baudelaire, "you

were the man to destroy all that''), a syntax that is sometimes confused, and an imagery that is often awkward or labored. Much of
his verse gives the painful impression of having been assembled, as
a recent critic put it, ''drop by drop.''[14]

T.S. Eliot once described Samuel Johnson as ''a secondary poet
at the end of a movement which had been initiated by greater poets
than he.''[15] Sainte-Beuve was a secondary poet at the beginning of a
movement that he helped initiate and that produced greater poets
than he. Even secondary poets, however, have their merits. The
fairest judgment of Sainte-Beuve's poetry was probably Vigny's:
''By applying his mind, he has written some excellent verse without
being a poet by instinct.''[16] His boldness and originality in both
content and form still commend him to our attention. But there is
little doubt that his appeal will continue to be to a very narrow
circle of readers, perhaps of somewhat perverse taste, who are willing to join Baudelaire in confessing him to be their weakness —
''Sainte-Beuve, c'est mon vice'' (quoted in Antoine, p. cviii).
Patience and good will are needed to do justice to his poetry, as
they are needed to discover the strange beauties of that other creation of the ''incomplete artist,'' his novel *Volupté.*

CHAPTER 3

A Singular Novel and Other Fiction

IN 1831, Sainte-Beuve informed his friend Victor Pavie of a "novel of the heart" ("un roman de coeur") that he was planning to write and that he approached with apprehension, not because he considered himself lacking in aptitude for the genre but because he was reluctant to divulge the secrets of his private life. Should he not rather confide the "oppressive feelings" that weighed upon him to poems that, for the time being at least, would not see the light? (*B* I, 266 — Bonnerot believes this to be a reference to the manuscript of *Livre d'amour*).

The 1830s were years of prolonged crisis in Sainte-Beuve's "moral life," years in which he continued "to suffer, to feel constricted, to lead a dual existence [*se dédoubler*]" (*Poésies* II, 126). *Une vie morale,* incidentally, was the title that he originally proposed for the novel that was to become *Volupté* (*B* I, 311). Novel, verse, and even criticism were closely intertwined at this point in his career; all provided him with an outlet for expressing his intimate feelings in various forms of disguise. Lyric poetry, he observed to Hugo, was the kind of poetry he preferred writing, and, above all, "le genre rêveur, personnel, l'élégie ou le roman d'analyse" (*Poésies* II, 7) — a remark that shows how he viewed the novel itself as a form of poetry. The "subtle matter" of his spiritual life, as he called it (II, 126), links his verse with his fiction and links both in turn with his critical portraits, conceived, as we shall see, as a form of prose elegy designed to compensate for his gradual abandonment of the writing of verse.

Volupté was, in his words, "a fairly peculiar book" ("un livre assez singulier" [*B* X, 477]). It is also "singular" in both senses of the word in English: his only novel as well as one that resembles no

other. The major part of this chapter will be devoted to a discussion
of this strange work. In the remaining portion we shall glance at a
handful of finished and unfinished short stories from his pen, as
well as his project for a second novel to be entitled *Ambition*.

I *Memory and Imagination*

A summary of the plot of *Volupté* will assist the reader in following my subsequent analysis of the work.

The story, set for the most part in Brittany and Paris during the
Napoleonic Empire, takes the form of a spiritual autobiography
written by a Breton priest, Amaury, as he sails from Europe to
America to resume his career as a missionary. By addressing his
manuscript to a young friend, he hopes to cure him of a spiritual
disease remarkably like that from which he believes himself to have
recovered: the *volupté* of the title. Orphaned of both parents while
a child and brought up by an uncle, young Amaury rejects the
possibility of marriage to the virtuous Amélie de Liniers in order to
pursue adventure and ambition — and a deeper love — in the circle
of the Marquis de Couaën and his young wife, Lucy, who reside in
a mysterious château near a remote, hidden part of the Breton
coast. When the marquis, who is engaged in a royalist conspiracy to
overthrow the emperor, goes to Paris with his wife and two small
children, Amaury accompanies them. There they are sheltered in
the little convent of the Feuillantines by the venerable aunt of the
marquis, Madame de Cursy, a former mother superior. Their first
stay in Paris is brief, but hardly have they returned to Couaën when
Amaury, called from their side momentarily to his uncle's deathbed, learns the news of the marquis' arrest and removal to Paris for
imprisonment.

Once again in Paris, Lucy stays at the convent, seeking her husband's release, while Amaury settles in a nearby hotel and begins
his strange dual existence: by night secretly frequenting prostitutes
and by day engaging in long walks and conversations with the Mar-
quise de Couaën in whom he places his hope of a purely spiritual
love that will free him from the bondage of sensuality and lead to
his salvation. His life is further complicated by his attempts to serve
another anti-Napoleonic conspirator, General Georges, and by his
affair with a friend of Lucy's, the semi-estranged wife of a government official, Madame R. His platonic relationship with Lucy

having grown ever more ambiguous, his passion for Madame R. having remained unfulfilled, and his attempts to latch on to someone with a political future having been thwarted, Amaury comes to realize the futility of his existence. This sense of void, reinforced by his discovery of the world of divine grace in the works of the philosopher Saint-Martin, the Jesuit preacher Bourdaloue, and the pious laymen (*les solitaires*) of Port-Royal, especially the saintly physician M. Hamon (like the critic who created him, Amaury is a voracious reader), prepares the way for his return to the Catholic faith. In this "conversion," the living examples of Madame de Cursy and of a saintly ecclesiastic are also instrumental. Instead of following the marquis and his wife into exile at Blois, Amaury enters a seminary.

Ordained as a priest and paying a final visit to his native Brittany before leaving Europe, he is surprised to find that the marquis and his wife, who is gravely ill, have returned to Couaën from Blois. The climactic scene of the novel is reached when Amaury is called upon to administer the last rites to the dying Lucy. Some years later the ship bearing him to America is wrecked off the coast of Portugal. Having vowed, if he escaped alive, to record his experience as a salutary example to his young friend before it is too late, he begins his manuscript-confession, which, once his journey to America is resumed, he completes within sight of the New World. It is this manuscript that his "editor," Sainte-Beuve, resorting to the device he had used for *Joseph Delorme,* now reveals to the public.

That Sainte-Beuve drew heavily on autobiographical elements in composing *Volupté* is obvious from this summary of the plot. The main theme, the erosion of will and character that *volupté* produces and that can be counteracted only by recourse to true (i.e., divine) love, is based on the disorder he experienced in his own moral life, although Amaury's solution to the problem was not his own. The story itself merely transposes to the plane of fiction the real-life drama, or *roman vécu* as the French put it, of his relations with Victor and Adèle Hugo. It was Sainte-Beuve's belief that most sensitive people whose youth has been the scene of strong emotions and who have the courage to record their experience faithfully could, with a minimum of inventiveness, produce at least one good novel. Such a novel, he hastened to add, might well be their first *and* last, since the distance was infinite from this kind of composition to the "creative, magic gift" of true novelists such as Le Sage

or Prévost, Fielding or Scott, who could invent "a variety of situations," "a whole world of characters," to embody their feelings
(*PC* I, 483–484).

In his comments on *Volupté* Sainte-Beuve tended to minimize the
fictional or novelistic aspects of the book and to stress what he
called its "reality" and "truth." To a clerical correspondent he
wrote that *Volupté* was "not exactly a novel," since it was drawn
largely from his observation and experience; even the episode of
Amaury's training for the priesthood, although necessarily
"invented," was based on scrupulously exact information about
seminary life furnished to him by the Abbé Lacordaire (*B* XIII,
69).[1] In a similar vein he claimed that Balzac's attempt to "redo
Volupté" in *Le Lys dans la vallée* was doomed to failure because
Balzac lacked the experience to create the required "moral atmosphere," whereas in his own novel, "which is hardly a novel" ("qui
est très peu un roman"), he had painted from real-life characters
and situations, his objective having been, despite certain "trans-
formations," to remain "strictly credible."[2] His reason for not
continuing to write novels, if we are to believe an entry that occurs
more than once in his journal, was that writing a novel had been for
him "merely an indirect way of loving and of saying so" (*PM*
44–45, 230).

At this point one may be tempted to conclude that *Volupté* is not
really fiction at all but a form of autobiography mixed with history.
But the temptation should be resisted. By playing down the novelistic features of the book, its author may have done an injustice to
the modest but nevertheless real power of imagination that he
possessed. Whatever his intentions concerning it, the resulting
novel has a scope and interest far surpassing those of a lover's
message to Adèle Hugo disguised as fiction. The limited personal
experience serving as its raw material has been enlarged into a number of themes that could hardly be more universal in meaning:
ambition, the role of the "great man" in the making of history,
fame and obscurity, the reality of the self, memory, the conflict
between flesh and spirit, between human and divine love, the
psychology of conversion, change and changelessness in human
nature. If the novelist is one who succeeds in telling his story so that
it becomes our story, *Volupté* is a better novel than most of its
critics, obsessed with the question of its factual accuracy as auto-

biography and indifferent or blind to its artistic nature, have been willing to grant.

To begin with, the "transpositions" of observed and remembered reality, as Sainte-Beuve called them, are much more profound than his recipe for a good novel of one's youth, referred to earlier, would lead us to expect. Their effect is to alter the literal or surface truth of "fact" in the interests of a deeper kind of truth related to the author's fears, wishes, hopes, and ideals, to what *might have been* as distinct from what was. The importance of these alterations as a system of disguises is certainly not negligible; but it is surpassed by their significance as fictional devices enabling the author to interpret his experience and to reveal it to us in its widest import. Here Victor Hugo's astute remark on *Volupté* in his welcoming speech to Sainte-Beuve at the French Academy is especially relevant: "You have succeeded in probing into new areas of what is possible in life" ("Vous avez sondé des côtés inconnus de la vie possible").[3] To say this was to recognize that the author of *Volupté* was not entirely lacking in the imagination of a novelist.

The most significant transpositions occurring in the work are, in ascending order of importance, those related to place, time, and characters. Sainte-Beuve's childhood and early education in Picardy became Amaury's in Brittany, and the genesis of his love for Adèle Hugo, in Paris, is transferred to the imaginary Château de Couaën. Why Brittany? For several reasons, one may presume: its greater poetic aura, and especially its association with Chateaubriand's *René* (Amaury reports his discovery of this work in words taken verbatim from Sainte-Beuve's own journal), its stronger religious traditions (the link with Lamennais, a Breton, may have influenced the author here), its history of royalist conspiracies, to lend credibility to the "second plot" dealing with politics, and its affinity, as a Celtic land, with the native Ireland of Madame de Couaën.

The transfer in time, roughly thirty years into the past, is even more significant. What is especially interesting about it, what may be rare in the history of the novel, is the author's projecting into the past an experience (his love affair with Adèle Hugo) that he was in the process of undergoing even as he wrote his novel. "When enjoying a keen happiness," noted Amaury, "I needed, in order to make it complete, to imagine that it had already fled far from my grasp, that one day I would return to the places associated with it and find a delightful kind of sadness in experiencing this happiness in the form of memory" (*Volupté* 181). Amaury's impatience for his present emotion to become a thing of the past, in order that he might better savor it as memory, was also his creator's, who used the resources of fiction in at least three ways to satisfy this need: by having the narrator himself record his experience twenty years after its occurrence, by projecting the whole story at least one generation back in time, and, most curiously of all, by imagining an "end" to this chapter in his life before it had in fact ended.

The greatest liberties that the author took with his *expérience vécue* were in the handling of the major characters. To attempt to find a "key" to these, as some critics have done, is an interesting but ultimately futile and misleading exercise. Most of the portraits, to begin with, are composite in nature, and almost all of them, not merely the hero's, contain traits of Sainte-Beuve himself, including even the melancholy, skeptical, and witty Madame R., the least angelic and most believable of Amaury's three loves, for whom no "model" has yet been found. Proponents of the *roman à clef* approach not only imply that Sainte-Beuve was incapable of even partial invention but also tend to overlook the degree of imagination required in the very creation of a composite portrait.

Lucy de Couaën is primarily Adèle Hugo elevated to the rank of the nobility and provided with more exotic antecedents, as well as with a Christian name linking her with Dante's Lucia, the symbol of hope. Infinitely more important than these details, however, is the fact that Lucy's love for Amaury, unlike Adèle's for Sainte-Beuve, is never physically consummated — an ennobling change from which Balzac seems to have taken a hint, in *Le Lys dans la vallée,* by sublimating Félix de Vandenesse's passion for Madame de Mortsauf (in "real life" Balzac's first mistress, Laure de Berny).

The Marquis de Couaën is based largely on Victor Hugo and Lamennais, and represents all the proud, ambitious men, believers in the exceptional individual's role in shaping history, to whom Sainte-Beuve–Amaury, in this "drama of friendship and pride," seemed destined to play the role of *âme seconde.*[4] From the leader of a literary movement (a "conspiracy" against Classicism?), Hugo has become a political conspirator; the young, handsome, successful demigod has been transformed into a far from attractive man, ten years older than his wife, and a "failure." His frustrated political ambition is but one of the many variations in the novel on the theme of *refoulement* — repressed political ambition, repressed physical desire, repressed desire for fame. It is the marquis, rather than the more *voluptueux* Amaury, who serves as the main vehicle for Sainte-Beuve's own "ambition rentrée" (Poux, I, xxxiii). Despite the sharp differences between the marquis and Amaury, however, they finally embrace, after the death of Lucy, in a gesture of reconciliation — a scene that was never to occur in the lives of the two writers.

To assume that Sainte-Beuve's humbling of Hugo in the character of the Marquis de Couaën was the product of envy or of the desire to denigrate would be a misreading of the novel, for the harsh and proud conspirator gradually wins the reader's sympathy and emerges in the end as a figure of considerable tragic stature.

Imagination plays no less a part in the creation of Amaury than in that of the other major characters. To limit ourselves here to perhaps the most important point, the *dénouement,* why did the author imagine a resolution of Amaury's spiritual drama so different from his own experience? His friend Ulric Guttinguer's conversion (in part brought about by the reading of Sainte-Beuve's own poetry!) may have influenced him, as well as the priestly example of Lamennais, whose exhortations to Sainte-Beuve are echoed in those of Amaury to his young friend. From the point of view of plot, what more dramatic way to bring the whole story to a climax than in the great *scène à faire* in which the priest-protagonist hears the confession of the woman who had been, if we may use the term, his spiritual mistress? There is, however, a deeper significance to be found in Sainte-Beuve's projection of himself into the role of priest, as Pierre Poux has observed. The priest Amaury corresponds to the priest in Sainte-Beuve himself, more precisely, to the moralist who was inseparable in him from the critic — the moralist not, of course, in the sense of the reformer and healer of human nature but in the sense of its observer and portrayer. In Amaury's final affirmation that man's passions remain basically the same whatever form of society he may live in, and in his recognition that the cause to which he could most successfully contribute lay in this "eternally arable field" of human nature (p. 352), Poux was right to discern the voice of Sainte-Beuve himself, "assuming consciousness of his real vocation, which was to be a moralist" (II, 368).

In one of his essays on the Abbé Prévost, Sainte-Beuve observed that those who, like this eighteenth century novelist, "combine a tender soul and lively imagination with a weak character" (he probably intended to include himself among them) should be judged by their writings rather than by their lives. For, he reasoned, "if our life reveals only too well what we have become, our writings show us at least as we would have wished to be."[5] This surprisingly Proustian observation on the relation between life and work applies to Sainte-Beuve more than one might suspect. Throughout his works, and no less in his criticism than in his poetry and fiction, runs the motif of an ideal image of himself, "tel du moins qu'il aurait voulu être." As critic, biographer, and historian, he was to some extent free — in his choice of materials and in his manner of arranging them — to "transpose" reality, and of this relative freedom, as we shall see, he took full advantage. But it was in the novel that this freedom was greatest. Here he could, and did, round out reality and transform it in such a manner that "the author alone, the creator of the characters" (to apply to *Volupté* a remark he once made about Madame de Staël's fiction), "would be able to point out the sinuous, hidden demarcation line dividing invention from memory."[6]

II *Aspects of Fictional Technique*

The novel consists of twenty-five chapters divided into two approximately equal parts. The narrator tells his story in largely chronological order, with occasional flashbacks to provide additional insight into the events being described. At the beginning of Part II he pauses to reveal for the first time his present circumstances and the turn of events that has led him to write his confession. Part I culminates with a farewell banquet for the marquis and his wife about to depart for Blois, and Part II with the scene of the last rites. Each of these climactic scenes also serves as a kind of "coda" for its respective part.

Of the two related plots, the main one concerns Amaury's emotional and spiritual life, and the subordinate one his involvement in political intrigue. These correspond to the two worlds that begin to open up to him with his discovery of the Château de Couaën, the world of love ("le monde intérieur"), and the world of ambition ("le monde du dehors") (*Volupté* 98). According to a more or less rhythmical pattern, these two plots alternate in occupying the foreground, and occasionally they coincide.

The stress on "psychological" action was an essential feature of the *roman confession* or *roman intime* upon whose traditions Sainte-Beuve drew heavily, as was also the choice of aristocratic characters of independent means able to spend much of their time exploring their feelings. "I have no adventures to relate to you," remarked Amaury to his friend (87), but instead, a life largely devoid of "events," at least visible events. Yet the long periods of introspection are frequently interrupted by flurries of activity. What is relatively new in the "action" of *Volupté* is the emphasis not so much on the hero's inaction as on his endless, ill-directed bursts of activity amounting to a kind of pseudoaction — *allées et venues,* flights and returns, abortive attempts to succeed as lover, conspirator, soldier.

The episodic nature of the narrative, together with the many abstract, moralizing passages, has led some critics to feel that the novel lacks unity as well as dramatic power.[7] Only on a second reading, perhaps, may one become aware that the apparent disorderliness is due less to Sainte-Beuve's inexperience or clumsiness as a novelist than to his calculated effort — highly original in itself — to convey the aimlessness of his hero *without* sacrificing coherence and intensity. Some degree of unity is conferred on the action simply by the fact that it concerns the rise and fall of a central protagonist as told from a single viewpoint, his own. But the author is also skillful in unifying his materials thematically. Pierre Poux notes three major themes, "ambition, love, and faith" (I, xxii), and Molho, in a variation on this in the introduction to his edition of *Volupté,* refers to "the three faces" assumed by the malady from which the hero suffers, namely *volupté, curiosité,* and *ambition* (*Volupté,* 20). To which I would add that the theme of love is really the theme of "three loves," three women, the most important of whom is "the sanctifying friend," Madame de Couaën, to the thought of whom Amaury constantly returns in the midst of his contradictions and confusions, "une pensée fidèle ... se retrouvant en chaque point" (*Volupté* 173). (Madame Arnoux will play a similar role for Frédéric Moreau in Flaubert's *L'Education sentimentale.*)

Despite the slow, sometimes laborious pace of the novel (Sainte-Beuve the moralist is not to be hurried in recounting every phase, every nuance of his hero's spiritual itinerary), it is not without a certain dramatic impact. From the outset the reader's curiosity is aroused as to what brought Amaury to his present situation, and as we are drawn further and further into the labyrinth of his experience the suspense increases. There is dramatic tension in the very conflict between flesh and spirit, the very *dédoublement* into which the disorder of *volupté* plunges him. The many passages devoted to analyzing and sermonizing, although in character (the narrator is after all a priest), tend to detract from the tension, to be sure; but they yield at strategic points to scenes of considerable dramatic force.

Most of the major characters are presented as mysteries to be unraveled. Direct dialogue passages of any length are rare, but conversations, especially on the subject of love, religion, and politics, play a decisive role in the action. By paraphrasing these, the narrator allows us to hear the voices of characters other than himself, though filtered through his memory. Monologues, resembling at times bel canto arias, are frequent. Speech, in this novel of *refoulement,* is used as much to hide as to reveal the truth. This is especially true of the narrator, who seems incapable of forthright utterance (it takes the blunt peasant conspirator, Georges, to tell him that he is in love with Madame de Couaën), and of Madame de Couaën herself, who attempts to hide her growing passion for Amaury and her jealousy of Mme R. by means of interesting subterfuges. Silences, or long-delayed responses, account for some of the most moving scenes. The physical reality of the characters and of the setting is seldom described directly or at length, but must be pieced together from suggestive details presented as though in passing — an approach in keeping with the tradition of the *roman intime.*

Unlike that type of novel, however, which usually had few characters, *Volupté* is peopled with a large cast of supporting roles. (Compare the loving attention given by Sainte-Beuve to secondary figures in his literary criticism.) Some of these, by virtue of the fact that Amaury is constantly seeking guides and mentors to help him, have a decisive influence on the course of the action. George Sand, in a judgment quoted in the Appendix, praised the author for "neglecting no role," however minor, and for the originality in particular of his portrayal of the Couaën children, Arthur and Lucy (*Volupté* 364–365), for children had rarely been encountered in French novels of any kind before this.

Without being a "regional" novel in the usual sense of the term,

Volupté is very much a novel of place, and it is the feeling for place as much as anything else that confers upon Amaury's confession the degree of concrete reality that we expect to find in works of fiction. The scenes, whether the farm at Gastine, the Château de Couaën, the Breton heath and seacoast, or the various *quartiers de Paris,* certainly lack "local color." Like most of the descriptive passages, they are short on what Hytier calls "matérialité" (p. 75). What gives them their power — the power, like so much else in the novel, of suggestion — is their combination of *le vague* and *le précis;* here the novelist is close to the "poetics" recommended by Joseph Delorme in his *Pensée* XV. The secret lay in providing just enough visual detail to stimulate the reader's imagination.

Places play an essential role in Amaury's spiritual drama. "Ame mobile et peu ancrée" (*Volupté* 217), he is forever on the move, forever given to flights and *déplacements.* His orphan's longing for a home (thus the surrogate family of the Couaëns) is contradicted by his horror of settling down. His adopted family is soon uprooted and forced into exile. The theme of flight is expressed through continual changes of scene, at times reaching dizzying proportions. Places also become like characters in conflict with one another. The idyllic charm of Amélie's La Gastine and the greater enchantment of Couaën are opposed to the corruptions of Paris, whose atmosphere progressively erodes the vision of spiritual love originating in the Edenlike *terre de Couaën.* All three places, in turn, as places of memory for the narrator, enter into conflict with his resolve to look only to the future as a man of God; the evoking of them in his imagination becomes a major source of temptation for him to fall back into earthly attachments, by indulging in what one of his spiritual guides (the author of the *Imitation of Christ*) called "the imagination of places [*Imaginatio locorum*]" (*Volupté* 297).

The various *décors* in *Volupté* are thus both settings for the action and forces involved in the action. They provide motifs associated with certain characters as well as possessing their own symbolic meanings.[8]

One of the most curious features of the novel is the way in which the narrator moves back and forth from real scenes — real paths (*sentiers, chemins, allées*), real landscapes and seascapes — to metaphorical ones, the paths of salvation or perdition, the stormy or calm seas of the soul's voyage toward God. The symbolic role assigned to places is merely part of the extensive use of figurative

language in *Volupté,* which must be one of the most densely metaphorical novels in existence. Small wonder that George Sand
referred to it as "le poème" (*Volupté* 364)! The dominant images
are those of light and shadow, of roads and paths, and most important of all, as Yves Le Hir observed, of water.[9] Some serve as
motifs for certain characters, for example, the lamp for Madame
de Couaën, or the dual image (a "grande image allégorique," the
narrator calls it) in which Madame de Couaën and her husband are
represented respectively as a calm lake and the rock dominating it,
which challenge the navigator Amaury to explore their mysteries
(*Volupté* 130–131).

Not content to seek figurative meaning in characters and
settings, Sainte-Beuve also extends it to crucial episodes and scenes.
The farewell banquet (Ch. XIV) becomes "an eloquent symbol" of
his own youth drawing to an end, as well as a "reflection" of the
supper at Emmaüs (the martyred marquis corresponds to Christ,
the guests number twelve). The striking episode in the park at
Auteuil where Amaury and Madame R. run in vain to the top of a
hillock to catch the last rays of the sun (Ch. XVI) becomes the
"emblème" (i.e., symbol) of their abortive attempt at love. Almost
all the scenes at Couaën have this figurative quality. From the
moment early in the narrative when Amaury on horseback nego-
tiates the almost impassable road leading to Couaën, like some
modern *chevalier* in quest of a holy grail, it is clear that his story
will have otherworldly implications. The whole novel of this man
without a home and without a country is in fact "une grande image
allégorique," a modern "pilgrim's progress," a modern allegory of
man's estrangement and exile from God.

III *A Flawed Masterpiece*

It was hardly to be expected that a novel of such subtlety of
subject matter and style would be a popular success, despite its
alluring title. Technically it was not exactly a failure, however, since
it enjoyed a certain *succès d'estime.* A sixth edition appeared in
1869, attesting to this modest success, and in it Sainte-Beuve published an Appendix containing critical opinions of the novel, both
negative and positive, from selected private and public sources.
Criticism of *Volupté,* from his own time to ours, has for the most
part focused on three problem areas: its style, the credibility of its
hero and action, and its religious significance.

From the beginning critics recognized that the language of the novel departed radically from established traditions of French prose, but were unable to decide whether the style deserved condemnation for its ponderous obscurity or praise for its originality. Prolixity or *bavardage* is certainly one of its most disconcerting features; in other words, lack of vigor and sharpness. George Sand complained of the excess of imagery (*Volupté* 366), and Balzac (not among the critics quoted in the Appendix), while admitting that there were "sublime things" in the "muddle [*le fouillis*]" of the style, sympathized with readers obliged to labor at extracting them from the tangled growth.[10] In our own time a much more impartial critic than Balzac, Jean Hytier, compared the style to a tapestry lacking in clarity and intensity of design and suffused with greyness — *la grisaille* (p. 46).

Though not unfair, such criticisms reveal only one side of the coin. The aristocrat soldier-esthetician, La Tour du Pin, whose views are probably the most perceptive of those quoted in the Appendix, foreshadowed in 1834 the more favorable approach that a later generation of readers formed on Symbolist poetry would take to this novel. He defended its vagueness and its tendency to communicate through "association d'idées, d'images et surtout d'impressions," rather than through direct statement, as the means best suited to touch the individual reader's feelings (*Volupté* 373). Had the term existed he would undoubtedly have called this style *symboliste* or *impressionniste*. He was obviously the first in a long line of "incorrigible lovers" of *Volupté*, to borrow a phrase from the most incorrigible of all, Baudelaire, who found little to quarrel with in "les longs enlacements des phrases symboliques" of this "livre voluptueux."[11] As for the famous "spineless sentence" ("la phrase molle"), with its meandering profusion of subordinate and parenthetical clauses, its deliberate interruption of the syntactic flow, and its avoidance of the Classical "periodical sentence" marked by restraint and balance, some critics have defended it as an original creation perfectly suited to the narrator and his subject matter.[12] *Felix culpa,* one might say: the indecisive style, which might have been a flaw in the author of a third person narrative, becomes a virtue in a confession by the weak-willed Amaury. Without denying the fact that the author of *Volupté* sometimes writes badly, one could well argue, as Bellessort has done, that the very

"corruption" of the style "is fully in harmony with the corruption
of the heart revealing itself to us" (p. 122).

Few critics have questioned the power of observation and analysis that the author applied to the moral paralysis of his protagonist,
whose affliction he saw as that not merely of an isolated individual
but of a whole generation. But are Amaury's conversion and
ordination credible, *vraisemblables?* A distinction should be made
between the former, which is convincingly enough prepared and
motivated, and the latter, which one suspects is arranged primarily
to make possible the spectacular scene of the last rites. But with the
credibility of the *dénouement* as with the style of the narrative, we
need to remind ourselves once again who is telling the story. If the
author had intended his narrator to end up as a sincerely repentant
sinner, then the novel might be unconvincing. However, it is clear
from the text, if not from the author's Preface, that the very
manner in which the priest relates his confession raises serious
doubts as to the depth of his supposed change of heart. Not only
does he tend to qualify his sinfulness but he appears less concerned
with saving his young friend's soul than with transmitting to him
the memory of his beloved Couaën, less ready to repent the sin of
loving another man's wife than to regret his lack of success in finding a real "Beatrice." (George Sand, objecting to the "cure by
cloister and priestly vow," suggested shrewdly that with a little
more perseverance and luck the hero might have carried off his
experiment in *l'amour pur* [*Volupté* 365].)

The very pleasure he savors in telling his story, the complicity of
his imagination in the very sin he is attempting to eradicate, do
more than anything else to undermine the reality of his repentance.
"Every novel more or less contradicts strict Christianity," noted
Sainte-Beuve on the subject of Guttinguer's *Arthur,* "for every
novel contains and cherishes some ideal either of happiness or of
sorrow on earth" (*PC* II, 411). His own novel, at least, seems to
illustrate his point.

The *dénouement* of *Volupté* is thus not false but ambiguous, and
deliberately so, like the whole story of which it is part. "Un livre à
deux fins," objected Lamartine, that is, "with two endings or pur-
poses" (*Volupté* 362), his implication being that Amaury ended up
with the best of both worlds — God and the memory of Madame de
Couaën. But the ambiguity that he considered a failing in the book
may in fact be its greatest merit. Molho put the matter most suc-

cinctly: "Is Amaury using 'pure love' to reach God or God to attain his goal as a lover?" The answer, if there is one, he wisely concluded, is hidden in the blurred atmosphere ("le flou") that remains one of the novel's chief attractions (22).

Volupté, to conclude our assessment of it, should be recognized as a bonafide novel, even though the moralist and critic occasionally overshadow the novelist in the course of its pages, and even though it was "the novel of a man who was not a novelist" (Poux, I, xviii). It belongs to a distinct tradition, that of the semiautobiographical *roman personnel,* often the creation of "authors who were not novelists." The plot in fact derives in part from one such precursor, Madame de Krüdener, whose *Valérie* (1803) the bookish hero at one point even advises Madame de Couaën to read as a signal of his intentions! But Sainte-Beuve's novel far surpassed the others in originality of style and form, in the importance attached to historical context, and in richness of poetic imagery and moral reflection. Yet once again, as in his poetry, the "incomplete artist" was less successful in creating his own masterpiece than in inspiring the masterpieces of others who took up the same or a similar theme after him: Balzac in *Le Lys dans la vallée;* Flaubert in *L'Education sentimentale,* written, he declared, "in part for Sainte-Beuve."[13] What a bold experiment Flaubert must have found in this attempt to render monotony and futility in fiction, in the "blank pages" and "empty days," "the immense intervals leading up to nothing," that Amaury describes as features of his adventureless story (*Volupté* 87) and that so clearly anticipate the *grisaille* of Frédéric Moreau's unheroic existence![14] "The most remarkable of failed novels" (Bellessort, p. 98), "a bungled masterpiece" (Hytier, p. 42), *Volupté* remains, with all its imperfections, far more interesting than many a "successful" novel whose author possessed greater technical skill.

IV   *Other Attempts at Fiction*

Toward 1830, just prior to undertaking *Volupté,* Sainte-Beuve had tried his hand at collaborating with Guttinguer on a "grand roman poétique" based on his friend's stormy and painful love affair with the coquettish Rosalie. The novel, to be called *Arthur,* was to consist of a first, "worldly" part written by Sainte-Beuve and a second, religious part by Guttinguer, recounting Arthur's conversion, which corresponded to his own. The thirty-two chapters completed by Sainte-Beuve are written in a spare, analytical style which bears a much greater resemblance to that of certain eighteenth century *romans intimes* than to the image-laden style of *Volupté.*[15]

In the years following the publication of *Volupté* Sainte-Beuve seems to have been especially interested in the short story form, both in verse (the "récit domestique et moral" of *Pensées d'Août*) and in prose. He planned but did not complete "une petite nouvelle" in verse, "L'Archiviste," to avenge his friend Victor Pavie's sufferings at the hands of a custodian of documents bent on frustrating his research at every turn (*B* III, 189), and also a short story in prose, "M. de Cerenville," based on a tragic love "triangle" about which he had learned during his stay in Lausanne (III, 305, 417–418). Of the stories conceived in the 1830s, only two were completed and published, both in the *Revue des deux mondes,* during his lifetime, "Madame de Pontivy" (1837) and "Christel" (1839).

The latter concerns the daughter of an impoverished invalid noblewoman in the Perche region of France who has been reduced to the humble circumstances of postmistress. The young woman falls in love with a local nobleman, Hervé, whose exchange of letters with a rival she is obliged to follow as part of her duties assisting her mother; by the time her love is finally made known to the young man and is returned, she dies of an unspecified illness. Rare among Sainte-Beuve's stories for having been "wholly invented" (so he claimed, *B* XIV, 397), this study in the psychology of the timid lover afraid of being scorned appears nevertheless to be a curious transposition of his own unsuccessful courtship of Frédérique Pelletier.[16] It is possible to agree with Maurice Regard in finding the story "touching," even though its plot is somewhat improbable.

A much more successful story is "Madame de Pontivy," a kind of prose sequel to *Livre d'amour.* In a footnote to the last poem in that collection, Sainte-Beuve admitted having written this story "to try to bring her [i.e., Adèle Hugo] back." A witty *nouvelle historique* set with precision in the Regency period of the early eighteenth century, it invents a purely worldly *dénouement* to their affair, as befitted the less "mystical" Sainte-Beuve of 1837: Monsieur de Murçay and Madame de Pontivy revive their expiring passion, he by acquiring greater "ardeur" and she by acquiring greater "subtilité." The theme — how to arrest the decline of love — belongs to the great tradition of the dramatized or fictionalized treatment of problematic aspects of love, "questions de coeur," that had produced so many fine works of French literature, especially in the Classical period.

In 1921 Troubat collected and published under the title of *Le Clou d'or (The Golden Nail)* the two stories just discussed, plus two other unfinished ones that had never been published, "Le Clou d'or" and "La Pendule."[17] "To possess, toward the age of thirty-five or forty, and if only once, a woman whom one has known for a long time and whom one has loved," observed Sainte-Beuve in his journal, "is what I call fixing the golden nail of friendship ("le clou d'or de l'amitié" [*PM* 151]). The metaphor has become famous. If he wrote "Madame de Pontivy" to win back Adèle, his aim in "Le Clou d'or" was to argue for the sexual fulfillment of his Platonic relationship in the 1840s with Madame Césarine d'Arbouville, whom he described as one of those spiritually attractive women that nature appears to have intended, but not quite managed, to make beautiful, thus producing something much more interesting than a merely beautiful woman (*Le Clou d'or,* vi). Technically a *récit par lettres* (only the man's letters are provided, however), "Le Clou d'or" is barely a work of fiction, since the letters are for the most part taken verbatim from the author's own correspondence with Madame d'Arbouville. But what it lacks in imagination it makes up for in the truth of the feelings expressed, in the intimate glimpses it gives us into Sainte-Beuve's tormented soul, and, surprisingly, in its touches of the comic. If Amaury occasionally reminds us of Molière's Tartuffe (an effect hardly intended by his creator), the relationship in "Le Clou d'or" may have been meant to evoke that between Molière's Alceste and Célimène, between the "misanthropist" threatening to flee into solitude and the "coquette" whom he accuses of preferring drawingroom society to the private conversation with him that might settle the issue between them.

In "La Pendule," written in 1844 as a tribute to the Swiss storyteller and humorist, Rodolphe Toepffer, the narrator is a clockmaker — no ordinary one, but a moralist given to comparing the "secret wheelworks of the heart" with those of his timepieces — who reconstructs the love affair of a young married woman by observing her behavior over a long period of time during his visits to repair the household clocks. As part of his spying he copies the texts of poems he finds hidden in the clocks, poems by Marceline Desbordes-Valmore and . . . Joseph Delorme! This slight but clever story, although more humorous than "Christel," resembles the latter in its "fictionalizing" of Sainte-Beuve's own passion, as a biographical critic, for prying into the intimate lives of his subjects. Christel's curiosity concerning Hervé's mail, however, is motivated by awakening love and then by jealousy, while the clockmaker, though he has a touch of the spiritual voyeur about him, is primarily a disinterested observer of the "human machine" in operation.

The hero of Sainte-Beuve's projected second novel, *Ambition,* on the other hand, uses his knowledge of human behavior to manipulate and exploit others in order to succeed in the world of politics.[18] Unlike the stories discussed so far, all of which offer so many variations on the theme of love unrequited or unfulfilled or expiring and in need of revival, the planned novel, reversing the priorities of *Volupté,* was to deal primarily with ambition and only secondarily with love. Fascinated by the political intrigues of the July Monarchy, Sainte-Beuve began taking notes for this project while still in Lausanne in 1837-1838 and referred to it frequently in his letters. He intended the work to serve as the "complement" ("le pendant") to *Volupté* (*B* III, 46). If unfulfilled love — "l'amour sans issue" (I, 203) — inspired most of his stories and many of his poems, clearly we owe this projected novel to his own disappointed political ambition. Finding no place in public life for men of his intelligence, he fell back on "private life" and on a novel about politics, as a *pis-aller* (II, 47) — an attitude that helps to explain his disenchanted, at times cynical, approach to the subject. His aim was to achieve a truth that would be "frightening" in the bitterness of its disillusionment, producing a book for the disabused, "les hommes revenus" (VI, 246-247).

The scene was to be Paris in the early stages of the July Monarchy, and the protagonist, a poet approaching thirty and "awakening" from his youthful idealism to total disillusionment with love, religion, and politics. He cultivates a different form of *volupté* from Amaury's, "not inward-turning and faint-hearted but based on activity and enterprise" (Sainte-Beuve, quoted in Molho, *Un Projet avorté,* 207), a pleasure more of the intellect than of the senses; the pleasure, in a word, of exercising power over others. "*Volupté,* roman intérieur et sensuel; *Ambition,* roman extérieur et intellectuel," observes Molho (p. 207). To achieve his goal, the hero becomes a man keeping not three women on a string, like Amaury, but three political parties. The seamier side of life under the July Monarchy — involving not only politicians but also professors, academicians, journalists, writers, the salons, even the crowds of the boulevards — was to be portrayed on a broad canvas of the kind associated with the historical novel.

Over the years Sainte-Beuve continued to refer to this project in letters and conversations. As late as 1864 the publisher Lacroix reminded him of his long-standing promise to furnish this "new novel" (*Un Projet avorté* 214), a sign, incidentally, that readers might have welcomed a second novel by the author of *Volupté.* His reasons for not finishing it, suggests Molho, were his uncertainty as to how to conclude the story, his greater ability in analysis than in the synthesizing power needed to shape a novel into a whole, and the "poverty" of his imagination (*Un Projet avorté* 214). I would agree with these, providing that by the last reason one meant that his was an imagination less suited to fiction than to biography and history. Lack of time was certainly also a reason, but even with more time available it would have taken something of a Balzac (*pace* Sainte-Beuve!) to carry out a project of the scope outlined in the notes published by Molho.

The amount of space that I have given to Sainte-Beuve's poetry and fiction is justified not only by their intrinsic merits, deserving of greater recognition, and by their influence on subsequent writers, but also by the fact that they are intermeshed with his criticism to form a single whole. "Sainte-Beuve was bent on deciphering the mystery of souls," wrote Yves Le Hir, "and his whole work is but one long inquiry into the inner life; poetry, novel, criticism were all so many stages in his acquiring knowledge of human nature."[19] "To separate the critic from the novelist," cautioned Pierre Poux (I would add "and from the poet" to make the thought complete), "is to risk understanding neither" (I, xxi). For over a decade, furthermore, from 1829 to 1840, Sainte-Beuve appears to have clung to the illusion that he might still become a great artist, or at least that he might succeed in combining a career as artist with a career as critic.

CHAPTER 4

Artist versus Critic:
A Conflict Resolved

I N Chapter 1 we paused to sketch a portrait of young Sainte-Beuve toward 1828 when he published his first book, the *Tableau de la poésie française*. Similarly let us pause now, as he approaches the middle years of his life some ten years later, to take stock of the direction in which his work is moving and, more precisely, to probe a bit more deeply into the reasons for his abandoning imaginative writing in favor of criticism.

I *Coexistence of Artist and Critic*

The explanation most commonly offered for this decision is that he "became" a critic because he "failed" as an artist. In point of fact, however, he wrote both poetry and criticism almost from the beginning, published as a critic before publishing as a poet, and experienced not failure but qualified success with his first two books of poetry and his novel. His hope in the 1830s was to reconcile his ambition as an artist with the necessity of earning his living as a critic.

His ambition as an artist was very real, and his talent as an artist was equally real. Joseph Delorme's "motto" in the concluding sentence of his *Pensées* — "L'àrt dans la rêverie et la rêverie dans l'art" — was his own. "I was above all a poet in 1829," he affirmed in 1863, looking back on *Les Consolations* and rejecting as false the view of his career that claimed that he had been predestined to be a critic, that the critic in him was bound to destroy the poet, or that the poet had existed merely to "prepare the way" for the critic (*Poésies* II, 126). The poems of *Pensées d'Août* were written (alas, a bit too doggedly!) to prove that he had not abandoned this "beloved art." A great part of his originality lay in his ironic ability, in his best poems, to turn the very theme of his uninspired sterile Muse, of his "soul orphaned of poetry" (*CL* XIV, 432), into matter for poetry. The failure of *Pensées d'Août* discouraged him from pursuing this kind of alchemy further. But although he ceased writing verse, probably toward 1848, he continued to think of poetry as an essential ingredient of his nature and his "first and last love," now became a "Platonic love" (*B* V, 83).

The important point is that for a period of approximately ten years, from *Joseph Delorme* in 1829 to the first volume of *Port-Royal* in 1840, critic and artist cohabited with reasonable harmony in this versatile writer, producing works in which he achieved a certain equilibrium of his diverse and sometimes divergent talents. Whatever their genre and whether imaginative or critical, the works produced during this period reflect in one way or another the various facets of his spiritual struggle as he confronted the end of youth and the onset of middle age: his frustrated ambition, his "poésie refoulée" and "amour sans issue" (*B* I, 203), his search for an absolute in faith or friendship or love, and the conflict within his nature between sensuality and spirituality, skepticism and belief, boundless curiosity for all forms of experience and the need for commitment to some cause. Poems, critical essays, and stories constitute so many variations on the central theme of self-discovery, so many transcriptions to different registers of thought and feeling of the search for self-knowledge. This "exercise in the awareness and creation of the self" ("Un exercice de conscience et de création de soi-même"), as Maurice Bémol called it, comparing it to a similar undertaking engaged in by Paul Valéry,[1] is carried out — I repeat — no less in Sainte-Beuve's criticism during these years (as we shall see in the next chapter) than in his poetry and fiction.

Artist and critic not only coexist in the Sainte-Beuve of the 1830s but enrich each other to produce some of the most original fusions of forms to come from a generation — the Romantic — that specialized in such fusions. The *élégie d'analyse* is but one example among many. At his best, the scholar-poet, *le poète studieux,* combined lyricism and analysis, fervor and intelligence, feeling and erudition. His verse, as Baudelaire perceived, provided "not only poetry and psychology but also history."[2] "Madame de Pontivy," the fictional transposition of his aspirations as a lover, was published in book form together with *Portraits de femmes,* critical essays on the psychology of women writers: what could have been more natural, since the two works overlap in inspiration? The projected novel, *Ambition,* grew from the same soil as the essay on La Rochefoucauld, also in the *Portraits de femmes,* and as the pages in *Port-Royal* on that other great seventeenth century *ambitieux,* the Cardinal de Retz.

In *Volupté* the collaboration between artist and critic, though at times uneasy, goes far to explain the unusually rich texture of that work, in which imagination is reinforced by critical analysis and prose takes on poetic qualities. Sainte-Beuve referred to himself in the Preface as not only the "depositary" and "editor" of his hero's confession but also his "rhapsodist," borrowing a term from epic poetry. Amaury both dramatizes in his life and reflects as a moralist upon the basic questions raised by Sainte-Beuve's own spiritual crisis. The most striking illustration of this is the farewell banquet scene climaxing Part I, where he contemplates the faces of those who have influenced his life, seeking to penetrate their mystery as well as his own: "What was I and what was I in search of?" ("Qu'étais-je et que voulais-je moi-même?" [*Volupté* 201]). Such questions are precisely the ones that the author of the *Portraits* and *Port-Royal* will raise, though much less directly, as he seeks to understand the innumerable *visages* of the men and women whom he portrayed as a critic. If this crucial scene is a "figure" of Amaury's youth coming to an end, it may also be read as a figure of the torments and consolations of Sainte-Beuve's own existence as an artist-critic. Amaury becomes a spokesman less for religious conversion than for Sainte-Beuve's love of the past and his fervor, amounting to a kind of piety without God, for interpreting the past, for keeping it alive by relating it to the present.

II *Conflict and Resolution*

This equilibrium between the artist and critic in Sainte-Beuve was almost bound not to last. Each year the possibility of prolonging what was in effect a dual career became more doubtful and difficult, until finally, toward 1840, he resigned himself to becoming a full-time critic.

His assessment of his chances of success as an artist was certainly a leading factor in this decision. How could he succeed as a writer, in the face of the greater public favor accorded to such contemporaries as Lamartine and Hugo, Vigny and Musset, *unless* he competed with them on his own ground and in a genre — criticism — where he clearly excelled? The failure of *Pensées d'Août* seemed to dispel all doubt on this matter.

In light of this failure it was natural enough, though not necessarily correct, for him to conclude that his sources of poetic inspiration, never very abundant, were drying up altogether. Thus we find him in letters and notebooks, even in certain poems, explaining that he ceased writing poetry and fiction when he ceased being young and in love. At thirty-one he believed that his voice was "too broken for song," and that his vision lacked the "light of love" needed if he were to continue as a poet (*B* I, 499). He persisted in claiming that he had abandoned poetry largely because "singing" for him was the same as loving and being loved, or at least the same as desiring and hoping for love; he compared himself to Buffon's swan, whose song was limited to "la saison des amours" (XI, 43). He even formulated, to fit his situation, a general rule according to which poetry is the product of youth, and criticism the product of maturity ("La poésie est proprement le génie de la jeunesse; la critique est le produit de l'âge mûr")[3] — a proposition which admits of too many exceptions to its first, if not to its second, clause to be of much value.

Without questioning the sincerity of this explanation (or rationalization) for his short-lived artistic career, one needs to view it with skepticism. His own poetry, permeated as it is with frustration, disillusionment, and premature old age, hardly fits the conventional image of youth to begin with. Is not the scholar-poet, furthermore, precisely the kind of poet whom we might have expected *not* to be dependent on youthful or amorous inspiration, but instead to renew himself into ripe old age? Would Sainte-Beuve have ceased trying to "sing" if *Pensées d'Août* had been better received by the critics? As for fiction, the very existence of his project for *Ambition* suggests that he was quite prepared to use the novel as much more than a means of indirect confession of love.

The real obstacle to his pursuing a career as an artist lay elsewhere, in what he called the "sad condition" of trying to collect his thoughts for poetry while working as a critic (*B* I, 171). In a revealing letter of 1856 to Jules de Saint-Amour he wrote that he was obliged to become a critic "to some extent by nature and vocation but even more by financial necessity" (X, 318). The invasion of his life by journalism, "l'invasion de la prose," he termed it (XI, 43), was as much responsible as any drying up of the poetic source for his abandonment of "the life of art." He would certainly have preferred this life, he confessed to Lamennais in 1833, but each day it slipped further from his grasp as he observed the inevitable happen: the "métier de critique" which he needed to survive was revealing itself as his true vocation and gradually imprinting its shape upon his mind (I, 334).

Had Sainte-Beuve been a less conscientious critic he might have found more time for poetry, a "jealous mistress who will tolerate no sharing with others" (*Poésies* II, 126). His dilemma, in other words, was a matter not merely of time but also of the zeal, the perfectionism with which he threw himself into his labors as a critic. The scholar-poet became the scholar encroaching upon the poet. As he worked on his *Portraits,* for example, the "demon of accuracy and detail" possessed him and made him willing "to go to the end of the world for a small fact, like a mad geologist for a stone." In the meantime "poetry lay idle"; biography and literary history had become its "natural enemy, the insect gnawing away at the strawberry bush" (*B* II, 47).

At first Sainte-Beuve viewed the abandonment of the "life of art" with sadness and a kind of stoic resignation. Criticism appeared to him in a somewhat negative light as "the raft after the shipwreck," a "last resource," though an "honorable" one (*PC* II, 527). But gradually, thanks to that immense resilience which was his, he adjusted to his second-best vocation and came to affirm not only its positive merits, but, more significantly, its *potential as a form of art.* It is true that in his well-known essay of 1835 on Pierre Bayle ("Du génie critique et de Bayle," *Portraits littéraires*) he argued that the gift for criticism was the opposite of the gift for poetry and creative art generally, "le génie créateur et poétique." But this was not the same, as we shall see in the following chapter, as giving up all claim to becoming an artist in his own criticism. He consistently denied, furthermore, that critics were nothing more than failed artists, impotent figures who, having betrayed the creative impulse in themselves, were incapable of recognizing it in others (see, for example, *CL* II, 455; *NL* VIII, 119–120). Unlike Pierre Bayle, Sainte-Beuve had been a poet, even a moderately successful one. Certainly he ceased being a poet in any traditional or conventional sense of the term. But if he could not continue to be a poet *and* a critic, he was resolved to be a poet *in* his criticism, or what Pierre Moreau called a "psycho-poète."[4]

Molho has summed up this evolution succinctly and accurately: "Discovering more and more clearly, toward the midpoint of his life, that the only literary domain left to him was criticism, Sainte-Beuve discovered at the same time the means of transforming criticism into something other than itself and of making it an instrument of creation for one who lacked the creator's gifts [*qui ne possédait point les dons du créateur*]."[5]

The shipwrecked artist, in other words, snatched a kind of salvation from the midst of shipwreck itself — "Le salut se retrouve dans le naufrage" (*PC* III, 390). What at first appeared to be a salvage operation turned into the much more positive, and highly original, enterprise of making criticism a creative art. The "poète-critique" became the "critique-poète" (Antoine, p. lx).

Many years earlier, in the 1820s, before the publication of his first volume of poetry and long before he concluded that he would never win fame as a poet or a novelist, Sainte-Beuve had already glimpsed the possibility of criticism as an art. This was, as we saw in Chapter 1, in his apprentice essays for *Le Globe*. In resigning himself to criticism he was thus really returning to an earlier vision of his potential as a writer. But he was doing so — a great difference — enriched by his experience as an artist.

CHAPTER 5

A New Literary Genre: The Portrait

T HE term "portrait" was the one that Sainte-Beuve chose to designate approximately 150 essays published first in *Le Globe, La Revue de Paris, La Revue des deux mondes,* and a few other periodicals, the earliest in 1827 and the last in 1849. He thus devoted twenty years of his life to perfecting this type of essay, in reality a new form of literary art, to characterize which is my main objective in this chapter. The individual essays he grouped into three collections: *Portraits littéraires* (1844), *Portraits de femmes* (1844), and *Portraits contemporains* (1846, revised and greatly expanded in 1869). The history of the editions of these various *Portraits* is actually somewhat more complicated, but need not detain us here.[1]

To analyze these works in a single chapter is hardly a less formidable challenge than that which will be presented later by the *Lundis.* Their immense range and diversity must first be taken account of. Although they deal almost exclusively with French literature,[2] they take us from the sixteenth to the nineteenth centuries, covering a wide variety of genres and many types of authors both living and dead, both great and small, including some who were "authors without our suspecting it" ("les auteurs qui le sont sans qu'on s'en doute" [*PF* II, 1393]). They emphasize now biography and "character," now thought, now literary art and the analysis of specific works. Their tone varies from the grave to the light, from the polemical to the meditative and detached. They constantly shift the viewpoint and change the approach in the treatment of their subjects.

Despite the element of chance that presided over their birth as periodical essays, they make, in collected form, far from disorderly

82

reading. The subdivision into three subject headings provides a certain degree of thematic unity to each collection. The *Portraits contemporains* are grouped to some extent in series ("Poètes et romanciers," "Historiens"). A further guarantee of order and unity lay in the critic's habit of taking stock at intervals of his literary and other opinions, a habit arising from his need to "liquider le passé" and "mettre ordre à ses affaires littéraires" (*PL* I, 654). Where a lesser journalist might have been content to react passively or in random fashion to the subjects proposed to him, Sainte-Beuve sought constantly to arrange and inventory his ideas. But what above all holds these miscellanies together is the author's consistent vision of the world together with the art that he devised to express it, or, as he put it, defending the unity of the *Portraits,* "le procédé de peinture et d'analyse familière qui est appliqué à tous les personnages," together with "le fonds de principes moraux et de sentiments auxquels on s'est constamment appuyé" (*PL* I, 653–654).

Before focusing more sharply on these organizing principles, it will be helpful to outline certain broad features that the *Portraits* have in common and to dwell for a moment on one of the most difficult problems Sainte-Beuve had to face as a critic: the problem of judging writers who were his contemporaries.

I *General Features*

In the interests of brevity I shall present these in schematic form:

A. *Fondness for secondary figures*

Sainte-Beuve, despite his reputation for preferring mediocrity to genius, had no real quarrel with greatness, either in the literary or in other fields. Great writers — Homer, Pascal, Diderot, Madame de Staël, Chateaubriand, and many others — are in no way sacrificed to lesser ones in the *Portraits.* The *Portraits contemporains,* in large part an assessment of the Romantic generation, overlooked very few of the Romantic writers whom posterity has sifted out as being major figures. Whatever we think of the critic's opinions of them, he at least gave them ample space.

It was not greatness but pseudogreatness that he questioned, and even more, the cult of great men at the expense of those less gifted or less favored by circumstances. As a philosopher of history he argued against the theory of "providential men" and the "apotheosis of geniuses," defending the indispensable role of "secondary figures." In a manifesto type essay on Mirabeau's *Memoirs (Portraits contemporains),* clearly echoing Amaury's conversations on this theme with the Marquis de Couaën in *Volupté,* he disputed Hugo's view of Mirabeau as a demigod of the French Revolution and argued that Mirabeau's genius — which he does not deny — grew out of the common roots of humanity.

His flair for bringing secondary and often minor figures to life was from the beginning, and remained, one of his specialties. Apart from their usefulness in helping the literary geographer, as he fancied himself to be, to measure the giant peaks around them, they appealed to him as worthy subjects in themselves. Sometimes, as with Charles Nodier, the problem lay in determining what made them fall short of greatness, or what made them, as in the case of Joubert, not so much "secondaires" as "grands dans leur incomplet" (*PL* II, 280). Minor figures (at least those who from our own vantage point have receded into minor positions) are often the springboard for major thoughts in Sainte-Beuve, as in his reflections on the dilemma of knowing and defining the self, apropos of an historian whom few but specialists in nineteenth century France will have heard of, Charles de Rémusat. Uncovering *talents méconnus,* not only from the past but also from among his contemporaries, was a matter of simple justice for him.

Most interesting of all, given the stress I am placing on Sainte-Beuve the artist in this study, was the opportunity that little known figures gave him to use his talent as a frustrated novelist. He himself saw an analogy between his penchant for rescuing half-forgotten figures from obscurity and the gift that enabled others, "luckier in imagination," to invent fictional characters from whole cloth (*PF* II, 1353).

B. *Role of past and present*

Portraits littéraires and *Portraits de femmes* deal mostly with writers from past centuries but include a few living ones; *Portraits contemporains* favor "les vivants" but include a few of the recently dead, "les morts d'hier." Past and present thus have an equal share in the *Portraits.* As a *critique-journaliste* Sainte-Beuve was concerned with commenting on contemporary problems, with recognizing, occasionally even heralding, contemporary writers of talent. As a critic of historical bent, on the other hand, he considered it his responsibility to "inventory" the past, to reassess its legacy from time to time, and to keep alive valuable traditions. This theme of the critic's dual role will recur in various guises throughout his writing.

"Ours is definitely the most retrospective of centuries," he wrote in 1846, noting that while industry and science looked largely toward the future, much of intellectual activity was bent on discovering the past (*PL* II, 894). Many of the *Portraits* were written while he was also working on his own greatest contribution to the magnificent flowering of historical studies in nineteenth century France: *Port-Royal;* like the *Lundis,* they are to some extent by-products of his research into the seventeenth century.

What attitude toward the past does one find in the *Portraits?* Often it is that of openly confessed nostalgia for what their author considered the more orderly and stable Restoration period, before the Revolution of 1830. Nostalgia for "les grâces," "les parfums" of a more remote past — the infinitely refined conversations of polite society under the *ancien régime* — is a dominant feature of *Portraits de femmes,* in which the author frankly admitted seeking "a temporary refuge" in the past from the "whirlwind" of the present (*PF* II, 1024–1025). There is also a tendency to judge contemporary achievements in the light of certain concepts of taste, sobriety, and perfection bequeathed by the past. In this sense Sainte-Beuve was a traditionalist, though a much less restrictive and dogmatic one than his fellow critic Désiré Nisard, for example. In an essay on Homer in *Portraits contemporains* he argued for the classical Greek tradition as a touchstone of greatness, both esthetic and moral. For him no real literary achievement was possible without a sense of that "gloire" that inspired the ancients and after them those more modern "ancients," the great writers of French Classicism; no enduring work was possible without the sense of a perfection that would meet the approval of the severest judges, the ancient masters who served less as models to imitate literally than as guides to emulate in spirit. From this point of view, which he called "ma vue *rétrospective* de postérité" (*PL* II, 839, italics in original), the judgment of "posterity" lay, paradoxically, not in the future but in the past.

This respect for the achievements of the past is accompanied in the *Portraits* by a sense of reverence for the memory of the dead. Historical knowledge becomes nothing less for Sainte-Beuve than a form of piety, a "piété littéraire" to be precise, as when he compared his essay on Fontanes (and there are many others like it) to "an urn placed on a tomb" (II, 278). Not all the past, to be sure, is worth preserving, even if it were possible to do so. Sainte-Beuve is no pedantic antiquarian. But whatever in his eyes has once struck its spark of poetry, has once possessed the dynamism of life, somehow lays claim to be remembered. The ultimate reason for pondering the past was simply the pleasure of understanding, for its own sake, that which was once alive. "Il est doux," as he put it, "de comprendre tout ce qui a vécu" (*PF* II, 1327). He would have agreed with Lytton Strachey's observation: "Human beings are too important to be treated as mere symptoms of the past. They have a value which is independent of any temporal processes — which is eternal, and must be felt for its own sake."[3]

C.   *Attention given to oral sources*

An essential part of "tout ce qui a vécu" was the spoken word of gifted men and women, either as recorded in writing or as transmitted orally by reliable witnesses. The manner in which Sainte-Beuve himself acquired knowledge of his father from conversations with his mother and aunt, or of the Revolution of 1789 and the Consulate from Daunou, or of many great figures from persons who had known them, goes far to explain both the emphasis he placed on oral sources in his criticism, beginning with his earliest essays, and his conception of the critic as a transmitter in turn of such testimony to posterity. This approach provides one of the most original features of his *Portraits*.

Some writers, he believed, citing the case of Joubert, put more of their talent into their conversation than into their writing. Madame de Staël, on the other hand, was the supreme example of brilliant conversation, "la parole improvisée, soudaine," overflowing into written form (*PF* II, 1061–1062). In trying to recover the spoken word, no one made better use than Sainte-Beuve of letters and memoirs; yet no one realized better than he the limitations of such documents or criticized more severely the "superstition" and "pedantry" of believing in them absolutely. Somewhat paradoxically for one who was supposed to be a literary critic, he claimed that the written word was but part, often a very small part, of the living character, the living mind, he was attempting to portray. In each generation there is something vital which perishes with that generation, some part of its finest thought. "Les écrits ne rendent pas tout" (*PL* II, 785). What was true of Pascal, whose fragmentary unfinished *Pensées* represent an extreme and dramatic example of a thought transmitted to us with tantalizing gaps, he felt to be equally true of all human beings: "What remains of their inner lives and thoughts, compared with the continual flow of their minds, is never more than the fragment of fragments" (*PC* V, 210).

D. *A multifaceted criticism*

The author of the *Portraits* is primarily neither biographer nor historian nor literary critic but a new, unclassifiable species combining all these roles and still others — *critique peintre, critique moraliste*. Biography as an end in itself interests him less than "psychological biography" whose purpose is to "prepare the way for reading an author" (*PC* II, 45–46). Thus, far from neglecting an author's works (part of the "myth" about him), he moves back and forth from life to works, seeking whatever light the one may shed on the other, "passant tour à tour de l'homme à l'auteur," as he explains in an early essay on Boileau, his first for *La Revue de Paris* (1829), setting forth his method and illustrating it in practice (*PL* I, 657). The result is a new kind of "intermediate genre" (*PC* I, 83) lying somewhere between biography and literary criticism. Historiography also enters into the picture, but again less as an end in itself than as an adjunct to these other disciplines.

The "poète-critique" who had delved into questions of literary style and form in the *Tableau de la poésie française* and the *Pensées de Joseph Delorme* continued to pursue such questions in the *Portraits*. The first eight essays of *Portraits littéraires* concern "points of art," "principles of art and literary criticism," raised by seventeenth and eighteenth century authors (*PL* I, 653, 706). *Portraits contemporains* contain numerous pieces devoted to specific analyses of works of poetry and fiction. The main emphasis, however, is placed not on the literary work as an end in itself but on "the relationship of the work to the personality, the character, the special circumstances" that lay behind it (*PL* I, 649). In a carefully shaded introduction to his manifesto type essay on Corneille (*Le Globe,* 1829), Sainte-Beuve explained exactly why he sought out "the man behind the poet" ("l'homme au fond du poète"): it was an attempt to isolate, from amidst historical and biographical circumstances, the specific talent which nature had given to this particular writer and to no one else (*PL* I, 678). This quest, in turn, was but part of a much broader literary reality that interested the portraitist: the writer as a phenomenon in himself, the "personnage littéraire" (*PC* III, 359), by which he meant not a character in a work of fiction but the writer himself as a character. From the only partially successful creation of characters in his own fiction (most are too pale to be truly alive) he turned to the brilliant re-creation of writers as characters in the world of criticism.

Here the biographer-critic merges into the role of the moralist. How writers behave interests him no less than what they wrote. A major aspect of the *Portraits,* and even more of the *Lundis,* as Thibaudet recognized, consists of this exploration of "l'éthos littéraire" resulting in a veritable "Comédie littéraire de la France" (p. 287). This realm in turn, I would add, is part of an even larger one, the "Human Comedy" itself. In Chapter 1 we noted the apprentice journalist's passion for the study of human nature and his ambition not merely to analyze it in his critical essays but, rivaling the great creators of fiction, to recreate it as felt life. In the *Portraits* he gives free rein to this ambition, seizing the opportunity that the framework of the literary review gave him to produce "une infinité d'aperçus de littérature et de morale." As he progressed he found "moral observation" tending to predominate, with "literature" becoming merely "a pretext" for it (*PL* I, 653). For "l'esprit moraliste," he observed, literary criticism could hardly be more than "un point de départ et une occasion" to pursue this broader inquiry into human nature (*PF* II, 1177–1178). (This emphasis will remain a constant in Sainte-Beuve's work: twenty-five years later we find him declaring in the *Nouveaux Lundis:* "Literary study leads me . . . quite naturally to moral study" [*NL* III, 15].)

II   *Judging Contemporaries*

Two kinds of problems beset Sainte-Beuve in his efforts to provide a fair assessment of contemporary writers: the first stemmed from his literary preconceptions and personal tastes, and the second, from difficulties inherent in the very act of judging those so close to him in time and in space.

A major part of the critic's duty, as he conceived it, was "to point out the new, wherever it came from" (*PC* II, 262) and to recognize talent or genius whenever it appeared among his contemporaries. He compared this to acting as "ship's lookout" ("la vigie"), greeting each sighting of new talent with joy (II, 200). Envy has no place in such an activity, for "the more talents there are for the critic to grasp, the more reason he has to declare that business is going well" (V, 457).

To Sainte-Beuve's credit, he recognized envy, especially on the part of an unsuccessful artist turned critic, as a possible obstacle to his just appraisal of contemporary artists. But envy played a much smaller part in his own judgments than has often been alleged, and a much less significant role than another factor, namely, his conservative literary tastes. His basically classical preference for sobriety in art, clearly manifested from his 1827 article on Hugo onward and unchanged by his brief flirtation with the Romantic movement, stood in the way of his full appreciation of the Romantics and limited that openness to new talents which he so often preached but so inconsistently practiced. Furthermore, he was not content merely to *record* his strictures. He imagined for himself a much more ambitious role, modeled on those of Boileau under Louis XIV or Fontanes during the First Empire: the role of mentor, first to the Romantic poets and later, in his position of authority with *La Revue des deux mondes,* to contemporary literary movements in general. The nautical comparison changed from "lookout" citing new talents to "coastal pilot" ("pilote côtier") guiding writers around reefs and into a safe passage (*CL* XI, 534).

Such was the thrust of a whole series of polemical articles reprinted in *Portraits contemporains* from *La Revue des deux mondes* of the years between 1839 and 1845, deploring the "industrialization" of literature and the destruction of literary standards and urging a closer collaboration between criticism and art as a means of preserving "tradition," "continuity," "doctrine."[4] Only by rallying around such a "clairvoyant and benevolent judge" as *La Revue des deux mondes,* he argued, could contemporary artists compensate for the lamentable disappearance of a public or publics of connoisseurs and avoid falling into complete "anarchy" (*PC* II, 486–487). In these articles, which read like a combination of sermon and medical report, "Doctor Sainte-Beuve" (so to speak), reviving the tradition of the critic as "médecin" (Boileau, Samuel Johnson, La Harpe are the examples he claims to follow [*PC* V, 269]), diagnoses the literary ills of his time and proposes his remedies.

Even had Sainte-Beuve been less restricted by his conservative bias in assessing his contemporaries, the very enterprise raised serious problems of which he was well aware; in fact they recur as motifs in his criticism. In the first place, "mobility" — the constant flux in which both critic and subject, both portraitist and model, find themselves. "Nous sommes mobiles, et nous jugeons des êtres mobiles," reads the great epigraph from Sénac de Meilhan introducing *Portraits contemporains* in the 1869 edition. To some extent this problem also arises for figures of the past whom we fancy as no longer "mobile" because dead, although the meaning of their lives and works may be far from "fixed" (we shall return to this point later). With the living the problem is more acute, however, and was magnified, as Sainte-Beuve saw it, by the rapid rate of change occurring in his century, its lack of stability and continuity, its cult of "progress," its endless "variations." Then there was the difficulty of the critic's proximity in time and space to his subject. How take the measure of a life or work that is unfinished, that one cannot yet grasp as a whole? How judge a literary scene of which one forms a part, acquire a perspective on it from within?

This last problem is related to still another: how tell the truth, that is the whole truth, about one's contemporaries? Disagreeing with the old adage from Tacitus that distance increases respect ("Major e longinquo reverentia"), Sainte-Beuve argued in an early essay on Walter Scott that there are certain familiarities with genius that one would dare take only from a safe distance (*Premiers Lundis* I, 249–250). The ideal of "frank speech" ("franc parler") that he held up for the critic had its inevitable limits, such as restrictions to freedom of expression in the periodicals themselves, or simple respect for the proprieties (*les convenances*), a respect that Sainte-Beuve, fundamentally a decent man despite his reputation, generally maintained. Comparing the portraiture of the dead with that of the living, he made this interesting distinction: we know less about the dead but can usually tell it all; we know more about the living but cannot tell all we know (*PL* I, 649–650).

To cope with the problem of telling the whole truth about his contemporaries, Sainte-Beuve devised a system of what one might call "levels of truth," ranging in degree of frankness from the vitriolic notations of his intimate notebooks to the politely phrased judgments of his signed public criticism, with his anonymous articles lying somewhere in between. The *Cahiers* he reserved for what

he called his "poisons," that is, concentrated substances which
when "diluted" ("délayés") become "colors." They provided an
outlet for opinions that he recognized as coming from too "black"
a palette, better suited to caricature than to considered judgment
("un fond de palette très noir et très. chargé"), from moods that
were often ill-humored or vengeful ("Ceci est mon arsenal des ven-
geances; j'y dis la vérité" [*PM* 236]). Between these private and
public judgments, however, there was considerable overlapping.
Many passages from the *Cahiers* appeared as "Notes et pensées" in
both *Portraits* and *Lundis,* and materials from them were frequently used by Sainte-Beuve as the basis for published articles.
The difference between the kinds of "truth" expressed by these
various texts is a difference less of essence (one seldom contradicts
the other outright) than of degree. The "poisons délayés" became
portraits; the art of the portrait consisted in great part of this very
process of dilution, a process (it should be noted) which still produced colors that were vivid, "des couleurs qui font vivre"
(*PM* 236).[5]

In the *reportage littéraire* (as it would be called today) of the
anonymous *Chroniques parisiennes* that Sainte-Beuve authorized
to be compiled from his letters of 1843–1845 to his Swiss friend
Juste Olivier, he had the best of both worlds. Free from the
restraints on frankness of the Paris reviews, able to view his subjects at close range in the French capital while seeming to speak
with detachment from Lausanne, he discussed with more candor
than in his signed criticism of the same period the literary, theatrical, and political highlights of those years.[6]

This is not to imply, however, that his signed essays were hypo-
critical. They, too, possess their own kind of truthfulness. He
became a master at enveloping in a courteous, sometimes convoluted style — not to be mistaken for insincerity — his sharp criticism of contemporaries, many of whom he considered hypersensi-
tive creatures prone to take any criticism as a personal insult. ("To
criticize an author," he quipped, "has become like breaking a mer-
chant's shop windows" [*PC* II, 529].) When he wished to do so,
Sainte-Beuve could write with unsurpassed sharpness (his *Cahiers*
and *Chroniques parisiennes* show this), but he usually chose to
soften the blow. Acknowledging his method openly, he described
how he used circumlocutions to swathe his negative criticisms, to
"dilute" them (*PC* I, 5 — the very word echoes from his *Cahiers*);

but their point was hardly lost on the attentive reader. "The praise is on the surface," he remarked, "the blame, beneath" ("la louange est extérieure, et la critique intestine" [*CL* XVI, 44]). In his *Cahiers* he added: "Squeeze the sponge and the acid is released" (*PM* 236). The *Cahiers* provided his thought "stripped of flesh" ("à l'état écorché"), as in an anatomical model (Sainte-Beuve never forgot his medical training); the *Portraits* covered it with flesh and even at times with a soft layer of padding (*PM* 236).

As for the problem of "mobility," his own no less than that of his subjects, he attempted to solve it by constantly revising his essays on contemporary writers and adding footnotes and appendices to the originals. This habit of revision dated from his first book, as we saw in Chapter 1, but nowhere is it more strikingly exemplified than in the original and revised editions of *Portraits contemporains* (1846, 1869). His "correctifs," "retouches," "repentirs," as he variously called them, were designed in part to correct errors of fact, for few critics have been so obsessed with factual accuracy. Seldom does he revise his style, however, or *radically* alter an opinion by way of "rétractation" (*PC* I, 5). There is a fundamental consistency in his views. He does use notes and appendices, on the other hand, to provide additional biographical facts, second thoughts, adjustments to the changing realities of his models. For Sainte-Beuve there was no such thing as a "portrait complet" or "définitif." The most one could hope for was a good likeness "for the moment" ("qui a ressemblé un moment" [I, 198]), or, if one had the opportunity to return to the same subject, an even greater approximation to the truth, "la ressemblance de plus en plus fidèle" (I, 654).

Besides throwing new light on their shifting subjects, the notes and appendices of *Portraits contemporains* also provide us with an absorbing account — for the most part a clarification and defense — of Sainte-Beuve's relations with many great writers of his time. They read like fragments of his own "psychological biography," like a portrait of himself as a "literary character," the erstwhile champion and now disillusioned critic of Romanticism. Significantly, it is the great Romantics who rate most of the appendices. Although the work contains much more than a reassessment of the Romantics, its central theme is the retrospective view of these artists from various vantage points subsequent to 1830: ten years later ("Dix ans après en littérature. 1840"), thirteen years later

("Quelques vérités sur la situation en littérature. 1843."), and over thirty years later in the appendices of 1869. The interest of the work certainly lies in the quality of the portraits themselves, but it may lie even more in the juxtaposition of original texts with retrospective notes and appendices. For here one may observe how the critic tempered his original enthusiasm for the Romantics, reducing it to something more closely resembling "justice and truth" (in his own eyes at least) while still confessing stirrings of sympathy for poets with whose aspirations he was once linked so closely (IV, 271).

III *Physiology and Poetry*

The *Portraits* were clearly intended by Sainte-Beuve to be a means of expressing indirectly in his prose a poetic talent whose direct expression, in verse, had been greeted with less than enthusiasm. He admitted that they were not criticism "in the strict sense of the word," but a very special form that allowed him to convey his "personal feelings about the world and life," to give voice to "a certain hidden poetry" in his subjects, and thereby to continue, in the pages of a literary review, the "interrupted elegy" of his verse (*PF* II, 1353). Here was the chance to combine his two conflicting vocations of poet and critic into a new "composite vocation, truer and more firmly founded" than the writing of verse (*PC* III, 364). More specifically, he viewed the *Portraits* as the equivalent in prose of the essay length verse compositions (such as the title poem or "Monsieur Jean") that had met with so little favor in *Pensées d'Août;* again he observed that they were not so much criticism as a form intermediate between poetry and criticism, "une moyenne composition poétique."[7]

By using criticism as a roundabout way ("un détour" is his term) to continue being a poet, he was in no way denying the "scientific" side of his nature. Why could criticism not share in the qualities of poetry and science alike, and succeed in being both personal and impersonal, subjective and objective, both expressive of the critic's feelings and accurate in its portrayal of the object under study? This dual objective is well summed up in a passage of the *Cahiers* where Sainte-Beuve declared that his purpose was to introduce into criticism "a kind of magic [*une sorte de charme*] as well as more *reality* than it contained before; in short, *poetry* as well as *physiology*" (*PM* 259, italics in text).

"Physiology" in the *Portraits* meant attempting, much more than past criticism had done, to relate the mind of the person being portrayed to his physical experience and endowment; it meant exploring the connection between the "physical universe" and the "world of the mind" (*PC* I, 8), seeking out "relationships and laws," "origins and causes" (III, 360). The term, like "reality," was thus broadly synonymous with Sainte-Beuve's quasi-scientific ambition to pioneer in "the natural history of literature" ("l'histoire naturelle littéraire" [*PM* 259]). Even before such investigations could begin, however, the naturalist critic had to establish accurate biographies, a relatively new enterprise in France, where ignorance and error persisted as to the lives of even the greatest writers and where the "official" biographer who made a monument of his subject ("la littérature monumentale," Sainte-Beuve called this) was preferred to the one who sought out "the natural and the real," not excluding wrinkles and warts (*PC* III, 329; *PL* II, 785). Curiosity, flair for finding and interpreting the relevant documents, respect for accurate verifiable facts — all qualities one finds exhibited in the *Portraits* — were of course also included in this "scientific" side of criticism.

Its poetic side, on the other hand, involved a certain degree of imagination, artistry, and intuition. The "poet," etymologically, is the "maker," the "creator." In his first essay on Diderot (*La Revue de Paris,* 1831), Sainte-Beuve described the pleasure he felt in "constructing," in "composing" the biography of a great writer for the first time, especially from intimate sources such as letters; he spoke of the joy of reaching the point where "analysis becomes creation, and the portrait lives and speaks, the man reveals himself" (*PL* I, 867). The *Portraits* mark his passage from unsuccessful maker of verse and of fiction to successful inventor of criticism as a form of creation. He conceded that his "characters ... were not really created, even when they appear most unpredictable, since they are true, they have existed." But he added that they cost him almost as much to "rediscover, study, and describe" as if he had invented them. This was by way of general comment on his *Portraits de femmes,* which he compared to "little short stories with a single character" ("petites nouvelles à un seul personnage" [*PF* II, 1353]).

Defending the kind of imagination that went into Mérimée's learned historical essays, he argued that imagination is much more than the ability to invent images and metaphors. To imagine the past is to represent vividly "how things were," or at least "how they probably were," and therefore in a sense to "create" them, or at least to "compose" them ("on les combine" [*PC* III, 471–472]). In describing Mérimée's gift as akin to the "impersonal, dramatic, narrative faculty" of a Shakespeare or a Walter Scott, Sainte-Beuve was indirectly describing his own use of the imagination in the *Portraits* and reaffirming his youthful ambition to emulate these creators in his criticism.

The many comparisons related to painting, engraving, and sculpture in the *Portraits* suggest that Sainte-Beuve saw an analogy between these other arts and his own. In the methodological introduction to the essay on Corneille quoted earlier, for example, he compares the biographical critic to the sculptor, the former achieving by "analysis" what the latter accomplishes by the divinely inspired "symbol." Artistry enables the biographer to rise above the level of a mere "chronicler" to become a "sculptor" of poets' lives, even a kind of "priest" in the temple of art (*PL* I, 679–680).

Apropos of Jean-Jacques Ampère (another poet turned critic and literary historian), Sainte-Beuve attempted to define more precisely what he meant by the "poetic spirit" ("l'esprit de poésie") as adjusted and tempered to suit the critic's needs. Such a spirit has nothing to do with rhetorical tricks or feelings of rapture. It *is* to some extent related to expression and sense of composition, to a "certain form of art." But essentially it is the intuitive gift of perceiving and rendering the precise individual nature ("le sens propre") of each object under scrutiny. If the critic is "he who knows" and the poet is "he who does not know but who intuits, feels, and renders," the "poet within the critic" ("le poète sous le critique") is "the one who intuits within the one who knows" ("celui qui devine sous celui qui sait"). For all his knowledge, and however indispensable such knowledge is to the pursuit of "reality," it is not the critic who in the end discovers and recreates the essence of his subject, but the poet within the critic; and he does so by virtue of a magic — a "sober-minded magic," as befits criticism — that by its very nature is elusive and indefinable (*PC* III, 362–363).

IV   *A Certain Form of Art*

As a critic Sainte-Beuve's task was not to create beauty himself but to awaken readers to beauty in the works of others. To perform this service well was to be inspired by the only "muse" he felt he could lay claim to, "la *muse* du critique" (*PC* V, 342). He acknowledged the danger that a critic like himself who conceived of criticism as an art might sacrifice to "the seduction of art" the interests of what should be his principal concern: "the true [*le vrai*]" (*PL* I, 652). The word "art" nevertheless occurs frequently with "truth" in his statements of principle and objective, and sometimes side by side with still another important term, "life [*la vie*]." One sure sign of the truth, in the portraitist's as well as the poet's work, is, he pointed out, that it lives: "C'est le propre du vrai de vivre" (*PL* II, 907). Some form of art was indispensable to release this living quality of the truth and to create the illusion of life in the critical portrait.

Given the great variety of subjects treated in the *Portraits* and the variation in form from one individual essay to another, it is difficult to make valid generalizations about Sainte-Beuve's artistic practice in these works. To read them carefully from cover to cover, however, is to discover certain patterns of form that recur frequently enough to be considered characteristic.

One such is his method of attack in the long preamble. Michaut compared this to the "portico" in architecture;[8] it might also be likened to the framework ("le cadre" is a term Sainte-Beuve often uses) of a painting or to an overture or symphonic introduction in music. In this introductory section, which varies in length from a few paragraphs to several pages, he presents the broad reflections that the subject has inspired in him and will serve to illustrate. Grave, slow, occasionally even ponderous, this initial section gives way to a quickened pace when the body of the essay is reached, reminding one of the passage from slow introduction to allegro in a classical symphony. In essays of the "life and works" type, the onset of the biographical sketch marks the turning point ("Or, quand Corneille, né en 1606 ..." — "Né, en 1621, à Château-Thierry en Champagne, La Fontaine ..."). We then pass from the broad, theoretical, at times abstract ideas of the preamble to the more concrete and precise aspects of the portrait itself. The reader becomes, in fact, so conditioned to the appearance of this formulaic phrase that he may be startled when it fails to appear or when the biographer shows uncertainty about the accuracy of a date.

The main body of the essay, typically, appears casual and meandering on the surface. The texture is composed of many loosely interwoven strands of various kinds, including biographical data, literary and linguistic analyses, quotations, direct critical judgments, personal reflections, images, lyrical passages. The perspective frequently shifts, in the manner of a "kaléidoscope" (Sainte-Beuve uses this very term to describe his efforts to capture the elusive "polygraphe" Charles Nodier [*PL* II, 324]). But beneath the sinuous course of the surface with its many changes in perspective and tangential remarks, a clear line of thought usually can be traced; a central viewpoint, "un point de vue dominant" (II, 366), guides the thought. The form is thus in reality far from haphazard. The various kinds of material appear to be arranged almost in contrapuntal fashion, so that subjective impressions contrast with objective facts, and broad general ideas run parallel with scenes, anecdotes, and other concrete details.

This quasi-contrapuntal effect is also discernible in the interplay between the critic's voice and the voice of the individual he is portraying. Thanks to his extensive use of excerpts from a given author's writings, both published and manuscript, his own judgments are counterbalanced by what amounts to self-portraiture — often self-judgment — on the part of his model. He claimed that good criticism, in fact, was nothing more than a framework ("une bordure") for quotations (*PL* II, 155). Too modest an assertion, surely: it is his commentary on these that brings out their full meaning. The choice of quotations was in itself part of the larger art governing the selection and arrangement of *all* his materials.

The endings of his essays are generally much lighter in touch and briefer than their beginnings. Once he has assembled enough traits to reveal the distinctive "form" (as he liked to call it) of a talent or character, the portrait comes to an end without fanfare, usually with a last telling anecdote, quotation, or image. A sense of openness rather than of finality characterizes these closures, in keeping with his belief that portraits require constant retouching and with his practice of returning to his subjects to view them from still another angle.

V *Obsessive Themes*

"Every writer," observed Sainte-Beuve in an essay on Senancour, has his favorite word [*mot de prédilection*] which occurs frequently in his speech and inadvertently betrays a secret wish or partiality" (*PC* I, 162). (Senancour's he found to be *permanence*.) Often, we might add, there is more than one such word, and the recurrent words (or images) serve to convey what may be called a writer's *thèmes de prédilection*.

Sainte-Beuve is no exception to the general truth of his own stylistic observation. A number of such themes, all involving contrasting if not opposing forces — continuity and discontinuity, fixity and mobility, measurement and mystery, the secret self and the public mask, youth and age — recur in the *Portraits* with an insistence of which he may not have been fully conscious. It is these themes, even more than the continuity of method and principle to which he referred in his Preface of 1832, that contribute to the unity and coherence of the *Portraits* as a whole. Closely interrelated, they spring from his preoccupation with two problems underlying all his criticism: the problem of grasping the reality of human nature and the problem of defining the truly creative life, particularly the literary life.

To discover the continuity beneath the "apparent breaks" in a literary tradition, collective movement, or individual life and work (he uses the above term apropos of Victor Hugo [*PC* I, 465]), was one of his major objectives, reflected in his repeated use of such words as *continuité, fond, suite, durée, déviations, écarts*. Lamennais, for example, a notorious case of radical shifts in thought, he compared to a meteor whose apparently erratic course was nevertheless "regulated by a secret compass" awaiting discovery by the critic (I, 249). At times, like Montaigne and Pascal, Sainte-Beuve was skeptical that any such underlying "fond solide" existed beneath the fluctuating phenomena ("l'ondoyant") of human nature. "Who can say the final word about others? Do we even know it of ourselves?" he asked. Do we possess true substance ("un fond véritable") or are we merely "unending surfaces" ("des surfaces à l'infini")? Yet in the same context he makes it clear that he is prepared, despite his skepticism, to persist in search of this fleeting reality (*PL* II, 802–803).

The search for continuity is related thematically to the search for a fixed point of reference. "Every day I change," wrote Sainte-Beuve in a *pensée* appended to the 1852 edition of *Portraits littéraires,* and he went on: "Before the final death of this mobile being who calls himself by my name, how many men have already died within me? You think I speak only of myself, reader; but ponder a moment and see if this does not also apply to you" (*PM* 47). A dizzying prospect, this implied absence of centrality or continuity either in the critic himself, in the object of his study, or in the reader to whom he would serve as a guide! But once again, despite the temptation to dismiss his investigations as ultimately futile, he persevered in them. Emily Dickinson begins one of her poems with these lines: "Each life converges to some center / Expressed or still; / Exists in every human nature / A goal...." Sainte-Beuve would have endorsed this belief. His work is pervaded by endless variations on the theme of fixity and mobility, centrality and dispersion, ranging from authors who quickly find their center and remain fixed within well-defined limits, through others who must search longer (and the critic with them as he recreates their self-discovery) or whose talent continually broadens out from their center, to those whose extreme versatility seems to suggest the absence of a fixed center.

Still another dual theme in the *Portraits* is the author's attempt to take the measure of his subjects while recognizing the mystery lying at the bottom of anything related to human beings. Terms such as *mesurer, fixer, saisir, borner, limiter, arrêter, circonscrire, définir, déterminer,* and the like abound, but, to remind us of the virtual impossibility of grasping the ever elusive substance ("le fond qui échappe toujours" [*PC* III, 98]), they are attenuated by a generous sprinkling of *je ne sais quoi, mystérieux, insaisissable, indéfinissable.* On the one hand, Sainte-Beuve pioneers as a biographer and literary historian in establishing a whole network of relationships within which to circumscribe the individual — family (both biological and spiritual), generation, group, circle, century, etc. "Man, according to Emerson," wrote Irving Babbitt, "is a bundle of roots, and a knot of relations. No one ever surpassed Sainte-Beuve in following out the finest filaments of these relationships."[9] On the other hand, few critics have been as aware as he of the factors limiting measurement. The nature of creative talent itself is the chief among these. The greater the genius, the greater the ultimate mystery: Sainte-Beuve's symbol of this immeasurable power was Molière (*PL* II, 8–11). But even less gifted figures raise problems that "psychological observation" alone is unable to solve; the best the critic can hope to do in such cases (Bernardin de Saint-Pierre is the example he cites) is to "particularize the mystery" (II, 109). "A soul is a whole world," he wrote apropos of Madame Roland, "an exceptional character can never be too thoroughly explored" (*PF* II, 1159). While recognizing that human behavior in all its variety may be reducible in the end to "a certain number of forms that reproduce themselves invariably," he confessed in the next breath that "the study of human nature is infinite: the very moment you think you have grasped the subject and can relax a bit, it slips from your grasp and must be undertaken anew" (II, 1265).

Part of the problem of defining an individual's nature, especially a famous writer's nature, was the contradiction that Sainte-Beuve often found between his public image and his private self. The search for what he considered the "true" or "natural" self behind the authorial mask was another of his obsessive themes. "You seem to be a confessor to the authors you criticize," the Swiss pastor and critic Alexandre Vinet wrote to him (*PL* II, 955). His own analogy for his approach was to compare it to a surgical probe, and he justi- fied it, so far as the delicate question of applying it to his Romantic contemporaries was concerned, by arguing that their own love of public confessions made it almost a duty for the critic to seek out the real man behind the celebrity and to compare the two (*PC* V, 278).

Sainte-Beuve's relentless pursuit of what he considered the inconsistencies and hypocrisies of a Chateaubriand or a Benjamin Constant has led many to conclude that he was interested only in unmasking great men so as to reveal their *misères* and rob them of their *grandeur.* In reality, the theme of the search for the intimate or secret self assumes many forms in the *Portraits,* of which unmasking is merely one. He was as keen to reveal unsuspected vir- tues and talents as to expose weaknesses, and took delight in dis- covering *personnages* (Madame Roland, for example) whose public roles and private selves appeared to correspond perfectly. His prob- ing of the hidden self was in fact part of a much broader theme: his unwillingness to accept stereotyped views, whether flattering or unflattering, of any of his subjects, his desire to release new cur- rents of life in portraits that had become *figés.* History, including literary history, he observed, is like the frozen surface of a river whose ice the critic must break from time to time in order to reach the living stream beneath (*PM* 109).

By referring to a real self that supposedly existed *before* the assumption of a role ("l'homme avant le personnage" [*PL* II, 677]), Sainte-Beuve implied a link between the foregoing theme and the final one to be described: youth and age, promise and fulfillment. He emphasized consistently in his *Portraits* an individual's origins and early formation, the source of his life and life's work, "la donnée première d'une destinée" (*PF* II, 1161). His theory, first set forth in detail in his 1829 essay on Corneille, was that the first masterpiece or substantial work of a writer provides an essential clue to the nature of his talent. The critical moment occurs in youth when native gifts, education, and circumstances join to make possible a "premier chef-d'oeuvre" (*PL* I, 678–679). In this first flowering, furthermore, a writer "fully reveals himself." (One encounters repeated variations of this formula in the *Portraits*.) Sainte-Beuve's attempt to discover the whole in a part is comparable to the figure of speech known as synecdoche — which might lead us to suspect that the poet in him is at work even here. Whether this approach is valid or not as a critical method (a question to which I shall return apropos of Chateaubriand), it at least provided him with an effective means of circumscribing his material.

His obsession with beginnings applied to character as well as to talent. Every individual, he believed, conceives in youth an ideal of himself, "un premier type" to which he aspires to conform and in the light of which it is not unfair to judge his subsequent development (II, 798). He compared this to a vision of Sinai, a glimpse of some finer potential destiny of which our subsequent works and deeds offer but a pale reflection (II, 930).

The interdependence of these "obsessive themes" should be obvious. If any one, however, may be considered to be central, it is this last — the theme of youth and age, of beginnings and subsequent development. Seeking the key to an individual's talent was above all for Sainte-Beuve a matter of determining how he used or misused his gifts before naturalness was overlaid with calculation and artifice. His emphasis on how a talent unfolds, or fails to unfold, from its earliest affirmation is clearly inseparable from his quest for fixed reference points and continuity. For him the crucial problem of character as well as of talent was how to negotiate without shipwreck the narrow strait leading from youth to maturity, the years between twenty and forty. This was essentially a question of wise husbandry of one's "premiers fonds," of successful adjustment to the loss of youthful power — a motif recurring throughout both the texts of the *Portraits* and the *pensées* appended to them. The ideal in the light of which Sainte-Beuve judged both individuals and collective movements (especially the Romantic movement) was growth consistent with first inspiration, change without betrayal of self, renewal without disruption of continuity; in short, "rester fidèle à soi-même sans s'immobiliser, se renouveler sans se rompre" (*PC* V, 353).[10]

VI *Indirect Self-Portrayal*

It should be obvious from what we already know of Sainte-Beuve's own life that these obsessive themes in his criticism arose from deep within his personal experience and had their counterpart in his inner personal drama. They sprang from his own struggle to attain maturity and fulfilment as a man and as a writer. His concern with the continuity of others mirrors his awareness of the breaks in his own career and his anxiousness to show that despite such *déviations* he had followed an uninterrupted path, that the critic in him had grown out of, rather than betrayed, the poet. The ideal he set for others, "se renouveler sans se rompre," was his own. The problem of change and permanence in others would perhaps not have been such a persistent motif in his criticism had he not been the most "mobile" of beings himself, the most "experienced in metamorphoses" (*PM* 47–48), in search of his own fixed center, his own anchor against shipwreck.

His consciousness of mystery in others reflects the mystery he found in his own nature, a mystery that, as with others, he nevertheless persisted in trying to "surround," to reduce, and to limit by taking his own measure (vis-à-vis the Cénacle, his predecessors among poets and critics, and the like) as he took the measure of others. He too had his private or secret self and various forms of disguise for concealing it from his reader. As for the theme of youth and maturity, the early glimpse of a "Mount Sinai" from which he hoped the inspiration for his life and work would flow was his vision as a young man of a life devoted to poetry and spiritually redeemed. His recurrent fear was that his "disgust with life," "that incurable disgust with all things that is peculiar to those who have abused the sources of life" (36), might destroy both his capacity for virtue and his creative powers as he sank into premature old age. Thus the special fascination with which he writes of poets who (literally, not metaphorically as in his case) died young (Millevoye, Louis Bertrand), moralists and critics who died young (Vauvenargues, Charles Labitte), writers whose lives were longer but whose destinies remained in some way or other unfulfilled (Léonard, Nodier). Thus also his fixation on the problem of how individuals manage the perilous transition from youth to maturity, a central theme in his own experience as a critic attempting to salvage, with as much dignity as possible, what he considered the wrecked hopes and squandered virtues of his youth.

Critics have long been aware of the subjective aspect of Sainte-Beuve's *Portraits.* As early as 1832, an anonymous review of *Critiques et portraits littéraires* appearing in *Le National* (Bonnerot suspects the author was Nodier) observed that his essays reflected his "moral state," his "hopes and sorrows," and that his method was "to seek himself in others."[11] Michaut believed it was this subjective quality that set his criticism apart from that of others, since he never ceased being "a lyric poet revealing himself" (p. 217). For Pierre Poux the *Portraits* were "confidential criticism" (I, xxxiii), and for Bonnerot, "a confession in disguise" (I, xviii).

Such critics were merely following in the footsteps of Sainte-Beuve himself, for no one called attention more repeatedly than he to the subjective aspects of his criticism. "Our opinions in every matter," he wrote in a maxim in honor of La Rochefoucauld, "result much more from the individual nature of our mind than from the things we observe" (*PF* II, 1265). This was the general philosophical principle; the most striking application to his own case is found in a passage of his *Cahiers* later used almost verbatim in his portrait of Magnin: "If I had to judge myself, pursuing self-love in all its disguises, I would say: 'S.-B. paints no portrait without reflecting himself in it; on the pretext of depicting someone else, it is always his own profile which he describes.'" He believed in fact that *every* critic really "prefers" and "celebrates" himself in others, seeking, by means of certain "favorite types" to which he returns again and again, to carry out his own "self-glorification" ("sa propre apothéose"); in their judgments of others it is not so much others that critics judge as themselves (*PM* 260; *PC* III, 398–399).

Whether this view of the inevitable subjectivity and even self-centeredness of criticism is valid as a generalization, its applicability to Sainte-Beuve's *Portraits* is clearly justified. However, it is also clear that his *manner* of self-expression is far removed from that of the "personal" or "familiar" essay of English tradition or from that of Montaigne. His "confession" is above all indirect, manifesting itself in his choice of subjects (insofar as he was free to choose them), selection and arrangement of materials, choice of quotations, and of course in his style.[12] The most revealing of his "retours indirects de l'auteur sur lui-même" (to use his own phrase about Senancour's *Libres méditations* [*PC* I, 171]) tend to occur in essays on other critics, historians, and moralists, either those with whom he had certain affinities (La Rochefoucauld, Bayle, Diderot, Joubert, Ampère) or those from whom he wished to set himself off more or less sharply (Joseph de Maistre, Nisard, and to some extent Magnin).

"It is your intimate thought, your true self that attracts me in your writings," wrote one of his most perceptive readers, Vinet, in a letter to him quoted in the *Portraits littéraires* (II, 956). To say this, however, is not to rob his *Portraits* of all objectivity and detachment or to deny them their function as a means of education and enlightenment. Paradoxically, they tell us as much about the subjects portrayed as about the portrayer. The inner personal world of their author is linked inseparably in their pages with the outer world. They provide a body of knowledge almost encyclopedic in scope and possessing a high degree of historical accuracy and truth, they offer an unfailing source of insight into others, while at the same time serving as an instrument of self-exploration and self-affirmation. To borrow a phrase from Thomas Mann on Goethe (a "man of letters" and "educator" much admired by Sainte-Beuve), there is in the *Portraits,* as in all Sainte-Beuve's criticism, "an interweaving of the inner and outer self, a simultaneous wrestling with the ego and with the outer world."[13]

To use Sainte-Beuve's own terms, *apothéose* or self-affirmation is with him, again paradoxically, inseparable from *métamorphose* or the temporary assumption of another's nature. "Criticism is for me a metamorphosis," he wrote, "I try to disappear in the character I am reproducing" (*PM* 263). It made little difference whether he admired or liked that character, felt an affinity with him, or agreed with his views. He accorded to almost all his subjects a generous degree of attention that was in itself, as Vinet again shrewdly observed, "a kind of affection" (*PL* II, 955). Probing their mysteries, he came to feel for them what he called "a certain emotion" (*PF* II, 1353) and to transmit to them something of the vitality of his own nature. The warmth of his curiosity, his imaginative sympathy, the disinterested passion of his love of truth, helped restore his subjects to life.

This life-restoring power, of a lesser magnitude than, but not unlike, the life-giving power exercised by a great novelist over the characters he invents, is in the end the most attractive feature of the *Portraits*. It assumes an even more impressive form in what was to be the central work of his career, *Port-Royal*.

CHAPTER 6

The Major Work: Port-Royal

T HIBAUDET compared Sainte-Beuve's history of Port-Royal
— the French convent that became the center of the seventeenth century Catholic reform movement known as Jansenism —
to his "Massif Central" (p. 289). Just as the mountain range
bestrides the interior of France, so *Port-Royal* dominates its
author's literary production. Conceived in the early 1830s, cast ini-
tially in the form of a course given at the Academy of Lausanne in
1837–1838, it was revised to make a book whose composition,
achieved in the face of endless distractions and difficulties, took
over twenty years, from his return to Paris (1838) and the publication of the first volume (1840) to the appearance of the fifth and
last volume (1859).[1] Nor does the story of its continued presence in
his life end there: hardly had the first edition appeared when, with
that drive toward perfection in the revision of his work that we
have seen to be characteristic of him, he prepared a second edition
(1860) and, only two years before his death, a third (1867).

In Sainte-Beuve's eyes this book was his favorite, his "Benjamin" (*B* XV, 254), the "most searching and personal," the one in
which he had expressed himself most fully and with the greatest
freedom (XVI, 129). From the midst of his *Portraits* with their
ever-shifting subjects, he looked forward with pleasure to "a less
changeable and calmer object of study" (*PL* I, 652), an allusion to
the book already taking shape in his mind. After the "miniatures"
of the *Portraits,* as Giraud put it, he was ready for the "fresco" of
this larger subject,[2] or for what he himself called (he was wary of
his ability to paint true frescoes) "le plus énorme de mes Portraits"
(*B* X, 525).

I *Choice and Conception of Subject*

In 1834 Guizot, considering Sainte-Beuve for appointment to a teaching position at the Ecole Normale, suggested to the critic, who lacked both the *licence* and the *doctorat* usually required for such a post, that the completion of "some book of literary history" would be acceptable in place of these university degrees. Describing this opportunity to Victor Cousin, in a letter of September 1834, Sainte-Beuve alluded to "un morceau d'histoire littéraire française" which he had long had in mind (*B* I, 453). *Port-Royal* thus originated as a response to the very practical need to find a steadier means than journalism of earning his living. (He failed, incidentally, to obtain the post.)

There were several reasons for his choice of subject. Seventeenth century French studies were enjoying a revival of interest in the 1830s and 1840s, especially with the rediscovery of Pascal. Sainte-Beuve both profited from this vogue and in turn reinforced it powerfully through the impact of his own contribution. Having already shown a keen interest in the field in his *Tableau de la poésie française,* in many essays of the *Portraits,* and above all, in *Volupté,* the conversion of whose hero is due in great part to his reading of seventeenth century spiritual writers (Jansenist and others), it was natural for him to wish to continue his exploration of France's Classical age.

His own search for a religious solution to his problems, furthermore, attracted him to what is both a great literary and a great religious era in French history. He had not yet settled into what he later called his "definitively skeptical frame of mind" (*B* X, 477), and still hoped to find in seventeenth century spirituality, as Amaury had found, a "moral authority" that might provide him with the inner peace and stability which he lacked as well as teach him how to renew his moral strength, "se retremper lui-même."[3] From this point of view *Port-Royal* followed upon *Les Consolations* and *Volupté* as the last in a series of works that Giraud aptly described as "expériences religieuses" (tests or experiments with religion) carried out by their author to determine his acceptance or rejection of the Christian faith (p. 259).

In addition to spiritual regeneration, Sainte-Beuve hoped through his subject to recover something of the discipline and order of Classicism as an esthetic ideal. The composition of *Port-Royal* coincided with his increasing disillusionment with Romanticism —

a disillusionment that was to culminate in another series of lectures, his course on Chateaubriand at Liège in 1848–1849. *Port-Royal* offered him a chance to withdraw for a moment from worldliness as well as from Romanticism, and to acquire a new perspective on both.

If all this were not enough to make the subject irresistible to him, it held out still another attraction, in some ways the strongest of all: its suitability as a vehicle of expression for the "poet in the critic." "I was drawn to this subject," he explained, "by my poetic feeling for hidden lives and by the current of religious inspiration I had already followed in *Les Consolations*" (*Port-Royal* I, 923). When a Swiss critic, Eugène Rambert, wrote that in Port-Royal the critic had finally found the perfect subject for uniting his poetic talent with his intelligence and curiosity, he replied that his intention had indeed been to use this theme as an "outlet" for the "hidden poetry" that had not ceased to exist within him simply because necessity had reduced him to writing prose.[4]

Sainte-Beuve quickly perceived that the history of a group of Catholic nuns and pious laymen accused of heresy and subjected to persecution would have to be broadened in scope if it were to appeal to the largely Protestant audience who would hear him at Lausanne, and eventually to the much wider public who would read his book. His chief means to this end was to use Port-Royal as a vantage point for viewing seventeenth century French literature as a whole, "an occasion and a method for making one's way across the era" (*Port-Royal* I, 201). But he took great pains in his *Discours préliminaire,* an ambitious attempt to justify Port-Royal as "un grand sujet," to set forth several ways in which he felt the subject presented great interest for modern readers.

He enumerates seven of these sources of interest, in fact: (1) in theology, for the contribution of Saint-Cyran, whom he presents as an original and neglected thinker, a kind of Calvin attempting his reform from within the Catholic church; (2) in law and administration, since Jansenism was an attempt at greater decentralization from the authority of Rome, greater freedom for the French clergy; (3) in politics, by virtue of the fact that the Jansenists, many of whom belonged to the upper middle class of parliamentarians, represented a potential counterbalance, if not a challenge, to the authority of the king; (4) in philosophy, for the place of Jansenism in the history of ideas; (5) in literature, for the great number of writers associated either intimately or tangentially with Port-Royal; (6) in morality, both for the examples of Christian virtue provided by certain Jansenists and for their psychological interest as character studies; (7) and finally, for the poetic appeal inherent in the tragic "destiny" of this great religious movement.

These various "points of view," as the author calls them (I, 106), correspond quite closely to the main aspects, if not exactly to the main themes, of the text itself. But although the enumeration appears to place all of them on an equal footing, some are actually more prominent and more fully developed than others. It could be shown, I believe, that the last three headings — the significance of the subject "littérairement," "moralement," and "poétiquement" — correspond to the aspects receiving greatest emphasis in the work itself. Of these three, furthermore, there is evidence that the "moral" aspect of his subject interested Sainte-Beuve more than any other.

In a letter of May 1838 to Charles Labitte, he wrote that he especially appreciated the opportunity Port-Royal had given him for the study of what he called, underlining the phrases as though to show their novelty, "the *natural history* and *natural classification* of characters" ("J'ai surtout fait de la morale, de *l'histoire naturelle* et de la *classification naturelle* des caractères"). Anyone, he added, could do a detailed history of Port-Royal; the distinction of his book would lie in its being "above all the work of a moralist" ("surtout oeuvre de moraliste" [*B* II, 367–368]). Though sketched out in previous writings, this kind of approach was first used extensively in *Port-Royal.* Early in the book, discussing the origins of the Arnauld family, which was to furnish some of the leading actors in the drama of Port-Royal, Sainte-Beuve claimed that just as there are species of plants in botany and of animals in zoology, so there is a "natural history of moral character," a method, still in its infancy, of classifying "natural families of minds" and assigning individuals to species (*Port-Royal* I, 129–130).

There is some doubt about how rigorously or systematically Sainte-Beuve applied this "method" in *Port-Royal,* but there can be no doubt about the dominant role played in the work by what he called "the moral science of souls" ("la science morale des âmes" [I, 453]), a body of knowledge to which he believed the Jansenist theologians and moralists themselves had made significant contributions. He insisted on the broad implications of this "moral science," not only for the light it shed on the psychology of various Christian types (priest and layman, penitent and saint) but also for its wealth of "more general moral observations applicable to all times" (*B* IV, 216). In what is perhaps the best single definition of *Port-Royal,* he summed it up as "a study of the human heart as perceived from within a religious group" (*Port-Royal* II, 630).

II *Construction*

The basic framework of *Port-Royal,* which is preserved from the original course of lectures, is the division into six books, presenting the history of the movement in chronological order and dealing respectively with (1) origins and rebirth, (2) Saint-Cyran, (3) Pascal, (4) the Port-Royal schools, (5) the second generation, and (6) the final years. The main thread of the narrative is the story of Port-Royal itself, of the nuns, spiritual directors, solitaries, and literary and other figures associated with it.

Thus outlined, the plan seems simple and easy to follow, and would raise no objections, were it not for the profusion of digressions and details, the "labyrinth of facts, quotations, anecdotes, and characters" that Giraud complained of and that caused him to remark "Sainte-Beuve does not compose very well" (p. 200). The author himself confessed that his knowledge and love of detail made him better at developing separate points one at a time than at embracing a large subject in a single grasp, and that he was a poor "peintre à fresques" (*B* X, 525–526; see also *PM* 165). Without questioning his self-judgment, it can be shown, I believe, that the disorderliness and lack of unity of *Port-Royal,* at least, have been exaggerated.

To begin with the digressions, Sainte-Beuve justifies them, poetically, by comparing them to visits to the side chapels from the nave of his "church" or "cloister," or to the ever-widening network of relationships that a human being develops as he matures and that a good biographer (he looked on the work as a biography of Port-Royal) will pursue at the risk of seeming to lose sight of his subject (*Port-Royal* I, 113–114). Once we accept his twofold objective in the book — primarily to portray Port-Royal for its own sake and secondarily to use it as a focal point for portraying the great writers of the period — the digressions for the most part fit naturally into the scheme. The "literary interludes," in particular, provide welcome relief (as the author well knew) from the occasional dryness and monotony of his austere main subject. Even Giraud admitted that one would have to be something of a Jansenist to object to the pleasure they give. Or to put it in slightly different but still seventeenth century terms, it would be like refusing to enjoy Corneille's great play, *Le Cid,* because it fails to observe the rule of the three unities.

There is a very conscious, and largely successful, effort deployed by Sainte-Beuve in *Port-Royal* to avoid too rigorous and systematic a method of construction in favor of the "artful disorder" ("la méthode décousue avec art") that he admired in Montaigne and La Bruyère (I, 828). Here Giraud was more appreciative of the compositional merits of the work, when he observed that what it lacks in "point de vue logique" it makes up for in "point de vue poétique." By constantly varying his approach and allowing for the unforeseen turn of event (*l'imprévu*), Giraud added, the author succeeded in making of this historical study "the most poetic and dramatic of novels" (p. 205).

Perhaps the most striking example of this "méthode décousue avec art" is his technique of developing characters by bringing them back at different points in the narrative, even at the risk of appearing repetitive. In defense of this approach, he noted: "I try with each new encounter of a figure already familiar to add some new trait or to sharpen an old one" (*Port-Royal* III, 104). Vinet spoke of his "painter's method" in developing characters through the accumulation of concrete details, "little by little, as the occasion arises ... retouching, adding, rounding out," and compared it to the art of the *mémorialiste* Saint-Simon, a great favorite of Sainte-Beuve.[5] Taken together with the (not so digressive) digressions, this piecemeal approach was bound to baffle nineteenth century readers. They were not prepared for what is basically an extension of the method used in the smaller *Portraits* to the "enormous portrait" of this large-scale subject. But readers of the post-Proustian era are likely to find such an approach less disconcerting; as Regard pointed out, there is in the whole composition of the work, which meanders and seems to lose its way without really doing so, already "quelque chose de proustien" (p. 103).

It would not have been surprising if a book that took so long to finish and that appeared in successive volumes over a period of twenty years had lacked unity of composition. But Sainte-Beuve's claim that it had been conceived and composed in a single burst of creative activity ("d'un seul jet")[6] is borne out by the real degree of unity manifested by the text itself.

However much he seems to wander from his main narrative thread, the author, like a composer of some immense symphonic poem skillfully working his way back to a central theme, manages to return "home." The motif itself of "le retour au cloître," the return "au fil de notre récit," recurs frequently throughout the work. But the unity of the external narrative is much less significant than that belonging to the inner story of Port-Royal's essential nature as the author conceived it. "It is not the history of Port-Royal which I am writing . . . it is the portrait of Port-Royal," he declared (*Port-Royal* II, 683). To reveal "the mind of Port-Royal" ("l'esprit de Port-Royal") unfolding historically was his aim. His skill in keeping this essential feature in view throughout all the changing circumstances of his narrative, from the initial reform of the convent to its final dispersion a century later, is what provides the book with its real unity. As Molho comments: "Sainte-Beuve constantly returns to this *essence* of the community he is depicting, as to a link joining together the various parts of his history." He likens this to the critic's awareness in his *Portraits* of "the 'center,' the unchanging point, the fundamental characteristic that consti- tutes each individual's nature" (pp. 301–302) — an observation whose truth our own analysis of the *Portraits* has confirmed. *Port- Royal,* however, is not, as Molho would have been the first to agree, a collection of portraits. It is something entirely new in Sainte-Beuve's work: a large-scale unified subject conceived as a portrait.

Among the devices that Sainte-Beuve uses to keep the whole structure in view and to create a sense of symmetry and proportion are key scenes echoing or complementing one another (Jacqueline Pascal's entry into the convent, for example, harks back to Mère Angélique's rigid enforcement of the cloister rule on the famous "Day of the Grating"); the highlighting of certain crucial years, which he compares to "knots tightening all the strands," such as 1656, the year of Pascal's entry into the dispute with the Jesuits over the orthodoxy of Jansenism; and codalike passages summariz- ing major developments at various points in the story.

Furthermore, despite the immense cast of characters, he never allows us to lose sight of the key figures, "those grave and holy characters who are our true, our only subject" (*Port-Royal* II, 51). These include Saint-Cyran and his disciples Singlin and Saci in whom the true line of succession is preserved, the true "spirit of Port-Royal" prolonged. Even more important in providing continuity is the Arnauld family, which, especially through Mère Angélique Arnauld, the original reformer of the abbey, and through her brother, Antoine Arnauld (le Grand), Jansenism's most ardent champion, played a central role in the story. The drama of Port-Royal as recreated by Sainte-Beuve is to a remarkable extent the drama of *la famille Arnauld,* just as so much of Greek tragedy centered on the tragic destiny of the house of Atreus. And towering above all these figures, in the structural center of the work — Book III, a kind of "book within the book" — is Pascal, the embodiment for Sainte-Beuve of all that was greatest in Port-Royal, "a great philosopher and the last of the great saints" (II, 312).

III   *Dominant Theme: Grace and Nature*

In conformity with Sainte-Beuve's conception of the work as above all *une oeuvre de moraliste,* he lays greatest stress on the theme of grace and nature, which in turn may be subdivided into at least three component motifs: Christian heroism, the conflict between grace and nature, and (let this be no surprise in what he admitted was "the most personal" of his works) his own growing commitment, as the book progressed, to nature.

The "Christian heroism" ("l'héroïsme chrétien") of certain men and women of Port-Royal, which he declared it was his main objective to do justice to (*Port-Royal* I, 88), is but another name for their saintliness, their heroic virtue. The saint, however, differs from other heroes in that his strength derives from the supernatural life ("grace") acquired through his love of God and often, in the eyes of the world, resembles weakness — if indeed it is ever *seen* by the eyes of the world, since it tends to remain in obscurity, visible only to spiritual eyes. Sainte-Beuve's interest in this theme antedated *Port-Royal* by several years. In a letter of 1830 to Eustache Barbe he confessed that "literary opinions" concerned him much less than "the purpose of life, the mystery of our own hearts, the nature of happiness, holiness" (*B* I, 193). In *Volupté* he had begun to explore the theme through characters of extraordinary virtue who were either imaginary (Madame de Cursy) or historical (Abbé Carron; M. Hamon, the saintly physician of Port-Royal).

His interest in saintliness was part of his lifelong fascination with men and women who embody vividly some particular form of human character, "parfaits exemplaires humains en chaque genre" (X, 462). It was also part of the Plutarchian vein that we have noted before in his writing. Parallels between the heroism of the ancients and that of the Christians, reminiscent of the esthetic parallels drawn in Chateaubriand's *Génie du Christianisme,* are frequent in *Port-Royal.* Mère Angélique's courage in not allowing affection for family to thwart her in her duty to reform the convent, for example, is termed "one of the great pages of human nature," unsurpassed by any in Plutarch's *Lives of the Noble Greeks and Romans (Port-Royal* I, 174). "Moral beauty in its heroic, stoic form" as realized by the ancients is seen as meeting its rival in the "inward-looking, totally veiled moral beauty" of the Christians (II, 326). The emphasis placed on these parallels between Christian and ancient heroism was part of Sainte-Beuve's design to show that the conduct of the nuns and solitaries of Port-Royal was admirable *from a purely human point of view,* even for those who might not believe in Christianity or in the supernatural.

For all the stress he places on the "human" side of his saints, however, Sainte-Beuve never lets us forget that the real source of their exceptional virtues, *from the Christian point of view,* was the love of God, and, more specifically, of the God incarnate in Christ. Nor, for all the common ground he shows them to have shared as students of human nature with the "natural moralists" of their day (such as La Rochefoucauld), does he close his eyes to the profound conflict between nature and grace that the Jansenists believed occurred in every soul obliged to choose between God and the world. In Book III, on Pascal, it is Montaigne who represents "nature without grace" (I, 836); it is the prestige of Montaigne's example as a "natural man" which the Jansenists feared most and that Pascal sought to destroy in his *Pensées* or Apology for the Christian religion. A rival morality, *la Morale des honnêtes gens,* based on the ancient Stoics, Skeptics, and Epicureans as well as on Montaigne, was offering itself in the seventeenth century as an alternative to Christianity for those who could not accept the supernatural. Its representative, according to Sainte-Beuve, was none other than Molière, the successor to Montaigne as proponent of the natural man. Viewed in this light, as an end in itself, as a self-sufficient source of moral order and happiness, nature appeared to Port-Royal and its allies as the very antithesis of grace, the arch-enemy to be relentlessly attacked.

If Sainte-Beuve could write with feeling of this conflict, it was because he was no stranger to it himself. When he began what was to be his long and intimate association with the Christian heroes of Port-Royal, he felt a certain affinity with their beliefs that made it less difficult for a skeptic like himself to see the world from their point of view and to accept, at least temporarily, their assumptions about the reality of grace and of its operation in their lives. A pessimist at heart, impatient with the optimism of the eighteenth century *philosophes* and of nineteenth century utopians alike, he accepted the Jansenist view — which he considered simply the Christian view — that man is *by nature* profoundly corrupt and severely limited in his freedom and capacity to reform either himself or his society. If one "left aside the religious explanation" of this condition, he claimed (referring presumably to the doctrine of the Fall, which he could not accept), "Christianity as a moral doctrine showed keen knowledge of human nature and its flaws" (II, 563). The Christian monks, he believed, knew much more about what made humanity tick than most contemporary politicians with their flattery of human nature. Nothing is closer to a Christian, he wrote, than a "melancholy skeptic unsure of his skepticism" ("un sceptique mélancolique et qui n'est pas sûr de son doute" [I, 845]). As such a skeptic himself, he readily accepted the Jansenist diagnosis of human weakness, the Jansenist unmasking of human self-deception and absurdity. What he could not accept, even when so great a mind as Pascal proposed it, was their supernatural explanation of *why* man was corrupt and their supernatural remedy for curing his ills.

Thus although he writes with respect, at times even with awe, of the manifestations of grace that occur in his story, he often finds himself, and increasingly as the work progresses, defending nature. The "miracle" of the Holy Thorn, for example, which Pascal and others interpreted as a sign that God was on the side of Port-Royal, he dismissed as a "gloomy, disgusting piece of superstition" (II, 198). With all his love of Pascal, of whom he writes with an understanding surpassed by few other critics, a "forceful murmur" arose within him (it was none other than the voice of "common sense and nature") protesting against the excessive acts of penance to which Pascal, already mortally ill, subjected himself during his last years (II, 295). He even grants — for once in agreement with the Jesuits, the chief opponents of the Jansenists — that the latter went too far in trying to prove how out of tune Christianity was with the human and the natural, adding that this was "one of the great pitfalls of Jansenism" (II, 334).

Most significantly of all, not content to suggest that nature should have a more honorable place in the Christian scheme, he went so far as to raise the bolder question, a century before Camus' hero, Doctor Rieux, in *La Peste (The Plague),* whether it might be possible to achieve some form of holiness within the order of nature alone, to become, in other words, a saint without God ("Conçoit-on qu'il se trouve encore des Saints, là même où il n'y a peut-être plus de Dieu?" [II, 311]).

The ideal historian, Sainte-Beuve had written many years earlier in an article for *Le Globe,* must not be afraid to let his own "heart-beat" be heard beneath his narrative (*Premiers Lundis* I, 230). In *Port-Royal* the reader often hears the heartbeat of this "skeptic un-sure of his skepticism" who, at least when he began to write his his-tory, still entertained some hope of recovering Christian faith. His story of the growth and decline of *l'esprit de Port-Royal* takes on an added dimension of interest by being also "l'histoire des varia-tions religieuses et morales de Sainte-Beuve" (Giraud, pp. 55–56). Begun with some degree of fervor, in an atmosphere whose associa-tion with religion (the living Protestant faith of his Swiss friends) was no less important to him than its literary associations (above all, the memory of his fellow historian, Gibbon, who had com-pleted his *Decline and Fall of the Roman Empire* in Lausanne), *Port-Royal* reveals a gradual disillusionment with and detachment from Christianity, a growing *a-christianisme* (rather than *anti-christianisme:* Giraud's distinction), a gradual reaffirmation of the author's deeply rooted skepticism and naturalism. This evolving attitude culminates in the masterfully written conclusion or epi-logue of 1857. Addressing the virtuous company of Port-Royal in a poetic, emotionally charged but also lucidly critical apostrophe, Sainte-Beuve apologizes to them for having "pleaded the cause of grace" without believing in it and for being obliged to conclude that their faith was, like all other attempts to grasp absolute truth, merely "a fleeting illusion in the midst of infinite illusion" (*Port-Royal* III, 673–675).

IV *Imagination in the Service of Learning*

Port-Royal, we recall, was composed, like many of the *Portraits,* during the years when Sainte-Beuve, frustrated in his ambition to succeed as a verse poet, decided to use prose criticism as an outlet for poetry. The very subject, as we noted earlier, provided a certain beauty in the muted poetic quality of the obscure lives he was portraying, a "poetry without sunlight and flowers," not unlike that of his own poems and congenial to the "former poet" (II, 719). But the poetry of the work; if I may continue to use the term in its broadest sense as a synonym for the creative imagination, manifests itself in less vague and more significant ways, namely, in the use of imagery and in the exploitation of the epic and dramatic possibilities of the subject.

The very assimilation of this vast topic to a portrait, to the biography of a single individual, is in itself metaphorical. The dominant type of imagery (Molho refers to it as the "matrix-image") is the Rembrandtlike one of light and shadow. It is the latter, *l'ombre, les ténèbres,* that tends to prevail. Here again was a quality in Sainte-Beuve's subject corresponding to the self-image he projected in his verse, especially in *Livre d'amour.* "Je suis celui qui aime l'ombre," he reminded Adèle Hugo (*B* VII, 440); and concerning the brief summary given of *Port-Royal* by Victor Hugo in his speech welcoming Sainte-Beuve to the French Academy, he remarked that Hugo had "lent too much of his own radiance [*son soleil*] to the Jansenists who, on the contrary, constantly sought the shadows" (*Port-Royal* III, 422).

But all is not *demi-obscurité* or *grisaille* on this verbal canvas. If M. de Saci is "a Rembrandt without light, all of one tone," M. Hamon is a "ray of light" in the darkening years of persecution and decline, the "night of Calvary" for the nuns deprived of all spiritual guidance except his. Pascal is a blaze of light in the very center of the whole composition, "la partie centrale et la plus brillante" (I, 33), the "côté lumineux" offsetting the many "côtés sombres" (I, 66). In the midst of the shadows, there are also many sharply drawn individual profiles. The author suggested that an edition with real portraits, an "Iconographie de Port-Royal," would have great interest (III, 892); but this was hardly necessary, so vividly had he sketched what one might call an iconography of the imagination.

If Sainte-Beuve was a verbal painter of Port-Royal, a modern successor to Philippe de Champaigne who painted it in reality, he was also its epic and dramatic poet. The theme of "Christian heroism" in itself provided an excellent opportunity for casting his thought in epic terms reminiscent of both classical and medieval traditions. The flashback to Pascal's origins after the long introduction in Book III, for example, is compared to the narrator's retracing of steps in the second or third canto of an epic poem. Pascal is a "Hercules" in his labor of defending the Jansenists, while Arnauld in combat is like a knight in a great "tournament of the mind," "le vieux guerrier, le chevalier croisé." But less emphasis is actually placed on this kind of exploit than on the hidden moral strength of the humblest nuns and solitaries. Molho makes the interesting suggestion that Sainte-Beuve may have intended to create a new kind of epic, "le poème épique de l'humilité," in opposition to Victor Hugo's brand with its spectacular, flamboyant heroes (312).

Some episodes in history, Sainte-Beuve believed, are inherently dramatic. His reference, in an early essay of the *Premiers Lundis* on Thiers, to the "great drama of the French Revolution over which fate hovered as in a tragedy of Aeschylus" (*Oeuvres* I, 230), foreshadowed his conception of Port-Royal as another such event. He treats it as a drama complete in itself, with its own equivalent of classical unity and even its chorus, in the form of the many sympathetic witnesses to its fate (*Port-Royal* I, 106). Mère Angélique's radical reform of the convent, so unexpected in the light of her previous history; Saint-Cyran's imprisonment by a Richelieu unable to corrupt him into submission to authority; the persecution, exile, and underground resistance of his disciples; the long "duel" of the nuns with all the powers arrayed against them, including Louis XIV himself; the conflict in Pascal between the genius and the would-be saint ("ce drame du Prométhée chrétien" [II, 391]) — in the light of these and many other examples it must be admitted that French history offers few more dramatic scenarios than Port-Royal. Individual scenes of a dramatic nature also abound, of comic as well as serious or tragic tone and often based on the very dialogue of the actors as preserved in eyewitness accounts. Such scenes are also plentiful in the *Portraits* and *Lundis,* but here they are enhanced by their integration into the larger context of a work conceived as a dramatic whole.

Given its huge scope, elaborate detail, and slow pace — more epic than dramatic in this respect — the "dramatic" qualities of such a work are hardly those of true theater. Even Sainte-Beuve, as he approached the final scenes, quipped that Port-Royal, like some character in a ponderous tragedy, was "slow to die" (III, 635). But once having made these reservations, one must give him high marks for the care he took to bring out and keep in view the progression as well as the dramatic unity of his story, and particularly the central core of the drama, which he correctly perceived to be nothing less than a struggle — here assuming Christian form but in fact of much wider applicability — to preserve "freedom of conscience" (II, 325).

The twentieth century French playwright Henry de Montherlant found the original idea for his drama, *Port-Royal* (first performed in 1954) in reading Sainte-Beuve's *Port-Royal.*[7] However, he was obliged to take liberties with his historical source to achieve the intensity required of a play, and was of course justified in so doing. Sainte-Beuve the historian, on the other hand, could never allow the artist in him to tamper in this manner with the facts of history. There is no mistaking the solid foundation of learning on which the work is based. The subject abounded in written sources of all kinds on which the historian could draw, thanks to the seventeenth century habit (something of a mania with the Port-Royalists, especially the nuns) of recording controversial occurrences in an endless flow of *relations, procès-verbaux,* and other documents. If the discriminating use of such "primary sources" is one of the criteria of the true historian, Sainte-Beuve easily qualifies for the title.

To discover and make good use of documents that provided "precise, positive data" (*Port-Royal* I, 88) and thereby to replace myth and conjecture about the controversial subject of Port-Royal by fact, was no less important to Sainte-Beuve than to become the "poet of Port-Royal." His quarrel with the Romantic historian Michelet arose primarily from what he considered Michelet's abuse of the imagination in historical writing. Of the latter's own portrayal of the seventeenth century, in his *Histoire de France,* he raised the question, "It is poetic, but is it true historically?" (*B* II, 195). He realized, of course, that the very choice of documents, especially of excerpts for quotation, is to some extent an act of the imagination ("Le choix des extraits est invention").[8] But he stood in such awe of what he called "the strict Muse of history" (*PC* V, 30) that the danger of his sacrificing accuracy and truth to poetic effect was very slight indeed, even if he had possessed, to begin with, as fertile an imagination as Michelet's.

The point is that he did *not* possess such an imagination, nor the imagination of a true poet either, and sought to compensate for this deficiency by demonstrating that life recreated from historical documents, scrupulously and soberly, could move readers as deeply as any poetic fiction. In *Port-Royal* the brilliant magistrate Antoine le Maître's withdrawal from the world is presented as the equal in beauty of Corneille's *Polyeucte* or Racine's *Athalie* in the theater, and the conduct of the Archbishop of Paris, Harlai, as a comic match for both Molière's Tartuffe and his compromiser with the world, Philinte (*Le Misanthrope*). The supreme example he offers of such powerful counterparts "from life itself" to great works "in the realm of art" (*Port-Royal* I, 399) is the "Day of the Grating" (*La Journée du Guichet*), which saw Mère Angélique first enforce the strict rule of cloister.

Imagination is thus placed at the service of learning in *Port-Royal* — or is it the reverse? An academic question, perhaps. Giraud was probably right in believing that erudition was not an end in itself for Sainte-Beuve but "a means of exercising his intelligence, his imagination, his fine literary sensitivity" (276–277). Who but the pedant, in any case, makes learning an end in itself?

V   *"My Least Imperfect Work"*

Most of the criticisms of *Port-Royal* have been directed to matters of style and overall composition. Balzac's ridicule of the style as flaccid, ungrammatical, and full of "embryonic images afloat on a sea of words"[9] is intemperate and would apply with more justice to *Volupté* or certain of the early *Portraits*. (His whole attack on the book is little more than a diatribe.) Although some heaviness and tendency to convoluted phrasing still persist, the prose of *Port-Royal* shows a marked advance over the author's earlier style in both variety and simplicity. It reveals (*pace* Balzac) a new found vigor and sharpness, a greater restraint in the use of imagery, a greater naturalness, which may be attributable to the oral form from which the book developed and which looks ahead to the *Lundis*. "What else is *Port-Royal*," asked Giraud, "but an immense *Causerie du Lundi*?" (199).

As for the weaknesses in form and structure, summed up in Giraud's phrase, "Sainte-Beuve ne compose pas très bien," I have attempted to show earlier in this chapter that they have been exaggerated. There is undoubtedly in the work an overgrowth of detail that tends to obscure its unity and coherence. "Woe be to details," exclaimed Voltaire, "they are a vermin which destroys great works."[10] Sainte-Beuve would have disagreed: "Nothing has life except by virtue of details" (*Port-Royal* I, 534). While he recognized, and even apologized to his readers for, the *longueurs* that these produced, he also defended them as the only means of doing justice to the ramifications of his subject and of bringing it to life.

A more serious charge brought against the author by Giraud (he calls this the book's "original sin") is that he distorts seventeenth century French religious history by glossing over the faults of Jansenism and presenting it as the only truly Christian movement of the time — in fact, as the quintessence of Christianity. Similar charges had been laid by Sainte-Beuve's contemporaries, to the point where he felt obliged to defend himself in the course of the book, pointing out that he had overlooked the flaws neither of doctrine nor of conduct in the Jansenists (see e.g., II, 298; III, 622, 634). How, he asked his friend Rémusat, could he possibly have created sympathy for them by declaring at the outset, especially of a five volume work, that they were "wrong"? (*B* XI, 551).

The text bears out his claim that the work was in no real sense an "apology" for Port-Royal. Frequently, either directly or indirectly (using the technique he so loved of attributing an adverse opinion to "a perceptive moralist," "a person of wit," "a bolder one than I"), he calls attention to what he considered the major weaknesses of Jansenism: the narrowness of its doctrine based exaggeratedly on Saint Augustine to the detriment of the Gospels, the excess of its attacks on nature, the joylessness of its spirit as compared with the Christian joy, for example, of a Saint Francis of Assisi. The portrait of *le grand Arnauld* is typical of the author's carefully balanced and shaded attitude toward his whole subject: as Arnauld's character unfolds, the granitelike intractability limiting his genius is clearly established, but it is not allowed to overshadow his real virtues of courage, loyalty, and greatness of heart.

Sainte-Beuve correctly assessed *Port-Royal* as his "major work" ("mon œuvre capitale" [XIV, 143]), the "least imperfect" because it is the one on which he had found time to lavish the most care (XVI, 553). It is in fact his masterpiece. It is also one of the greatest books of literary history and criticism in any literature. Far from suffering from "literary myopia" (another curious charge by Balzac), the author broadened his subject in many ingenious ways and revealed its universal relevance as a drama of conscience and courage in the face of persecution.

As history, the book has dated remarkably little and remains, in the words of one of the great specialists on the subject, "eternally young."[11] Thanks to the infinite pains taken by Sainte-Beuve to establish his facts (he compared his scrupulousness as a researcher to the scrupulousness of his Jansenist friends in morality), the structure of learning on which it is based remains sound. Although it has been subject to correction and completion, it has not been superseded. What it lacks in the kind of breadth associated with "l'histoire générale," as the French call it (for example, it gives only passing hints of the social, political, and economic factors involved in the history of Port-Royal), it more than makes up for in its probing of the psychology of the characters. Taine stressed its uniqueness as a work of history in which the psychological conflicts of the actors, and not merely the actions resulting from them, are revealed and documented.[12] In this respect it is to some extent a precursor of the "psychohistory" of our own time.

One stands all the more in awe of Sainte-Beuve's achievement when one remembers that he lifted his subject almost single-handedly out of obscurity, "inventing" it, so to speak. "Port-Royal was at the time something brand new and demanded a kind of creation in criticism [*une sorte d'invention en critique*]," he remarked in a letter of 1857 to Adèle Couriard (*B* XI, 75). He was especially proud, and rightly so, of his discovery and rehabilitation of Saint-Cyran. "Ronsard and Saint-Cyran will one day be credited to me," he remarked to Labitte (II, 318). Although he did not "discover" Pascal in quite the same sense, his assessment of this "Archimedes in tears at the foot of the Cross" (*Port-Royal* II, 403), is marked by a high degree of originality and remains indispensable for its insight into both the man and the writer.

He displayed an even bolder originality by daring, as a literary critic, to take on a subject in which religious history figured as prominently as literary history. By doing so, as Giraud pointed out (Chapter VI), he annexed a whole new province for the critic and demonstrated beyond all doubt (if readers of his *Portraits* could still be skeptical) the breadth of which criticism was capable. In the *Portraits* he had created a new type of essay. In *Port-Royal* he launched a new kind of religious history, not only by bringing the subject within the competence of the literary critic but also by showing that the historian could treat a religion with understanding and respect while remaining detached from the faith on which it was based. By writing of Christianity "from the outside" but almost as if he were a Christian, he opened up the way for a long line of nonbelievers or ex-believers, "apologistes du dehors" as the French call them, from Renan to Montherlant, to treat this subject in comparable manner.

As a literary work, finally, *Port-Royal* represents the culmination in Sainte-Beuve's career of the concept and practice of criticism as a creative art, an ideal whose steady growth toward fulfillment we have followed from his earliest essays onward. By a happy conjuncture of circumstances, Port-Royal was the right subject at the right time for its author: he had developed mastery of his powers as a critic but was still close enough to his experience as poet and novelist to be able to integrate this into his critical writing. Port-Royal was the ideal subject for achieving the long-sought fusion of his imaginative and critical talents, "l'équilibre des forces poétiques et critiques," as his fellow historian of Jansenism, Hermann Reuchlin, so well expressed it (quoted in *B* V, 544).

In subsequent works (I am thinking especially of *Chateaubriand* and the *Lundis*) Sainte-Beuve will refine criticism as a creative genre and will use it to explore still further the nature of the human animal, and of the literary animal in particular; he will not add anything essential to *Port-Royal* as an artistic achievement. Yet it is a tribute to his genius that these later works, if they do not surpass *Port-Royal,* possess their own excellence and appear in no way to be anticlimactic.

CHAPTER 7

Confrontation with Chateaubriand

A second sojourn abroad, following ten years on Sainte-Beuve's course at Lausanne, enabled him to produce a second very substantial book on a unified theme. In 1848, apprehensive that the February Revolution had introduced a new barbarism into France and concerned with his own fate because his name had appeared on a secret list of persons receiving payment from the government of the deposed monarch (Louis Philippe), he resigned his post as librarian at the Bibliothèque Mazarine and accepted an appointment to teach two courses at the University of Liège for the academic year 1848–1849. The courses, which he gave concurrently, consisted of three lectures per week, two on French literature from the Middle Ages through the eighteenth century (open to students only) and one on Chateaubriand and the literature of the Empire (twenty-one lessons, open to students and public alike).

The first of these courses he never assembled in book form; the second he published in November 1860 as *Chateaubriand et son groupe littéraire sous l'Empire.*[1] The delay in publication was caused mainly by the new responsibility that Sainte-Beuve assumed on his return to Paris in 1849, to furnish the *Constitutionnel* with his weekly *Causeries du Lundi.*

As a theme for the more modern of his two courses, the subject of Chateaubriand could hardly have been more timely, since he had just died in July 1848 and since his memoirs began to appear in serial form in *La Presse* in October of the same year. Thirteen years later he still remained very newsworthy, thanks to the recent appearance of the long awaited memoirs of his beloved Madame Récamier. In 1860, with all the authority that Sainte-Beuve had accumulated as a critic, his book lost none of its impact, especially since his sharp reassessment downward of Chateaubriand's stature coincided with the more critical approach to the "Sachem of Romanticism," and to Romanticism as a whole, taken by the younger generation. In fact his *Chateaubriand* succeeded in creating an image of that great writer — a "myth" if one will — that was to dominate the criticism of Chateaubriand almost down to our own day.

I   *Crisis and Renewal*

Writing to Guttinguer in 1838 apropos of *Port-Royal,* Sainte-Beuve remarked that he considered his life "from the human point of view" a failure, but that he still might "redeem himself from the literary point of view" ("Humainement la vie est manquée, je le sais. Il ne me reste qu'à me sauver littérairement" [*B* II, 450]). He was implying that the void in his life which he had been unable to fill with a great love or adherence to a creed or cause could perhaps be filled with the creation of literary works that would justify his existence.

The ten years separating Lausanne and Liège, even for this inveterate pessimist, were relatively happy years marked by literary productivity, the cultivation of friendships, access to the polite society (*le monde*) he enjoyed frequenting, some degree of financial security thanks to his library post, and recognition as a writer in the form of election to the French Academy. The Revolution of 1848 put an end to these "happy years" (so he explained in his preface to the 1860 edition of *Chateaubriand*) by raising doubts in his mind as to whether literature itself might not be suppressed by the new régime as a "luxury industry" (*Chateaubriand* I, 5). Unlike the crisis of his thirties with which we dealt earlier in this study and which was primarily a *crise de vocation,* this "crisis of second maturity," as he called it (*B* XVI, 510), was largely political in origin. But it also partook of the understandable anxiety (aggravated in this case by political instability) of any productive writer approaching forty-five and faced with the need to renew his inspiration as he entered upon the "second half" of his life.

Just as Lausanne had assisted him in resolving the earlier crisis, Liège provided the opportunity to resolve this one. In this new "retreat," resuming the quasi-monastic routine that he had already acquired in Lausanne, he laid the groundwork for what he considered his "second career as a critic" (XVI, 520). The materials he amassed for these courses became the "currency" on which he was to draw again and again for his *Lundis*. What the professor, having chosen too vast a subject to complete within a year, was unable to finish, the journalist would continue, "in detached chapters and in fits and starts [*à bâtons rompus*]" (*Chateaubriand* I, 27). The course on Chateaubriand he described as "the natural preface of the *Causeries*," adding, "I gave a lesson regularly every Monday in the academic hall of Liège just as I published my article each Monday in the *Constitutionnel*" (I, 6). Furthermore, the informal oral cast that he gave to this course, even closer to conversational style than the prose of *Port-Royal*, prepared the way for the language of the *Lundis*. It was in Liège also, far from the turbulent atmosphere of Paris, that he believed he acquired "the strength to criticize and to judge" (*B* XVI, 520).

His criticism, of course, had never been lacking in sharpness of judgment, but what he viewed as his "customary manner" before the course on Chateaubriand was "to paint rather than to judge" (*Chateaubriand* I, 13). Now his sole ambition, though it did not exclude description and explication, was to practice criticism as judgment ("la critique judicieuse"). Here his lectures on Chateaubriand foreshadow the role he will play in the *Lundis* as a judge of contemporary writers and an arbiter of taste during the Second Empire.

As a subject, Chateaubriand suited the needs of the critic-judge as perfectly as Port-Royal had suited those of the poet-critic, the skeptic unsure of his unbelief, ten years before. With the intimate knowledge he had gained of Chateaubriand through access to l'Abbaye-aux-Bois and to a number of the great man's close friends, Sainte-Beuve could use him as a test case, so to speak, of his cherished concept of "the man behind the work." He could reveal "the other side of the canvas" ("le revers de la toile" [I, 255]). Since Chateaubriand had been an important public figure as well as a writer, and also a writer profusely engaged in establishing his "image," the time had come, with his recent death, to compare the public with the private man, the *personnage* with the *personne*. And since his death had put an end to his work, the time was also ripe to view his achievement with greater detachment and to reassess it.

Such a reassessment was all the more necessary, in Sainte-Beuve's opinion, because a cult had grown up around Chateaubriand, a dangerous form of idolatry, which no critic interested in truth could afford to leave unquestioned. Even he, though in no sense a cultist (one finds serious reservations about Chateaubriand's stature dating back to his essays of the early 1830s), had "suspended his judgment" for many years out of deference to Madame Récamier and had dared at the most to "insinuate" polite criticisms of the great man, in the manner of "a cricket singing in the lion's jaw" (I, 14). He was now eager to tell the truth as he saw it, to speak his whole mind; to use his own vigorous phrase, he was "bursting with truths" ("Je regorge de vérités" [I, 15]). By 1848 he had stripped himself of almost all his illusions, retaining only a belief — but that, it should be noted, amounted almost to a religious belief — in literary study itself and in the search for truth, as affirmed in his opening lecture (I, 30–31). Chateaubriand was to be the beneficiary (given the severity of the judgment, some would say the "victim") of this renewed zeal.

II *Dual Role: Professor and Critic*

The approach taken by Sainte-Beuve to his subject was actually more complex than the foregoing remarks might suggest. He conceived of his responsibility to his students as consisting of two functions: that of professor and that of critic. The main theme of his opening lecture is the distinction between these two roles.

The professor, or *maître,* is another word for the literary historian. His path, *la grande route,* is largely traced out in advance for him to follow, in the sense that he has only to guide his students to the established masterpieces, the literary "monuments" of the past. But he is also responsible for transmitting from one generation to another the traditions of the past worthy of preservation and for forming the literary consciences of the young. The critic, on the other hand, is the "lightly armed reconnaissance scout," free to range wherever he will, not only through contemporary literature, where the professor is less at home (we are speaking of 1848 and not the 1970s!), but also into the past, where he may seek to revise accepted judgments and to prevent traditions from becoming fossilized. Because he is a writer, he often succeeds better than the professor in "receiving and communicating the sense of movement and life" belonging to his subject (I, 22).

Chateaubriand, like most of Sainte-Beuve's critical works, is both literary history and literary criticism. But in the text, as distinct from the opening lecture, he stresses the role of the critic, so much so, in fact, that Chateaubriand appears at times to be the pretext for a meditation on criticism. The subject lent itself beautifully to exploring the nature of the critic: not only had Chateaubriand himself made what Sainte-Beuve considered a major contribution to literary criticism in his *Génie du Christianisme* (especially Parts II and III), but also, two of the key figures in his "literary group" were the critics Joubert and Fontanes, his close friends and literary advisors. The latter symbolizes in the book two essential components of the ideal critic: the ability to acquire and to make wise use of authority in matters of taste, and the ability to recognize genius among the writers of one's time. The final chapter (Lesson XXI), after a brief coda summarizing Chateaubriand as man and as writer, concludes with reflections on these two aspects of criticism as represented by Fontanes.

Authority of judgment and the courage to maintain one's position with independence, dignity, and a certain pluck (*le cran*) are, Sainte-Beuve believed, hallmarks of the true critic. He placed Fontanes in the tradition of authoritative critics, beside Malherbe, Boileau, and Doctor Johnson. He stood prepared himself, in an age when he felt that critics were getting too soft, to revive that tradition. He especially admired the sharp wit (*le mordant*) of Doctor Johnson and appears at times to be emulating it in this the most caustic of his works.

The critic must expose false talents (*les faux succès*) among his contemporaries, but he must also be able to discern and to promote true ones. The highest excellence of the critic, in fact, lies in this power to recognize genius in his midst (I, 215–216). "The true critic," writes Sainte-Beuve, "anticipates public taste, directs and guides it; and if the public goes astray (which often happens), the critic stands firm and proclaims: They will come back to my view" (I, 95–96). Fontanes' merit as a critic was to have recognized a master in Chateaubriand (nine years his junior) when pedants like the Abbé Morellet were heaping ridicule on his innovations. Although timid in his own poetry, Fontanes was bold in the counsels he gave to Chateaubriand, persuading him, for example (such was the authority of his taste), to prune the overgrowth of the original *Génie du Christianisme* while leaving its stronger passages intact.

Yet every critic, however perceptive, has his limitations

("Chaque critique ... n'a que sa portée" [II, 108]), which are usually revealed with advancing age. The mature Fontanes, observes Sainte-Beuve, recognized Chateaubriand's genius; the old Fontanes failed to recognize the genius of the much younger poet, Lamartine. It is tempting to think here that Sainte-Beuve may have been anticipating his own inevitable lapses in later years as a critic of younger writers. With the same hindsight that permitted him to find Fontanes an inadequate judge of Lamartine, we look back today on his own myopia concerning Baudelaire, for example. Whatever the case, there is clearly an implied comparison intended between Fontanes' role in Chateaubriand's circle and his own in the Romantic school. Both were "timid poets" who found their true gifts as critics; both academicians; both, basically neoclassical in taste, though sympathetic (Sainte-Beuve much more so than Fontanes) to certain aspects of Romanticism. If only Hugo and his friends had listened to Sainte-Beuve's advice on how to keep their imaginations within the bounds of good taste, as Chateaubriand had listened to the advice of Fontanes!

III *A Large-Scale* Causerie

As in the *Portraits* and *Port-Royal,* Sainte-Beuve uses a wide variety of approaches and adopts a kind of artful disorder in the organization of his materials. Basically these fall under two headings, those related to the man (*l'étude de l'homme*) and those related to his works (*l'étude du talent*). The portrait of the man and the analysis of his works are presented in such a way as to imply a causal relation between his character and his writing: the quality of the fruit depends on the tree that bears it, "Tel arbre, tel fruit" (II, 94).

Chateaubriand the man is recreated by reconstructing the complex of relationships, "le tissu historique," that conditioned his life, such as historical circumstances, the salons of 1800, his circle of friends at La Vallée aux Loups, his family, with special emphasis on his sister Lucile (the occasion for a development on the significance of "les soeurs des grands hommes"). Continuing to believe that a writer's essential features are formed early in his career, the author has hardly brought Chateaubriand out of his adolescence in Brittany (third lesson) when he is ready to sketch the "essential moving forces" ("les mobiles essentiels") of his nature — tendency to reverie and ennui, cult of youth and of prolonged desire, sense of honor. In the study of the man, he attaches great weight to contemporary testimony, especially unpublished documents and oral accounts. Since Chateaubriand was very prone to self-display ("l'homme de parade"), the critic is keenly interested in what he said or what others said of him behind the scenes — "dans les coulisses" — as compared with the figure he cut on center stage.

Analysis of Chateaubriand's major works, including detailed discussion of his language, style, and composition, is given extensive space, further evidence that Sainte-Beuve cannot justly be accused of sacrificing literary criticism to biography. He was especially conscious of providing his students, through his "readings" ("lectures") of *Atala, René, Le Génie du Christianisme,* and *Les Martyrs,* with a model of literary analysis. "To know how to read a book well," he told them, "judging it while at the same time enjoying it, is almost the critic's whole art" (I, 189). As part of this art, he often uses the comparative method, as, for example, when he compares Chateaubriand's descriptive technique with those of Rousseau, Bernardin de Saint-Pierre, and Lamartine. Skilled in the use of biographical and historical sources, he was no less skilled in the close reading of literary texts.

In overall form, the book preserves the character of the course, which in turn represented a sharp break with the tradition of the public *cours littéraire* as established by La Harpe in the eighteenth century and carried on by Villemain in Sainte-Beuve's own time. The traditional course had been highly organized in form and rhetorical in style. Sainte-Beuve, wisely recognizing that rhetoric was not his strong point, nor oratorical delivery either, deliberately chose a leisurely informal manner, "speaking" his subject rather than "reading" it (I, 12). He regarded his lectures as conversations in which he alone spoke but his listeners replied in thought. A reviewer of the book considered it more a "familiar lecture" ("une conférence familière") than a course (quoted in *B* XVI, 514). His relationship with his listeners at Liège foreshadows that which he will enjoy with the readers of his *Lundis. Chateaubriand,* even more than *Port-Royal,* resembles an extended *causerie.* Comparing the two books derived from courses, Regard observes: "His sentences, while retaining their allusive graces, have gained in clarity and firmness" (141). His use of imagery is marked by an even greater restraint than in *Port-Royal.*

A certain affinity is evident with the essays of Montaigne. In Lesson XIII Sainte-Beuve refers to this great writer, whom he always considered to be one of his "masters," as a fine literary critic without intending to be one, and as the creator of a whole critical tradition, very French in nature, that carries its learning lightly, avoids too much theorizing and systematization, excels in analysis rather than in synthesis, and allows room for the play of the imagination. As a worthy successor to Montaigne he cites none other than Chateaubriand himself, on the basis of his "Poétique du Christianisme."

The "disorderly" surface form is, however, as so often with Sainte-Beuve, deceptive. As in *Port-Royal,* he may appear to wander from the central theme (thus the wealth of observations on literary questions of all kinds) but he never loses it from sight. In *Port-Royal* he had coped, for the most part successfully, with the organization of a much larger subject. Here his canvas was more limited: a major author and his circle, less than half a century of history, with greater emphasis on the purely literary and esthetic aspects of his subject. The result is a more concise, better unified, less slow-moving work, though it lacks the dramatic qualities that Sainte-Beuve was able to exploit in the rise and fall of Port-Royal.

IV *Breaking the Magician's Spell*

Most critics rank *Chateaubriand* below *Port-Royal* as a work of criticism, not because of any failing in literary talent or lack of stimulating ideas but because of what they consider the author's unremitting bias against his subject. Victor Giraud, fairly representative of this point of view, argued that Sainte-Beuve might have produced a "new masterpiece" if only he had treated Chateaubriand with the same scrupulous fairness, the same blend of criticism and sympathy, that he had brought to Port-Royal; instead, claimed Giraud, he produced a witty but malicious "livre manqué" (168, 269).

It must be admitted that Chateaubriand is one of those authors — ironically, Sainte-Beuve is another! — who make impartiality difficult. If his egoism and vanity, his theatricality, the pompousness of much of his style, his often questionable truthfulness and sincerity, make up what might be called the case for the prosecution, Sainte-Beuve has stated such a case forcefully. But does he go too far? Is his *Chateaubriand* a polemical pamphlet disguised as criticism?

To engage in systematic denigration of Chateaubriand was certainly not his intention. What this was, we learn from two epigraphs introducing the book: one (from Chateaubriand) tells us that "the time has come to admit that most contemporary writers have been ranked too high"; the other (from Voltaire) points out that to distinguish between an author's "faults" and his "true beauties" is not the same thing as to destroy his reputation. Sainte-Beuve's real intention, as he explained in a *Lundi* on Madame Récamier, was to express a "twofold opinion," namely, "persistent admiration for the writer and complete truthfulness about the man"; to interpret this as the desire to belittle Chateaubriand, he added, merely showed the inability of French readers to deal with more than one idea at a time (*CL* XIV, 314).

The fact remains that his reassessment of Chateaubriand falls far short of doing justice to a writer who has come to be recognized as one of the greatest in French literature. As a writer he has benefited from the greater willingness of criticism in the post-Sainte-Beuve era to accord a certain autonomy to literary works of art and to judge them on their own merits apart from the man who produced them. His imagination, to which he gave supreme expression in *Mémoires d'outre-tombe* (a work that has come to be recognized as his masterpiece but for which Sainte-Beuve could find only begrudging praise), was an instrument not for the fabrication of lies (as his critic was tempted to believe) but for artistic creation of the highest order. The "myth" of himself upon which he lavished such care has come to be seen not as something to be placed, as his critic constantly places it, in scandalous contradiction to some supposedly "real" or "natural" self, but as a literary creation in its own right possessing its own order of truth.

In the light of Chateaubriand's emergence as one of the giants of French literature, Sainte-Beuve's criticism (to turn against him one of his remarks about the Abbé Morellet) appears in retrospect to be "a web of sound, just observations woven in with others that are obviously false, a continual mixture of judiciousness and incomprehension" (*Chateaubriand* I, 217). The judiciousness reveals itself in many fine, original observations, expressed in striking formulas that still deserve currency. The errors in judgment, on the other hand, seem to me to stem not so much from personal bias against Chateaubriand (though this accounts for much of the unfairness) as from biases in Sainte-Beuve's critical method and in his taste.

His preconceptions about an author's growth and development which we noted in Chapter 5 — that the first work reveals a talent in essence, that continuity in change is a seldom attained ideal, that the promise of youth is rarely fulfilled, and when it is, that a mature talent is quick to "spoil" — all these are applied with a vengeance to Chateaubriand. He is judged almost exclusively in the light of works he wrote before the age of thirty-five, one of which, *René,* masterpiece though it is, is exaggeratedly presented as revealing all one needs to know about the author's "method and secret" (I, 220). After that, "decadence" sets in, the style becomes forced, the talent repeats itself. The fact is, however, that Chateaubriand showed an extraordinary power of renewal, with his *Mémoires,* begun at the age of forty and completed in first draft at seventy-three, and his *Vie de Rancé,* a minor masterpiece in a vein new for him, written at seventy-five.

Nor do his breadth and versatility fare much better at Sainte-Beuve's hands than his creative longevity. As a poet (that is, a poet in prose), his entry into politics is viewed as disastrous, according to still another preconception on the critic's part (it also distorted his judgment of Lamartine): poetry and politics do not mix. He is willing to grant that Chateaubriand was a brilliant pamphleteer, even "a great journalist"; but his straitjacket formula of the "poet-dreamer" ("le poète-rêveur") will not allow him to take Chateaubriand seriously as a political thinker and statesman.

In dealing with the problem of Chateaubriand's "sincerity," Sainte-Beuve betrays another weakness of his method: his near inability, with his contemporaries, to focus on the writer without being distracted by the man, whether that man was Chateaubriand, Stendhal, Balzac, Hugo, or Baudelaire.[2] In his mind there existed an ideal, natural Chateaubriand who revealed himself in occasional moments of intimacy when the "pose" ceased and the "mask" came off; it was this Chateaubriand he looked for in the works, largely in vain. His error consisted in the failure to distinguish between "sincerity" in the usual sense — openness, candidness, spontaneity — and *literary sincerity,* a quite different and more complex matter, involving a writer's faithfulness to his vision of the world and to his artistic (as distinct from moral) conscience. He gives only fleeting recognition to this kind of sincerity, by conceding that the mask worn by Chateaubriand was a "noble mask" and that he possessed his own "sincerity as an artist and writer" (I, 148). For the most part, however, he seems to have expected from him a probity that would have done credit to a Jansenist. From this point of view, Chateaubriand's undeniable vanity, his ambiguous religious stance, and his sometimes questionable veracity so far as facts were concerned were bound to disappoint him.

A final *parti pris* that prevented his giving Chateaubriand an unbiased hearing was his incorrigibly neoclassical taste. There was, to be sure, in much of Chateaubriand's best work a fusion of the Romantic and the Classical, and this he admired. But his "ideal" Chateaubriand (once again) would have been a kind of "Goethe in the French manner" (II, 353), who would have set an even stricter example of sobriety to his young Romantic disciples of 1830 instead of encouraging them in what Sainte-Beuve considered their worst tendencies: abuse of force, lack of naturalness and refinement, overindulgence in the grandiose.

Like *Tableau de la poésie française* and (even more) *Port-Royal,* Sainte-Beuve's *Chateaubriand* was a pioneer work in its field. The view that he held of this author, furthermore, dominated the field for several generations, thus providing an excellent example of the very kind of authority that he believed the true critic should be able to exert. Much of the progress in Chateaubriand studies in our own time, it should be admitted, has consisted of refuting Sainte-Beuve and vindicating Chateaubriand. The major flaw of the book is the author's failure to achieve his professed and not unreasonable goal of "taking the measure" of Chateaubriand without "reducing him in stature" (I, 23). Despite its deficiencies, however, the book contains more than enough knowledge and insight to maintain a valid place in the canon of Chateaubriand criticism. As a literary work it is one of the most forceful to come from Sainte-Beuve's pen. To compare it, as Giraud did, with *Port-Royal,* a unique blend of critical acumen and poetic artistry, is not entirely fair. Its problems were different and its virtues are different. Barbey d'Aurevilly, a master among polemical critics, who admired the book while disagreeing with most of its views, correctly sensed in its manner something new for Sainte-Beuve, a sharpness of tone, a brightness of glow ("fulgurance" was the term he used), which were very different from the *clair-obscur* in which he had enveloped his negative criticisms in previous works.[3]

Much of this increased firmness of judgment may be attributed to Sainte-Beuve's determination to shake off once and for all the spell of Chateaubriand and of the Romanticism that he symbolized. Maurice Regard points out that in writing the book he was struggling against himself, against his own past (140). The resulting work was thus, characteristically, both criticism and indirect confession. Sainte-Beuve had much to admire and to be grateful for in Chateaubriand, above all, *René,* in whose torments he had discovered as a youth a mirror of his own feelings (was not his Joseph Delorme a "René des faubourgs"?), and *Le Génie du Christianisme,* which had provided a model of creative criticism that helped inspire his "Génie de Port-Royal" (as Thibaudet called it).[4] But his conception of truth and beauty was irreconcilably opposed to what he considered the theatricality of Chateaubriand and his Romantic followers. His book is thus much more than the mere reassessment of a great contemporary: it is the record of his struggle to exorcise the magic spell of a writer so seductive (at least so Sainte-Beuve claimed) that he could make even his faults pass for virtues. The spectacle of this struggle, in the end as interesting to readers as anything he has to say about Chateaubriand himself, takes its place beside those other confrontations between great minds that are so marked a feature of French literature: Pascal coming to grips with Montaigne (as so eloquently described in *Port-Royal*), Voltaire with Pascal, or Proust with Sainte-Beuve.[5]

CHAPTER 8

The Lundis: *A Critic's Human Comedy*

I *Approaches to the* Lundis

O N October 1, 1849, an historic date in French literary history,
there appeared in *Le Constitutionnel* the first of the Monday
causeries or "chats" that Sainte-Beuve was to produce each week
(beginning in 1865, every other week) almost without interruption
until his death. To the articles published from 1849 to 1861 (in this
journal and in *Le Moniteur,* the official government organ of the
Second Empire) he gave, when they appeared in book form, the
title *Causeries du Lundi;* to those written from 1861 to 1869 (again
for *Le Constitutionnel, Le Moniteur,* and finally for the opposition
paper, *Le Temps*), the title of *Nouveaux Lundis.* Although there are
a few significant differences between the two subdivisions, as we
shall see, they constitute basically a single work. Taken together,
they represent a literary renewal on Sainte-Beuve's part that hap-
pily contradicts his own theory of the improbability of authors'
prolonging their creative powers into the second half of their lives.
Not only did he successfully renew his career, he also established
himself beyond any doubt as *the* critic to be reckoned with in the
1850s and 1860s, a leading "maître à penser du Second Empire," to
use Maurice Regard's term. The honors bestowed upon him cul-
minated in his being named sénateur by Emperor Napoleon III, an
appointment which, thanks to the modest income it provided, freed
him for the first time in his life, at the age of sixty-one, from financial insecurity.

Whatever one thinks of such honors, the *Lundis* alone certainly
would have sufficed to establish Sainte-Beuve as a major writer and
as a giant of journalistic criticism, though his modesty would have
rebuffed such a grand term as "giant," which is more often used of
poets and other artists than of journalists. The production of the

136

Lundis represents one of the most extraordinary feats in intellectual history, especially when one considers that he carried it out while preparing courses for the Collège de France and then the Ecole Normale and while bringing out revised and expanded editions of his earlier works. In his last few years, furthermore, he continued to meet his deadlines despite grave illness and extreme physical discomfort. Only death succeeded in interrupting his labors.

An approximate count of the contents of the twenty-nine volumes in which the *Lundis* were collected reveals some six hundred separate titles, and, allowing for the recurrence of a given subject at separate intervals and for the treatment of a subject in two or more consecutive articles, almost four hundred different topics. The majority concern French literature and history, and within that field (vast enough to begin with!) the seventeenth, eighteenth, and nineteenth centuries; a smaller but still significant number deal with the French Middle Ages and sixteenth century, Greco-Roman antiquity, and foreign authors (English, German, Italian, Spanish). The quality of these essays is no less astonishing than their quantity. There is surprisingly little that is dull or repetitious. The author managed to kindle excitement even in subjects not of his own choosing or at first glance unpromising of interest. Like his master, Montaigne, he possessed the secret of repeating himself without saying the same thing. Thanks to their immense variety, there is something for every reader in the *Lundis* and more than enough to sustain the interest of either the reader who browses in them or who reads them from cover to cover.

Sainte-Beuve would never have achieved this feat without imposing upon himself the semimonastic discipline that has become no less a part of literary folklore than the night-long vigils that permitted his archenemy Balzac to create the *Comédie Humaine.* Once his subject was chosen, in concert with the director of the journal (a newly published book or new edition of an old one that would serve as pretext for an original essay; an idea developed from his incessant reading and marginal notetaking; a topic growing out of another already treated; the recent death of an author, or some kind of literary anniversary), from Monday to Thursday he would research it with the help of his secretary, discuss it with him, and write or dictate his essay. Friday morning, a reading of it to the director, followed by planning of the next week's *causerie;* Saturday morning, correcting proofs; Sunday, a second revision and the approval of the final text; then a brief breathing spell before the next *Lundi* (Regard, pp. 175–176). For twenty years, as Sainte-Beuve put it, he "descended into a well each Tuesday morning, not to emerge again until the following Friday evening" (*B* XIII, 486).

Given the massive and varied nature of the *Lundis,* one is obliged, in a single chapter such as this, to limit one's presentation rather severely to certain selected aspects, hoping thereby at least to suggest the richness of this unique work. Few are the critics who have done justice to the multiplicity of viewpoints one finds in the *Lundis*. Most of them have tended to stress, if not to exaggerate, Sainte-Beuve's attempt to lay the groundwork for a "science" of literary criticism, a "natural history" of literature; or they have viewed these essays above all as a collection of opinions on poets, novelists, and other imaginative writers, based largely on the biographical and historical interpretation of their works. Literature in the traditional sense, from the Homeric epic to the novels of the Goncourt brothers, of course plays a central role in the *Lundis,* as it did in the *Portraits*. But the concept of literature has been enlarged in them to greater breadth than ever before by the *moraliste* in Sainte-Beuve. More than ever before, literary criticism has become for him a vehicle for exploring the human universe, "a series of chapters in which I insert my ideas on morality, on mankind, on the literary and social life of my times" (*Cahiers* I, 297) — and of other times, one should add.

To limit one's interest to the more purely literary questions raised by the *Lundis,* as most critics have done, is to distort and diminish their author's achievement. A princess of the royal blood, or a general, a magistrate, a politician, or a scholar, were as important in his scheme of things as Racine or Lamartine. Only by reaching an understanding of *why* this was so, of why persons who wrote little more than letters or memoirs or possessed slight literary talent meant as much to him as major literary figures, can one grasp the full meaning of his work.

The way to such an understanding is not to read the *Lundis* by eliminating "minor" or "nonliterary" figures or by selecting and arranging the texts according to century or genre, but to read them in their totality and in the order in which they originally appeared. "To rearrange my *Portraits* according to the chronological order of the subjects treated," Sainte-Beuve pointed out, "is to misinterpret them; the true order is that in which I wrote them, according to my feeling and fancy, the particular nuance of my state of mind at the moment" (*B* II, 384). This remark was certainly intended to apply also to the *Lundis*. Implied in this caution to future editors about the best order of presenting his essays is sound advice about the best order of reading them. My earlier chapter on the *Portraits* was based for the most part on such an approach, and I have used it again for the *Lundis*. To read them in this fashion is to become sensitive to the unfolding of Sainte-Beuve's thought from moment to moment. But even more important, it is to discover a vision of the world far surpassing in scope the mere formulation of literary opinions and to appreciate more fully the artistry that this "poet in the critic" brought to his journalistic task.

II   *From* Portraits *to* Lundis

As a genre, the *Lundis* grew out of the *Portraits,* while assuming a distinctive flavor and emphasis, a certain "newness" of their own. The essays of the 1850s and 1860s share many features in common with those of earlier years. Women continue to play a major role in them, since their author does not hesitate "to claim for literature all those women who belong in some way or other to it, either through their reputation for wit, the fame of their salons, or the posthumous publication of their correspondence" (*NL* IV, 163). Secondary figures are frequently spotlighted, both as "representatives" of their time and as nature's way of making "sketches" (*ébauches*) for greater talents who will emerge later. As in the *Portraits,* the critic divides his attention more or less evenly between the present and the past, the living and the dead, although in the *Nouveaux Lundis* contemporary subjects outnumber historical ones. More acutely aware than ever before of the difficulties involved in judging one's contemporaries equitably, Sainte-Beuve has nevertheless not retreated an inch from his view that such assessment is a primary duty of the critic and that the display of foresight in this exercise is one of the marks of the "born critic" (*CL* VII, 287). But the past continues to maintain its hold on him, especially the recent past which is beginning to recede from memory.

The need to serve as a kind of "recording secretary" of a world on the verge of disappearing gives Sainte-Beuve still another affinity with Balzac and with other novelists (they have been numerous) who have conceived a similar role for the novel.[1] By piecing together his own recollections of the first half of the nineteenth century (he wrote in 1854) with those of much older witnesses born in the mideighteenth century, he could reconstruct "an almost continuous chain of memories" dating back at least to the last years of Louis XIV! As he "closed his eyes" and summoned up these "scenes and perspectives" (*CL* XI, 6–7), he might well have marveled, like Balzac, at the thought of carrying whole societies in his head.

The "obsessive" themes that we noted earlier in the *Portraits* receive further variation and development in the *Lundis,* often in terms of the same characteristic vocabulary or "mots de prédilection." Direct self-portrayal occurs in the form of excerpts from his *Cahiers* (*CL* XI), autobiographical notations (*CL* XVI), and personal reminiscences of the literary life of his century. The *Lundis* from this point of view, like so many of the *Portraits,* are a substitute for the memoirs that Sainte-Beuve never wrote ("Ce sont nos Mémoires que nous écrivons" [*NL* III, 101]). Indirect self-portraiture is even more frequent, for he continued to believe that "every critic gives us his profile or a 'three-quarters' view of his face in his works" (*CL* XI, 465). Yet though he often "depicts himself while depicting others," to use his phrase about Feletz, a literary critic under the First Empire, he almost never distorts his subject to fit his own image or allows his presence to obscure the reality of his model, so unfaltering was his respect for the nature of the individual, so insatiable was his desire to bring out "the form of talent and mind" peculiar to each gifted person in a world offering "an infinity of forms of talent" (XV, 211). He had the skillful painter's sense of the exact color and light needed for each subject.

In this great diversity of approach, however, there is a single point of view that dominates and lends unity to the *Lundis* as it does to the *Portraits:* the point of view of the *moraliste* ("Nous autres critiques moralistes . . ." [VII, 282]). Widening his concept of literature even beyond that found in his earlier works, his ambition had become to create nothing less than a "galerie morale" in which as many forms of human experience as possible would be represented, each in its "meilleur exemplaire" (V, 479).

There is no doubt that Sainte-Beuve hoped, thanks to this vast collection of specimens, to lay the foundations for the "moralist's science" (*NL* III, 17), much as Balzac envisioned the novels that he grouped under the heading *Etudes de mœurs* as lending empirical support to others labeled *Etudes philosophiques* (Regard, p. 184). More specifically he considered himself a pioneer in the advance toward a more accurate, objective, and systematic form of literary study. For this reason it has sometimes been claimed that the *Lundis* are more "scientifically" oriented, less "poetic" than the *Portraits*. Much can be said in favor of such a view. One of the most famous *Lundis,* originally published in 1862, "Chateaubriand jugé par un ami intime en 1803" (*NL* III), is a methodological statement, indeed almost a manifesto (unusual for this critic who shied away from both kinds of writing) of the naturalist approach to literature. A few years later he expressed a large measure of agreement with his young colleague Emile Deschanel's attempt, in his *Essai de critique naturelle* (1864), to apply "the physiological or natural method" to literary criticism (*NL* IX, 80–81).

Nevertheless, the assimilation of criticism to a science is neither so new to the *Lundis* (it had been more than adumbrated in Sainte-Beuve's earlier works) nor so dominant a feature of these essays as has often been claimed. The article on Chateaubriand, brilliant landmark though it is in the history of criticism,[2] should not be allowed to distort the total impression made by the *Lundis,* of whose richness and complexity it provides a very imperfect microcosm. In reality, throughout the *Lundis,* "physiology" is constantly balanced by "poetry," the ambition to make criticism a "science" is constantly tempered by the realization that it must remain basically an "art," as even the essay on Chateaubriand affirms (*NL* III, 17).

Far from accepting the thesis that the *Lundis* are dominated by scientific ambition, one could with cogency argue that as the scientific claims made on behalf of criticism by Sainte-Beuve's contemporaries, especially by his disciple, Taine, became more insistent, he was compelled to express ever sharper reservations about them. Quite prepared though he was to bless Taine's efforts to describe and define an author in terms of biographical and historical factors, he drew the line when it came to "explaining" creative genius by means of such causes. He recognized that the desire to find the "formula," the ultimate secret, of a mind may well be the force that moves every true critic; but he was shocked at Taine's implication that the "last word" might one day be said about any great talent, or that given such and such "starting point" and adding such and such circumstances, writer "X" was bound to become what he was, no more and no less, and could not have been anything else (*CL* XIII, 272–273 — article dated March 9, 1857). Criticism, whatever progress it might make in refining its instruments of measurement, must remain a matter of conjecture. Its attempts to define a given literary genius must remain just that, "attempts," "testings" of the critic's skill against a superior power rather than true "explanations" — *épreuves* rather than *explications* (*NL* VIII, 96, apropos Taine on Shakespeare, article dated June 6, 1864). Nor are less gifted figures so easy to "explain," either. The more one explores *any* individual, in fact, the less inclined one becomes to consider his dossier closed ("tirer la barre à son sujet"), so clever can nature be in outwitting our observation (V, 101). Beyond a certain point of intimacy reached by the critic as anatomist lie secrets that only "the great anatomist of hearts" can penetrate (*CL* IX, 261).

Sainte-Beuve's position in this matter is basically consistent with the one adopted in earlier essays, and provides a further example of continuity between the *Portraits* and the *Lundis*. Given so much common ground between the two sets of collections, what, then, apart from choice of new subjects, can be said to be the "new" aspects of the *Lundis?*

To begin with, the style is much lighter and quicker in tempo than in any previous work of Sainte-Beuve except the course on Chateaubriand. Much of this difference is attributable to the change from *revue* to *journal* as a vehicle of thought: "Necessity, that great muse, forced me to change my style" (*PM* 54). With less space for his articles and less time to prepare them, he was obliged to cultivate this "more concise and unencumbered manner" in his essays; he had "no time to spoil them" (*CL* I, 3). Bonnerot, in his *Bibliographie de l'oeuvre de Sainte-Beuve,* claims that the fact that he often dictated his essays and "talked them out" with his secretary or friends also enhanced their lively spoken quality (III, 408). The tone of the "elegy continued under another form" has been replaced by a sharp wit that Jules Levallois (one of his secretaries) thought was a sign of Sainte-Beuve's "Picard nature" rising more openly to the surface.[3] The imagery has been severely curtailed: "I, too, like images, or used to like them, but now it is the truth above all that moves me" (*CL* XV, 282).

This firmer style was also part of his greater emphasis in the *Lundis* on the judicial function of criticism. After battling for various causes in *Le Globe* and *La Revue de Paris,* after practicing "a more neutral, impartial, analytic and descriptive criticism" in *La Revue des deux mondes,* he explained in the 1850 Preface, (*CL* I, 23), he was now emboldened to undertake a "third form" of criticism, in the guise of forthright, authoritative judgment. The great arbiters of taste and preservers of standards whom he admired, such as Malherbe, Boileau, Pope, and La Harpe, are cited frequently and approvingly in the *Lundis.* To have become a kind of Boileau of the Second Empire, with Napoleon III as his Louis XIV, would certainly not have made him unhappy. But if firmness of judgment appealed to him, dogmatism and rigidity remained as alien to his nature as ever. "Let us not allow our thought to congeal; let us keep our minds lively and fluid" (*NL* VII, 50). What guided him above all was the effort to be fair and just, and this meant a constant process of review, calling for judgments to be revised sometimes downward (as with Béranger), sometimes upward (as with Gautier).

The greater insistence on frankness and on the unadorned truth in the *Causeries* is carried forward with even more fervor in the *Nouveaux Lundis,* for Sainte-Beuve believed that the time had come in the 1860s to expose what he considered the "charlatanism" of his century with its merchandising methods applied to things of the mind (V, 253). There can be few key words that recur with higher frequency in the *Lundis,* especially in the *Nouveaux Lundis,* than "vérité." Never before had he been more determined to acquire "the knowledge of things according to their real value" (I, 248). This usually meant discounting a large part of the inflated claims made by others. He especially deplored the contemporary habit of using "words greater than the things they represent" ("les paroles plus grandes que les choses") as La Rochefoucauld put it (*CL* XI, 418). A true Classicist in this respect, he believed that truth lay in the direction of understatement.

A final relatively new aspect of the *Lundis* is their disguised political content. I say "disguised" because Sainte-Beuve repeatedly claimed that his criticism was above politics and that his aim was to "neutralize the republic of letters" by removing literary studies from the often bitter partisan atmosphere that (so he thought) had harmed them during the years immediately before and after the Revolution of 1848 (*NL* VII, 308). Although he appears to have been sincere in professing such "neutrality," the fact remains that the *Lundis* contain more political bias, of both a direct and indirect nature, than any of his previous works. By choosing to write for the Bonapartist *Le Constitutionnel* and later for *Le Moniteur,* by accepting a post as sénateur, the critic was lending his support to the new authoritarian order. Roger Fayolle, by analyzing in depth his attitude toward the eighteenth century revolutionary tradition in the *Lundis,* has shown how he used literary questions to insinuate his opposition to revolution and his basically middle class conservative views.[4] His support of Napoleon III, based on his belief that a "stable orderly government" could alone provide the conditions necessary for the "development of the mind" (*CL* XV, 308), emerges more and more openly as the *Lundis* progress.

However, this great skeptic and empiricist had not refused conversion to so many other creeds merely to end up as a devout Bonapartist. He considered himself not a "convert" to this "temporary dictatorship" (as he called it in 1862) but a supporter for reasons of common sense (*NL* II, 327). In his last years he moved to *la gauche de l'Empire,* the opposition from within, so to speak, and took up a courageous stand in the Senate against repressive forms of clericalism.[5] Politics may have distorted his views occasionally; they did not succeed — he was right to assert this — in depriving him of his "taste for truth" or his "independence of judgment" (*CL* XVI, 44).

III   *Literature and the Writer in the* Lundis

If Sainte-Beuve would have been shocked to hear anyone suggest that his *Lundis* were in any way a *cours de politique* disguised as literary criticism, he freely recognized, indeed he insisted upon, their function as a "Cours public de littérature" (VII, 187) and affirmed the critic's responsibility as an educator, an enlightener, indeed a civilizer of the public.

He has much to say about literary matters in the *Lundis,* including the evolution of French as a literary language, the style of individual writers as well as of whole eras, the nature of genres, the role of tradition and taste, the definition of a "classic," the relationship between art and morality. In general he attempted to reconcile respect for tradition with openness to innovation, respect for certain moral standards with recognition of the autonomy of art. While continuing to uphold a more or less "Attic" ideal of sobriety, clarity, and refinement (*l'urbanité*) in art, he was fully aware that curiosity for new forms of beauty was abroad, that emerging studies in comparative literature (which he welcomed) were widening critical horizons, and that no tradition, not even Atticism, was worth preserving if it meant stagnation and lifelessness. In his "Qu'est-ce qu'un classique?" (*CL* III) he recommended enlarging the "temple of taste," and defined a "classic" in terms broad enough to include Dante and Shakespeare, whose genius the French had been slow to appreciate. In "De la tradition en littérature" (the text was that of his opening lecture at the Ecole Normale in 1858), he reaffirmed his distinction, set forth ten years earlier in the course on Chateaubriand, between the critic as professor, "maintaining tradition and preserving taste" and the critic as journalist, "seeking out and discovering fresh talent" (XV, 356).

On the whole, however, the *Lundis,* like most of Sainte-Beuve's other critical works, are less esthetically than morally oriented. "Literary study," he confessed, "leads me quite naturally to moral study" (*NL* III, 15). Few critics have been so reluctant to separate talent from character, a writer's art from his spiritual nature, his "taste" from his "soul." In an extremely revealing letter of 1863 to the philosopher Ernest Bersot that throws great light on the *Lundis,* he argued that since all men of letters were at heart "actors (*comédiens*)", the critic had every right to seek out what kind of human beings they really were and how it affected their work, to find "the vulnerable point in their armor," and to reveal (here the former medical student hit upon an especially striking image) "the suture points joining talent and character" (*B* XIII, 153).

One must be careful in discussing Sainte-Beuve's moral bias as a critic not to suggest that he was especially interested in dealing with the *moral views* of writers or in judging them according to a specific ethical code, either his own or society's. The word "moral," as usual with Sainte-Beuve, has the broadest psychological and sociological connotations. What interested him above all was the study of the qualities inherent in the writer's situation *as a writer,* the specific nature of *the writer as a species.* The *Lundis,* in this respect confirming and consolidating the whole trend of his prior criticism, constitute nothing less than "une Comédie littéraire de la

France." This term, as we noted in Chapter 5, was Thibaudet's, and he explained it thus: "Sainte-Beuve is the only critic with a profound and detailed sense of what used to be called literary mores [*les moeurs littéraires*], the literary ethos. . . . He was the Montesquieu of the writers' republic, from whose *Lundis* one could draw a *Spirit of Letters* more flexible but no less rich in observation than *The Spirit of the Laws* [*L'Esprit des Lois*]" (pp. 287–288).

In these few pages I can merely suggest the abundant ramifications of this aspect of the *Lundis,* which has largely been neglected by scholars in favor of the more conventional kinds of literary criticism contained in the work. I have singled out for comment here three facets of the "comédie littéraire" to which Sainte-Beuve devotes most of his attention: the writer as critic; the situation of the "man of letters" in his own time; and, growing out of this second theme, the ideal writer as he conceived him.

Of the writer as critic, he possessed, of course, knowledge of the most intimate kind, from the inside. Beginning with the first volume of the *Causeries* (with the inaugural *Lundi,* in fact, on the dramatic criticism of Saint-Marc Girardin), he granted ample space to the "criticism of critics." The gallery is further expanded in subsequent volumes, with critics old and new, great and small, occasionally grouped in "families," but no individual quite like another. The critic is viewed at various moments of history, as poet-turned-critic, as continuing and successful poet, as scholar, as literary historian, as journalist, as professor. Models of great critics are proposed for emulation (Goethe, Pope, Boileau, with amends being made to the last for the cold treatment given him in the *Portraits*), and examples of poor critics are cited to be avoided (Laprade, Pontmartin). What makes a critic "complete" or "incomplete," his function and role, the various types of critical judgment that are possible, the kind of imagination needed in a critic and how it differs from "l'imagination créatrice" (*CL* VII, apropos of Grimm), the risks incurred by criticism as it became ever more learned and complex, the importance of "word of mouth criticism" (especially in Paris), the critic's ideal relation to contemporary authors, to his readers — these are but a few of the aspects of the "critic as species" treated in the *Lundis.*

Sainte-Beuve's study of the "man of letters" was based both on extensive historical knowledge and on close observation of almost all the important writers of his time, from Chateaubriand to the

Goncourt brothers, from the Cénacle of the 1830s to the Magny Restaurant dinners of the 1860s. He was convinced that the literary manners of his time had entered on a phase of corruption, and this conviction was as much responsible as his neoclassical susceptibilities for the severity with which he judged most of his great contemporaries. Writers no longer constituted a "class apart," held to certain standards of refinement by an élite readership or by enlightened patrons. Everyone had now become a "man of letters," and success meant selling oneself to an amorphous and no longer so demanding public. Exaggerated claims of worth, inflated reputations, were the order of the day, as literature became more and more "industrialized." In such an atmosphere, vanity (*l'amour-propre littéraire*), of which he considered Balzac to be the most monstrous example, counted more than sincerity, self-glorification more than truth. The writer had become essentially a *comédien*; his works mattered less than the legend that an adulatory public, assisted by the members of his coterie and by the author himself, had fabricated around him (here Sainte-Beuve had his eye on Victor Hugo; see *CL* XIV, 282–283).

Given this pessimistic view, it is hardly surprising that Sainte-Beuve appears at times to despise literature itself, at least as practiced by the professional men of letters of his time. These *littérateurs* (the term is decidedly pejorative with him) sacrifice truth to the display of their talent for making brilliant but empty phrases.

From this "antiliterary" or at least "anti-*littérateur*" stance on his part, two corollary attitudes derived. The first was his tendency to reserve his highest praise for writers who least resembled contemporary men of letters — for example, Bossuet, all the greater for having been "not an author but a bishop and doctor of the church" (*CL* XII); Le Sage, whose *Gil Blas* he considered the best French novel because "a completely natural book" (*CL* I); Buffon, "very little the author either in his life or in his correspondence" (*CL* XIV), Montesquieu, "a great mind from up close as from afar" (*CL* VII). One finds countless variations in the *Lundis* on this theme, which is in itself a variation on Pascal's famous *pensée:* "One is surprised and delighted to come across a natural style, for one expected to find an author and instead one finds a man." Or it may be a woman, like the contemporary poet Marceline Desbordes-Valmore, whose poetry Sainte-Beuve admired as the natural expression of her soul. The second corollary was his respect for so many writers of secondary or minor stature whom one would hesitate to call writers at all, individuals like the Maréchal de Saint-Arnaud ("the first among bivouac letter writers"), who were "writers without knowing it," and often had more of value to say and said it better than professional writers (*CL* XIII). Many women appear in the *Lundis* as illustrations of this "littérature involontaire," as he called it (*B* XI, 228).

If Sainte-Beuve devoted so much space to such "nonliterary" authors, it was not because of any inability to deal perceptively with conscious literary artists, either great or small (another myth about him that needs to be dispelled). To claim this is to fly in the face of the texts themselves and to reveal insensitivity to his real achievement. The host of "writers without knowing it" form a logical, integral part of his grand design in the *Lundis*. To dismiss them as less important than the others is like ignoring a whole category of characters in Balzac's novels. They belong to the work not only as antidotes to the "professional writer" but also by virtue of the light they shed on the human condition generally. For the "comédie littéraire" to which Thibaudet referred is merely one aspect of a much larger subject, a veritable "comédie humaine" contained in the *Lundis*. It was inevitable that Sainte-Beuve, more a moralist at heart than a literary critic, should have expanded the framework of criticism to encompass this larger subject.

IV   *The Broader Human Drama*

The range of human types portrayed in the *Lundis* far surpasses that found in the works of many novelists, let alone those of critics. In this section I hope to give some idea, first of this immense cast of characters, and then of the vision of the world underlying their presentation.

Some of these figures belong to the world of literature in the broadest sense or to the world of art. Historians interested Sainte-Beuve keenly, as did scholars, journalists, translators, orators, preachers. Few essays are devoted to philosophers; composers, sculptors, architects are even rarer; but painters received more and more attention as the *Lundis* progressed and as Sainte-Beuve discovered their qualities as writers (Horace Vernet and Gavarni, for example). A long essay on Gavarni opens with a plea for extending the concept of literature to include those whom men of letters used to dismiss with contempt as mere "artisans." "My real ambition in my genre," wrote Sainte-Beuve in a letter of 1867, "is to extend literary criticism to embrace all those who have *written,* whether painters, architects, naturalists or others" (*B* XVI, 54–55, italics in original). From the same letter we learn of his cherished desire, which death left unfulfilled, to devote a study to a painter he much admired, Delacroix.

A large number of figures, on the other hand, belong only very marginally to literature: kings and queens, princes and princesses of the royal blood, lesser aristocracy, magistrates, diplomats, administrators, financiers, politicians, statesmen, soldiers, ecclesiastics, women of polite society (*femmes du salon*), saints, scientists. Not only are they an essential part of the "human comedy," but the essays devoted to them (what a pity so many readers of Sainte-Beuve ignore this fact) are among his finest. The *Lundis* on soldiers are among the most fascinating, for Sainte-Beuve was a fine *peintre des militaires* and psychologist of "the warrior's virtue and genius." In recognizing that skill in warfare has its own kind of "poetry" (*CL* XIII, 49), he was following Napoleon, whose remark, "In the military profession, as in literature, each one has his genre," serves as an epigraph to introduce the essay on Count Friant, a general in Napoleon's army (*CL* XIV). Napoleon himself is viewed as "the Goethe among soldiers," General Jomini as the "Malherbe," and the like.

To recreate the host of "nonliterary" characters who appear in the *Lundis* Sainte-Beuve drew heavily on a type of writing in which he believed that the French had been especially prolific and successful and which had intrigued him since his early days as a contributor to *Le Globe:* namely, memoirs. For the moralist, the memoirs of even the least known authors, providing they had left a faithful portrayal of themselves, were a valuable contribution to "moral science." Furthermore, memoirs were rich in situations as dramatic as any found in imaginative literature. Bossuet's funeral oration for the Duchesse d'Orléans, for example, Sainte-Beuve found to be but a feeble echo of the scene of Bossuet kneeling at her deathbed as recorded in the *Memoirs* of Cosnac (*CL* VI). He exercised his own gifts for the dramatic by recreating from memoirs the tragic misfortunes of historical figures such as the Grande Mademoiselle, the Duchesse d'Angoulême, and Marie-Antoinette. Were not the sufferings of this last, he asked, comparable to those of

Hecuba or Andromache, whose history and legend the Greek play-wrights had drawn upon for their tragedies?

Thanks to their huge cast of characters, the *Lundis* cover a wide range of human experience. Their author succeeds in portraying with understanding many forms of happiness and misfortune; of success and failure; of love, friendship, and enmity; and many moral and philosophical views, not all of which by any means were close to his own experience or beliefs. To accomplish this was in itself a feat of the imagination. Yet throughout these "meta-morphoses," as he liked to call them, he retained his own point of view on human life. Here again I can but suggest the broad outlines of a subject that would certainly not be too small for book length treatment.

Sainte-Beuve believed that man's nature has remained basically unchanged throughout the ages, so that the modern reader, for example, could recognize himself essentially in the pages of La Bruyère, of whose *Caractères* he said: "He provided the text; we need only add the variants" (*NL* V, 427). The *Lundis* provide the text; we need only add the variants! At first glance the view of human nature proposed by this largely sedentary and largely Parisian critic might seem to be based on too narrow a field of observation. But if he rarely left Paris (some might say the Rue du Montparnasse!) his learning and imagination traveled widely for him both in time and in space. To reject his assumption that his compatriots were an adequate mirror of mankind is to suggest that a comparable criticism could be laid against Shakespeare or Balzac, Chekhov or Faulkner — a patent absurdity. A truly universal writer — and Sainte-Beuve is one of these — can make any people serve as the mirror of mankind.

The view of mankind that emerges from the *Lundis* is on the whole pessimistic, as one would expect from the historian of Port-Royal who agreed substantially with the somber Jansenist assess-ment of human nature. Man's propensity to evil remains fairly con-stant from one generation to another; like certain physical illnesses, his moral disorders merely assume a different form at different times. Given this pessimism, it is easy to understand Sainte-Beuve's scorn for philosophies of human perfectibility, such as Turgot's and Condorcet's in the eighteenth century, and for nineteenth cen-tury utopianism. Even his beloved Montesquieu, he complained, put too much faith in man's capacity for civic virtue and needed to be "corrected" by consulting Machiavelli. Similarly, one should "cure oneself of Condorcet" by reading the memoirs of the Cardinal de Retz and *Gil Blas.* To believe, with Condorcet, that by changing institutions one could "change the motives of the human heart" seemed to him the profoundest error (*CL* III, 346). Revolutions tend to produce more evil than good; at best they allow us to "change masters" and to replace one form of idolatry with another. The age of Louis XIV worshipped royalty; his own (according to Sainte-Beuve), the popular will. He would have agreed with Orwell that "in politics one can never do more than decide which of two evils is the less."[6]

Yet for all his pessimism he recognized, with Pascal, whose thought left its imprint upon him in so many ways, that man is a creature of greatness as well as wretchedness. For all the scarcity of virtuous men and women and the paucity of true wisdom, virtue and wisdom are not illusions but realities. He was as critical of cynics or extreme pessimists like Chamfort as he was of optimists and utopians. It is amusing at first, but then perhaps touching, to hear the disillusioned bachelor Sainte-Beuve taking that other disillusioned bachelor Chamfort to task for allowing his disappointments to blind him to the possibility that marriage and the procreation of children might well be a "method of hoping," a reason for belief in the future (*CL* IV, 558). Although he generally agreed with La Rochefoucauld's analysis of self-love as the primary human motive, he noted with pleasure that the great moralist had contradicted himself by shedding a "disinterested tear" when he learned of the heroic death on the battlefield of the Maréchal de Turenne (*NL* V, 391–392).

The text of the *Lundis* does not seem to me to bear out Gabriel Brunet's contention that their author's view of human nature was "bitter" and "cruel."[7] As in the *Portraits,* and of course as in *Port-Royal,* there are many examples of virtue, even heroic virtue, chosen from the most varied social origins and walks of life — Vauvenargues, Malesherbes, Madame Roland, Marceline Desbordes-Valmore, to name but a few. "Let us learn to appreciate every form of heroism, the invisible as well as the visible," he wrote, echoing the thought of *Port-Royal* (*CL* VIII, 511). As for greatness, his chariness in using the term about his own century (a century actually richer in great men and women than he realized), his love of demythifying supermen, his distaste for the "embellished, ennobling portrait" (*NL* II, 17) — none of this should mislead us. His real position on the matter is best summed up in his paraphrase of Frederick the Great, who believed that the critic, in judging great men, should raise himself up "to the point within their being at which they themselves rise above their contradictions and failings" (*CL* III, 185).

If Sainte-Beuve believed, *au fond,* in virtue and greatness, he also believed in happiness. There is a whole "art of happiness" (he had used the term earlier in an essay on La Rochefoucauld in *Portraits de femmes*) to be compiled from the pages of the *Lundis.* We noted a moment ago his skepticism concerning politics as an instrument of happiness: he refused to believe that if only we found the right kind of constitution all would be well. Pessimist that he was, he tended to view happiness as consolation in misfortune and the art of happiness, paradoxically, as "the art of doing without happiness" (VI, 47). Yet his view of this condition did possess certain very positive elements. He stressed the need in one's life for what he variously called a "mainspring," a "spur," a "fire," for the shaping of one's character or talent. It is not always the happiest people, in the conventional sense, who are gifted with or manage to acquire this driving creative force, and sometimes it resembles a "demon." But better this demon than an excessively cautious "good sense" that robs life of all passionate drive.

Another basic ingredient of happiness for Sainte-Beuve was the ability to endure. Although this may seem negative, especially when couched in his favorite metaphor of life as an inevitable shipwreck that one must seek to survive, *l'art de durer* takes on a very positive meaning in his pages. One could also compile from the *Lundis* a veritable "art of growing old" based on the many *vieillards* who are portrayed therein. If there was a key to happiness for Sainte-Beuve it lay in knowing how to grow old — *savoir vieillir;* and the secret of this art, in turn, lay in finding an interest designed to outlast the span of one's life, "une occupation plus longue que la vie," in the words of Madame de Tracy, one of those who had mastered this art of "growing old without ceasing to hope" (XIII, 204). Sainte-Beuve recognized many possible solutions to this problem. His own, however, he found, as had Montesquieu before him, in what he called "study (*l'étude*)," which is but another name for the vigilantly maintained activity of the mind. A man who had known love and friendship and the pleasures of society (his bookishness was never of the kind to lead him into solitude), he found no source of happiness to be more reliable than that increase of awareness and understanding which, in Montesquieu's words, "renders an intelligent being more intelligent" (VII, 58–59).

V *The Artist in the Critic*

With age and experience, Sainte-Beuve remarked a few years before embarking on the *Lundis,* "physiology" had tended to gain ground in his criticism over "poetry" (*PM* 259). While there is no reason to question his judgment, it would be a mistake to conclude that he was any the less an artist in the *Lundis* than in previous works. In an early *causerie* on Diderot (1851) echoing a *portrait littéraire* originally published in 1831 (see our Chapter 5, III), the great eighteenth century writer appears as the patron of poets disguised as critics, and Sainte-Beuve implies that literary criticism was for himself what art criticism had been for Diderot, "a pretext for reverie and poetry." He suggests that like Diderot he was a "demi-poète" who became fully a poet only in his criticism, when a literary work or historical document (a painting, for Diderot) provided the needed stimulus for making criticism a form of creation ("Il y a dans un tel mode de critique toute une création" [*CL* III, 306, 309]).

This essay deserves to be better known, for it provides the theory of what might be called "la méthode poétique en critique" to counterbalance "la méthode naturelle" of the 1862 article on Chateaubriand. Nor is it an isolated instance. Throughout the *Lundis* Sainte-Beuve insists on the critic's need to imagine and to create, in his own special fashion. The year before his death, in an essay on Jean-Jacques Ampère (it was his last piece devoted to a critic), he throws further light on this question. He points out that Ampère, whose gifts as a literary historian he esteemed highly, fell short of being an "artist" because he put all his "fire" into his research, leaving none for "execution" (*NL* XIII, 225). Of himself, on the other hand, Sainte-Beuve remarked: "I put together my article as a tailor puts together a suit."[8]

This craftsmanship reveals itself not only in the composition of single essays but to a surprising extent, given the circumstances of publication, in the pattern of the whole. The fact that no single essay structure is quite like another makes it difficult to generalize about this aspect, and so I will limit myself to a few remarks about the overall pattern.

Sainte-Beuve kept in mind the reader's need to be guided through what might easily appear to be a maze of disparate, unorganized fragments. A *critique feuilletoniste,* he tried to keep in view (as would a good *romancier feuilletoniste*) the whole work that he was constructing. Here his model was to some extent La Bruyère. To use the term "architecture" of the *Lundis* as he did of the *Caractères* would probably be an exaggeration: the latter is a book, the former a collection of articles. But one might well apply to the *Lundis* Sainte-Beuve's description of La Bruyère's concern for order "beneath the appearance of disorder" and for providing a "thread" to guide the reader through the "labyrinth" of his short prose pieces (*NL* I, 134).

In fact there are many such "threads" in the *Lundis.* Certain characters "reappear," as in the novels of Balzac, some (for example, Thiers and Chateaubriand) providing an especially strong element of continuity. Some are recalled or anticipated in connection with others, or first evoked briefly in one *Lundi* before moving to center stage in a later one. Thanks to what Regard called Sainte-Beuve's "genius for comparisons and contrasts," one subject engendered another in his mind, and this very manner of arriving at his subjects contributed powerfully, in the finished product, to their interdependence and cohesion, no matter how diverse they appeared on the surface. "As with Balzac," observes Regard, "one character calls forth another." The resulting product may not exactly "follow the same laws as in the creation of a novel" (even granted the novel has "laws," this claim on Regard's part seems exaggerated), but it certainly resembles in many ways "la création romanesque" (147).

But individuals also reappear collectively, so to speak, in the guise of their profession, their generation, their century (for example, the eighteenth century French *abbé,* usually a comic type for Sainte-Beuve). Other groupings that recur as motifs cut across centuries and occasionally national boundaries: brothers and sisters of great men; women admirers and correspondents of great writers; individuals who link one century with another, or who are the last of a type on the verge of extinction, or who died young, or who survived as *vieillards* either of the feeble or of the robust variety. Political behavior alone furnishes a wealth of subgroupings, such as courtiers fallen from favor, unsuccessful men of action become accomplished moralists, *femmes politiques,* writers contrasted for their comportment in times of revolution, restorers of order following on revolutionary upheaval.

If the *Lundis* are a vast well-ordered gallery, they are also, to borrow a phrase from Bonnerot's *Bibliographie* (III, 33), a gallery "on the move." The sense of movement that they communicate is at times almost dramatic. Sainte-Beuve's *comédie humaine,* even if he had possessed an imagination as powerful as Balzac's, could never by the nature of the enterprise have been dramatic in the same sense as what Balzac called, in the preface to his *Comédie Humaine,* "le drame à trois ou quatre mille personnages que présente une Société." Once having recognized this, however, it is interesting to note how frequently Sainte-Beuve, like Balzac, refers to his work in theatrical terms and how often he does succeed in endowing both individual essays and the work as a whole with dynamic, quasi-dramatic qualities. Some of these are simply the kind that one finds in any story well told, though there is nothing simple about the art involved. More than once Sainte-Beuve refers to the *Lundis* as "tales" (*contes*) or "short stories" (*nouvelles*) and compares the lives he is recreating to "novels" (*romans*). Regard writes perceptively of the "Thousand and One Nights" atmosphere of the *Lundis* and of how the critic developed *l'anecdote* and *l'historiette* into a whole new "literary genre" (pp. 148–151).

In more specifically dramatic terms there are many fine "scènes de comédie" (Sainte-Beuve's phrase), though always well documented. He was not free, like the full-fledged artist, to invent such scenes, and the historian in him rejected "the scene without witnesses" (*CL* I, 396). From a broader perspective, the whole of French history became for him "a play [*un spectacle*] with a thousand aspects" (*NL* V, 149). Some individuals played leading roles and others smaller, but never totally insignificant, ones. The Marquis de Lassay, for example, is "a bit player in the seventeenth century" ("un figurant du Grand Siècle"); Duclos, a "utility player of the first rank" in the "great comedy of the eighteenth century." Tocqueville's role in the nineteenth is compared to that of the *raisonneur* in "high comedy." The drama of France becomes in turn a microcosm of the universal human drama.

Like the artist, finally, Sainte-Beuve had an imagination for concrete detail. His characters appear to us not as abstractions but in their bodily presences, with their physical mannerisms, their gestures, the sound of their voices. Few are the essays that do not contain a verbal portrait based on a visual work of art (*peinture, gravure, buste*) or on a description reconstructed from other sources. With living authors, Sainte-Beuve often arranged a "sitting" ("une séance de pose"); for those recently dead, the "sitting" took place with witnesses who had known them intimately. In his sense of visual detail Sainte-Beuve might be compared with such portrait painters as his compatriot from the north of France, the *pastelliste* Quentin de Latour (see *NL* IV, 163; VIII, 295–296). His insistence on the truth, warts and all, suggests an analogy with Rembrandt. Among his contemporaries, the *Légendes,* lithographs accompanied by maximlike inscriptions, of Gavarni appealed to the *peintre-moraliste* in him and might be considered to some extent the visual equivalents of his essays (see *NL* VI). But his imagination was "auditory as well as visual" (Regard, p. 169). He could not have chosen a better title for his essays than *Causeries:* not only does he converse with his readers, whom he often refers to as his "listeners," but he converses with his subjects and they converse among themselves. The masterful use of quotations from written sources as well as from well-authenticated oral sources enabled him to bring all these voices to life.

VI   *Assessment*

There are some stretches of the *Lundis,* especially in the last five or six volumes of the *Nouveaux Lundis,* where Sainte-Beuve's earlier, more rhetorical prose manner returns and the style tends to be mechanical and verbose. The pressure to furnish copy goes far to explain these lapses, a pressure aggravated by the strain of illness and fatigue felt by Sainte-Beuve, who compared himself in 1864 to a "pieceworker" and to "an actor obliged to go on performing at an age when he should have retired" (*B* XIII, 485–486). Some subjects he treated more in the line of duty than out of pleasure, and the reader inevitably senses this. But his inspiration could always be counted on to be recharged on contact with the subjects he loved best, such as the Duc de Saint-Simon, author of the great memoirs of the court of Louis XIV (*NL* X). Most of these six hundred or so essays can be read and reread with interest more than a century later; many are literary masterpieces. Of how many journalists can such a claim be made?

Barbey d'Aurevilly found the *Lundis* long on anecdotes and details but short on ideas and compared their author to a collector of gossip disguised as a critic.[9] But this is to ignore not only his habit of accuracy and reliability as a biographer-historian but also the tact with which he selected anecdotes for their revelatory effect — "non pas l'anecdote futile mais celle qui caractérise" (*CL* I, 282). Furthermore, the reader who is willing to collaborate with the author discovers a whole wealth of general ideas suggested by the text. What is rare in the *Lundis* is not ideas but *abstract* ideas, for Sainte-Beuve, as his criticism of Tocqueville in particular makes clear, distrusted these. "Truth, no matter how elevated," he had written in *Port-Royal*, paraphrasing the Bible, "must become *man* in order to touch the hearts of men" (I, 638, italics in original). This insistence on clothing his ideas in visible, tangible human form may well have been a sign of the poet's and novelist's instinct surviving in the critic.

Other critics have objected not to an absence of thought in the *Lundis* but, on the contrary, to an abundance of ideas so divergent as to be confusing and contradictory. Fayolle, for example, alleged a serious contradiction between Sainte-Beuve's scientific aspiration and his conception of the critic as judge.[10] Such charges would be more disturbing had the *Lundis* been intended as a logical, systematic argument, a work of theory. Because they are essays, however, their contradictions (assuming these cannot be resolved) reveal all the better the tensions occurring in the author's mind. Nor should we allow his obvious biases to detract from our pleasure. That his undeniable effort to be impartial did not succeed with writers whom he clearly detested (his "haines," as the French expression goes), such as Condorcet, Saint-Just, Constant, Vigny, and of course his "favorite quarry," Balzac,[11] might be alarming had he written a dissertation; but again, like his contradictions, they merely add to the piquancy of critical essays.

Other perhaps more serious weaknesses that critics have found in the *Lundis*, indeed in Sainte-Beuve's criticism as a whole, are the abuse of the biographical approach to literature, the excessive amount of praise lavished on "mediocre" figures, and above all, the failure to recognize great writers in his midst. Insofar as he claimed that biography provides *the* key to the interpretation of a literary work and even appeared to postulate some kind of causal relationship between the two, he is open to the charge that Proust among others laid against him, namely, that he misunderstood the nature of artistic creation. Nevertheless, it seems not entirely reasonable to accuse him of devoting too much space to lives and too little to works when by his own admission he was as much a biographer and moralist as a literary critic. As for his alleged inability to deal perceptively with the greatest writers, his pages on Montaigne, Pascal, Diderot, and Goethe, and his many illuminating remarks on other major writers, simply do not bear out the truth of that charge.

In his assessment of his contemporaries he is clearly more vulnerable to attack. To be sure, for a critic whose career spanned forty years of almost uninterrupted activity, who wrote on an incredible variety of subjects, and who never claimed infallibility to begin with, his score for recognition of new talent (Louis Bertrand, Maurice and Eugénie de Guérin, Marceline Desbordes-Valmore, Renan, Taine, to name a few) was hardly contemptible. But all this makes no less painful his view that Stendhal had no talent as a novelist, his prediction that Balzac would soon be forgotten, or his willingness to devote essay after essay to poets each more mediocre than the other while managing only an appendix for the author of *Les Fleurs du mal*. Instead of stretching his mind so often to reveal the unsuspected "literary" vein of obscure and not very exciting figures like the astronomer Sylvain Bailly, one regrets that he did not reach out to discover, for example, what it was about Balzac or Hugo that made them great *despite* their objectionable traits.

His failure to perceive the true stature of these and other contemporary writers was due less to envy, however, than to the fact that his conception of beauty was in some ways very narrow. His esthetic horizons were restricted both by his neoclassical bias and by certain assumptions he held concerning the moralistic and idealistic nature of art.[12] But if the esthetic universe of the *Lundis* appears narrow, their moral and psychological universe is marvelously broad. If their author failed to show the kind of insight into the great writers of his time that characterized such critics as Boileau and Baudelaire, if he sometimes proved inadequate as a literary critic, he more than redeemed himself in other ways. As a literary historian, few have equaled his command of French literary history or his skill, rising at times to that of a true virtuoso (he belonged, after all, to the generation of Chopin and Liszt), in sketching the precise historical context needed for a given subject. With something of that "hypercreativity" that enabled Stendhal or Balzac to suggest the germ of a whole story in a passing remark,[13] he constantly throws off ideas for further research. By broadening literary criticism so that it became a means of inquiry into human nature, the *critique moraliste,* the *critique peintre,* provides delights that make us willing to forgive the deficiencies of the *critique littéraire.*

Among the most impressive features of his criticism as broadened in the *Lundis* are his ability to grasp characters who were very unlike himself and very unlike one another, and his equally great ability to arouse our sympathy for them, to make us appreciate their merits, while clearly bringing out their limitations and flaws. Both kinds of accomplishment, I would argue, are the mark of criticism of the highest order.

The *Lundis* are the final flowering in Sainte-Beuve's career of that gift which Thiers, seeking to define the chief attribute of the historian, called "l'intelligence," that is, the ability "to enter into the spirit of situations and views that differed widely from one era to another" (*CL* XV, 270).[14] He was not, of course, referring to Sainte-Beuve and had primarily in mind flexibility in understanding different statesmen and their circumstances and policies. Sainte-Beuve's "intelligence" goes far beyond this to embrace the broadest spectrum of human types. How great the scope of his sympathies could be, only a person who reads widely in the *Lundis* can fully appreciate.

CHAPTER 9

Other Writings

I *Studies on Virgil and Proudhon*

F EW French writers have been more ardent admirers and assiduous interpreters of ancient Greek and Roman literatures than Sainte-Beuve. One of his most prized possessions was his father's annotated copy of Virgil. In addition to Virgil, he especially loved Homer, the *Greek Anthology,* Theocritus, Tibullus, and Horace. Although not a classical philologist, he was an accomplished Latinist and a lifelong student of Greek (we recall that his main reason for leaving Boulogne-sur-Mer for Paris as an adolescent was to pursue his study of Greek), and frequently consulted scholars with the expertise that he lacked in the field of Greco-Roman antiquity. He devoted a substantial portion of his published criticism as well as many a passage of his notebooks to the "immortal spirits of Greece and Rome," acknowledging them as models of true maturity and as sources of renewed health and vitality for minds made weary by modern civilization (*PM* 39).

The most ambitious of his critical works in this field was his *Etude sur Virgile,* published in 1857 and based on the course on Latin poetry that he had undertaken to give at the Collège de France in 1854–1855 but had been unable to complete because of politically motivated student opposition.[1] Appended to this work are a study of the late Greek epic poet, Quintus of Smyrna, who subsequent to Virgil also treated the theme of Aeneas and the Trojans, and an essay on Horace viewed as the poet par excellence of good sense, taste, proportion, and restraint, a poet especially suited to French culture and a welcome antidote to counteract Romantic excesses. The major portion of the book, however, belongs to Virgil.

In his opening address Sainte-Beuve sketches the history of the chair of Latin poetry and evokes the memories of the eminent scholars who had occupied it before him. This *discours d'ouverture* also provided him with the opportunity to renew his profession of faith in the cause of the Muses and of literary study in a fervent tone reminiscent of his opening lecture for the course on Chateaubriand at Liège. His intention was to follow in his predecessors' footsteps by being not merely a teacher of Virgil but a "priest" in the enlightened and intelligent cult of that great poet, and of classical antiquity in general (*Etude* 23). The study itself is divided into two parts. The first consists of chapters on Virgil as a poet of his time, on the epic poet as conceived by Virgil and Homer, on the genius and art of Virgil, on pre-Virgilian traditions concerning Aeneas, and on the epic poem as a genre; it concludes with an analysis of the *Aeneid* as a whole. The second part is devoted to a detailed analysis of Book One of the poem, followed by a historical survey of the comparative reputations of Homer and Virgil in France.

Sainte-Beuve's Virgil is the poet of reflection, of "study," the polished artist, as well as the poet of restrained but deep feeling, of a melancholy that was (in the critic's view) still healthy and had not yet become a form of sickness, "la *maladie* de la sensibilité," that it was to become with the Romantics (so he alleged, underlining the word for emphasis [100]). The chief traits of *le génie virgilien* he found to be "the love of nature, the cult of poetry, respect for and imitation of the masters, learning, patriotism, humanity, piety, sensibility, and tenderness"; the chief characteristic of his art, his sense of proportion and harmony in the work as a whole, and his never-failing taste (102).

Sainte-Beuve lost no opportunity to relate Virgil to the literary and political scenes of France in the 1850s. The Roman poet's taste and restraint, his impeccable workmanship, his sustained excellence, are contrasted with the "gigantic feats of prowess" followed by "catastrophic failures" on the part of the "monsters" of contemporary French literature (105–106). (No names are given, but the reference to the "Cyclops" makes us think inevitably of Victor Hugo.) Allusions to contemporary politics are much less direct, but there can be no doubt that the Virgil who championed Roman imperial authority and stability as a guarantee against civil disorders also had exemplary value for the critic who had supported the Second French Empire formally established in 1852.[2]

The *Etude sur Virgile,* though by no means a neglected masterpiece, is marked by a number of original insights into its subject. Few classical scholars would probably include it on a short list of indispensable works on Virgil, but the experts continue to cite it occasionally on points of detail and laymen will still find it a readable and useful guide. The Virgilian scholar R.D. Williams credits Sainte-Beuve with launching a much-needed revaluation of Virgil's achievement in the wake of the Romantic (particularly the English Romantic) depreciation of his genius; he also recognizes that Sainte-Beuve "gave a new meaning, a new depth to the appreciation of Virgilian pathos."[3] These were perhaps the book's major achievements.

From the poet of classical refinement and restraint to the pioneer socialist and anarchist, the fiery, rebellious prose writer, Pierre-Joseph Proudhon (1809–1865) — if further proof were needed of Sainte-Beuve's versatility, it is provided in the juxtaposition of his *Etude sur Virgile* and his *P.-J. Proudhon, sa vie et sa correspondance (1838–1848),* published first in 1865 as a series of articles in *La Revue contemporaine* and then posthumously in book form in 1872.[4]

His interest in Proudhon, whom he first met in 1856 at the publishing house of Garnier Frères, was due to some extent to the affinities he sensed with this writer but perhaps even more to the attraction of opposites. Proudhon admired *Port-Royal* and the *Lundis* greatly. He shared with Sainte-Beuve a love for Pascal and for Virgil as well as a common interest in the moral implications of literature, a common belief that modern literature had become "decadent." His ambition to make politics and economics into a science was analogous to Sainte-Beuve's similar (though qualified) ambition for literary history and criticism. On the other hand, his defiance of the established order, his lack of prudence, his pluck (*crânerie,* Sainte-Beuve calls it) in fighting for a cause that he believed just, all appeared to fascinate the cautious, conciliatory bourgeois critic. Beneath the uniform of the academician and senator still beat the heart of Joseph Delorme, who understood and sympathized with the oppressed. Proudhon's humble origins, his poverty, his dream of social reform reawakened in the former fellow traveler of the Saint-Simonians a sense of injustice that had been repressed but never destroyed in this recipient of official honors and friend of the powerful. Proudhon's courage sparked his own, and although he was not quite courageous enough to defend the "Anti-Christ" (as the respectable bourgeois viewed Proudhon) during his lifetime, his courage in "avenging the memory of this great victim of persecution"[5] was none the less genuine. His *Proudhon* offers "perhaps the finest proof of his independence of mind and his human charity."[6]

His purpose in the book, Sainte-Beuve explains, was not to plead the cause of Proudhon or of his doctrines but to "perform a literary act" ("faire acte de littérature"), that is, to integrate this "great revolutionary" into literature by attempting to discover the truth about the man and to define his personality and talent (*Proudhon* 12). This objective was related to the project outlined for the *Nouveaux Lundis* but only partly realized — the goal of "neutralizing the field of literary criticism" by writing as dispassionately as possible about political figures of the extreme left as well as the extreme right (*CL* XVI, 42 — Proudhon is in fact mentioned in this passage).

Sainte-Beuve provides us with what is essentially an intellectual biography of Proudhon based on his own letters and interspersed with the testimony of those who knew him well and with the critic's analyses. "The true title of my work," he notes, "might well have been: Proudhon's story told and commented upon by himself," ("Proudhon raconté et commenté par lui-même" [115]). This method, which the critic had used in miniature in many of his essays and had experimented with at greater length in the "Chênedollé" section of *Chateaubriand et son groupe littéraire,* here received its most ample and masterful application. But Sainte-Beuve had additional reasons for basing his study on Proudhon's letters. He believed that these revealed the "true thought" of Proudhon (233), expressed, furthermore, in a moderate form that made it more attractive to those who might be repelled by the intransigence of his published writings (278). He even went so far as to claim that Proudhon's correspondence was his most important work, "son oeuvre capitale" (274).

As a judge of Proudhon, Sainte-Beuve reproached him for "his reduction of political questions to economic questions" (67) and for an excess of "combativité" that contradicted his claim to be a scholar, *un savant* (148). But he admired the integrity of the man and agreed with many of his views, including his conception of political science as "metaphysics in action" (Proudhon quoted, p. 212).

In the *Etude sur Virgile* Sainte-Beuve brought his contribution to a historic tradition of commentary on a poet long recognized as one of the greatest of classical antiquity. In this "first appreciation of Proudhon,"[7] a work of much greater originality, he broke new ground and opened the way for the serious and impartial study of a much maligned and misunderstood contemporary. Although the work is "unfinished" in the sense that the sequel which he planned on Proudhon's life and correspondence from 1849 to his death was never completed, it is by no means unfinished in the artistic sense: it is written in a vigorous prose that captures something of Proudhon's own forcefulness.

II   *Notebooks and Letters*

As a very young man Sainte-Beuve jotted down sporadic notes on his reading, his projects, and his moral and intellectual growth. Published posthumously by Charly Guyot and others, they provide a valuable source on which I have occasionally drawn in the early chapters of this book. It was not until 1834, however, that he began systematically to keep such notebooks. During his lifetime he included samples of these *notes et pensées* in collections of his published essays, and he was planning to publish a whole volume of such writings, to be entitled *Pensées ajournées (Postponed Thoughts),* which never materialized.[8] The published portions of the notebooks, according to Raphaël Molho's estimate, comprise only about one third of the total manuscript, now preserved in three *Cahiers* belonging to the Spoelberch de Lovenjoul collection housed in the Bibliothèque de Chantilly. Molho had begun the publication of the complete *Cahiers* and had brought out the first volume, *Le Cahier vert (1834–1847),* before his death in 1975.

In Chapter 5, I discussed the notebooks in the context of the problem of judging contemporary writers and showed how Sainte-Beuve used them to record what he called "thoughts too truthful for any eyes but one's own" (*Port-Royal* I, 971), extremely severe critical notations that he recognized often to be the product of his blacker humors. Here I would briefly characterize the notebooks as a whole, basing my remarks both on the portions published during his lifetime and on the *inédits* presented by Molho.

What the notebooks, first of all, *do not* offer us is much detail concerning the events of Sainte-Beuve's life or much by way of intimate confession. They are very rich, on the other hand, in notations intended to serve as the basis for articles (they give us a precious glimpse into the critic's "workshop," as Molho describes it), in portraits and judgments of many writers, in self-assessments, and in broad views of his century and of human life in general.

Despite Victor Giraud's assignment of the title *Mes poisons* (based on Sainte-Beuve's own metaphor) to his famous edition of selected entries (1926), despite the acrimony of many of the critical judgments and views of life expressed in the *Cahiers,* they "contain fewer poisons than one had been led to believe" (Regard, p. 207). The overall impression they give is not one of a morbid pessimist complacently denigrating everyone and everything around him, but that of a very human individual, at times very *sympathique,* adjusting with courage and intelligence to what he considered the shipwreck of his life, determined to save something of value from the wreckage, determined above all to free himself from the bonds of illusion. Friendship, love, and most of all, literary study ("la passion littéraire," the only passion he acknowledged in himself and the only passion he believed could last [PM 238]), recur as consolatory themes, and are epitomized in a single striking *pensée:* "A good day today, I read Homer in the morning and saw Madame D... [D'Arbouville] in the afternoon" (38). As for his judgments of individuals, they are by no means uniformly cruel, and the harsher ones often come accompanied by their own corrective, as when he recognizes that they may be more witty than true (*des boutades*) or that they constitute not so much "judgments" as "elements of judgment," components of a larger picture which would take account of other points of view (90). An important redeeming feature of the notebooks, furthermore, is that their author is hardly less severe in his self-assessments than in his assessments of others.

Lucidity of self-judgment, sharply drawn portraits, reflections on human existence no less true for being occasionally astringent in their pessimism, a language polished often to the point of lapidarian perfection ("In my youth I thought in sonnets, but now in maxims" [15]) — these are but a few of the qualities that contribute to making Sainte-Beuve's notebooks one of the most readable of private journals.

If he may have entertained the ambition, through his notebooks, to leave a collection of *pensées et maximes* not unworthy of the great moralists whom he so admired (La Rochefoucauld, La Bruyère, Vauvenargues), there appears to have been no similar ambition on his part to rival the great letter writers of literature, such as Cicero, Madame de Sévigné, or Horace Walpole. One could hardly say of his correspondence, as he claimed of Proudhon's, that it was his real masterpiece or that it contained, in quite the same way, "the story of his mind." He expended much less artistry on his letters than on his notebooks. They do form, however, an extensive collection whose importance is far from negligible.

That he was a prolific letter writer is clear from the great edition of his correspondence begun by Jean Bonnerot in 1935, brought forward after his death by his son Alain Bonnerot, and only now nearing completion with the publication of Volume XVII in 1975 — almost six thousand letters spanning half a century from 1818 to 1868, with at least two final volumes projected to bring the record down to Sainte-Beuve's death.

The most interesting of these letters throw further light on how his projects took shape, his reading and research, the roles played by numerous persons who became to some extent his collaborators by assisting him in his research or providing him with first-hand information about his subjects. A special relationship developed between Sainte-Beuve and his reader-correspondents, a kind of friendship of which he wrote: "Rien n'est plus doux que de penser qu'on se fait des amis par ses écrits" (*B* IX, 532). The letters are also interesting for the many literary opinions contained in them which supplement those of his essays and notebooks. They occasionally serve as literary bulletins for the benefit of friends absent from the Paris scene (the letters to Juste and Caroline Olivier later published in *La Revue suisse* are the best-known example). Finally, they give us an occasional insight into the inner man. No less reticent here than in his notebooks, he nevertheless reveals his intimate thoughts and feelings from time to time to such friends as Eustache Barbe, Lamennais, and Victor Pavie, and to a whole series of women correspondents from George Sand, Césarine d'Arbouville, and Hortense Allart to Adèle Couriard, Madame de Solms, and the Princesse Mathilde. His is an image that gains in attractiveness by being reflected in the eyes of his friends.

André Billy has published a selection of these more intimate letters with the intention of highlighting "l'homme amoureux, malheureux, tourmenté que [Sainte-Beuve] a été."[9] Sadness is certainly one of the dominant notes in the correspondence of a man who claimed that his lifelong melancholy could be traced to the fact that his mother had become a widow when she still carried him in her womb (*B* X, 115). Yet Billy is the first to admit the risk of distortion in such an approach and to remind us that a less unhappy Sainte-Beuve would be revealed through a different choice of letters. One could, for example, demonstrate equally well the strength of character revealed in them, a strength that allowed Sainte-Beuve to offset the void in his heart (*le néant*) by activities of the mind and to compensate for what he considered the "human failure" of his life (that is, emotionally and spiritually) by faith in his work. It was this same strength upon which he drew in his last years (the letters of 1866–1868 are especially moving in this respect) to accept stoically the painful illness that he knew to be irreversible and, as a matter of honor, "to do his job well until the end" ("bien faire jusqu'à la fin" [XIV, 73]).

For those acquainted only with the mean-spirited and weak Sainte-Beuve of caricature, it is a surprise to discover this strength of character, as it is to discover his paradoxical ability, morose though he could be, to bring pleasure and even joy to his friends, and his kindness in intervening repeatedly with the authorities on behalf of the humblest victims of poverty or persecution. After reading these letters one understands why those who knew him best referred to him as *le bon Sainte-Beuve*.

CHAPTER 10

Conclusion

I *Myth and Reality*

"P ASCAL, like all famous men who appeal to the imagination, has had his legend," wrote the author of *Port-Royal* (I, 913), and the same can be said of him. Some writers benefit from their legends, which make them greater than they were; Sainte-Beuve, on the other hand, is one of those whose myth has reduced his stature. His is above all what Leroy has called "la légende anti-beuvienne" (*Oeuvres* I, 10).

It is not hard to understand why this has been the case. The foibles of the man, the frequently clumsy style of the writer (of the artist more so than of the critic), made him an easy prey to caricature. As an unsuccessful artist turned critic, he aroused the hostility of those, like Balzac, who felt that he brought to criticism a bias against true creators. As a successful critic, the very authority that he wielded was bound to make him hated by many. A few generations ago he was the much-lauded symbol of so-called biographical criticism; now, in an age when this type of criticism tends to be dismissed as irrelevant and even harmful and to be replaced by various forms of direct analysis of the literary text, he has become the *bête noire* of the new style critics. His blunders of judgment concerning some of his great contemporaries, though exaggerated, have caused his very competence as a critic to fall under a cloud of suspicion.

The result of all this is that his true stature has been belittled, as in a distorting mirror that renders objects smaller. Yet although he has been "attacked from all sides," in Pierre Moreau's words, he is still "a strong presence, standing up irresistibly to attack."[1] Thanks to such leading *Beuviens* as Moreau, Jean Bonnerot, André Billy, Maurice Regard, Gérald Antoine, and Raphaël Molho, who have restored a more authentic Sainte-Beuve as he helped restore a more authentic Pascal, the true nature — the true greatness — of both the man and his work are becoming better known. He has been shown to be "better than his myth" (Regard, p. 198) — as a man, full of complexities and paradoxes, with weaknesses that only the pharisee in us prevents our embracing with fraternal understanding, and with unsuspected strengths and a curiously attractive kind of charm; as a poet and novelist, no longer deserving of contempt; as a critic, more versatile and wide-ranging in method, more shrewd in his judgments, than his current reputation suggests.

His most serious fault was a certain timidity of taste. His chief virtues were modesty (all the more unusual in a member of the Romantic generation), keenness of self-appraisal (no *contre Sainte-Beuve* can match his own self-criticism), integrity, devotion to truth ("If I had a motto, it would be *truth and truth alone,* and let the beautiful and the good manage as best they can!" [*B* XIV, 486, italics in original]), productiveness, fertility of mind, and "a marvelous psychological finesse in seizing and rendering the living individual."[2]

"The best reply to slanderous attacks," he once wrote, "lies in the totality of one's life and work and in the spirit emanating from them" (*B* X, 105). Not all the negative criticism, by far, that has been directed against Sainte-Beuve is slanderous or even ill-willed, but much of it is based — not very solidly — on the ignorance of those who accept stereotyped views of his achievement instead of looking into it first hand. It is my hope that the present book will have conveyed something of the spirit of this great and much maligned figure.

II *Summary of His Achievement*

In a passage of his notebooks outlining his intentions as a critic, Sainte-Beuve confessed to holding two opinions about the nature of criticism that appeared contradictory but were really not so: "First, the critic is merely someone *who knows how to read and who teaches others how to read,* and second, criticism . . . is a constant form of *invention* and *creation* [*une* invention *et une* création *perpétuelle*]" (*PM* 49, italics in original). The first half of the statement seems disarmingly modest; the second, provocatively ambitious. Together they form a proposal that can only be called revolutionary: for perhaps the first time in the history of criticism, it is advanced that the critic should be both the interpreter of the creations of others and, with their works as his springboard, a creator in his own right.

To appreciate Sainte-Beuve as master reader and teacher of reading, one must be prepared to know what *not* to expect as well as what to expect from him. He will disappoint those who turn to him for the minute kinds of textual analysis that contemporary criticism has accustomed us to, although he occasionally anticipated these and other forms of "new criticism."[3] But these same readers will be surprised to find how perceptive a guide he is to an impressive number of authors, to their works as well as their lives, for his approach was by no means limited to the biographical or the historical.[4]

There was some truth in Proust's famous attack on Sainte-Beuve as a critic who failed to do full justice to the artist *qua* artist, to "le *moi* qui produit les oeuvres" as distinct from "le *moi* extérieur."[5] But whether we like it or not, the curiosity to know something about an author's life, the desire to seek in his life a means of better understanding his work, will continue to be natural tendencies on the part of readers, needs that Sainte-Beuve stands ready to help satisfy. We will continue to inquire, as Henri Peyre so well phrased it, "how a certain individual with human frailties has created a work which far transcends him,"[6] and to such an inquiry Sainte-Beuve's criticism has lost little of its relevance.

With all respect for his achievement as a guide to the writings of others, however, it is the second basic component of the critic's art as he conceived it — criticism as "invention" and "creation" — that I believe provides the clue to the real strength and originality of his work. From the twenty year old journalist pondering the tragic image of Marie-Antoinette as reflected in the memoirs of her dressmaker to the patriarch of criticism, a few months before his death, attempting to unravel the complexities of Talleyrand, the concept and practice of criticism as creation runs like a golden thread through his work, giving it both continuity and durability.

This creativity manifests itself in many ways: in content, with his penchant for opening up new fields (Ronsard and sixteenth century French poetry; Port-Royal; Chateaubriand; Proudhon; countless subjects of *Portraits* and *Lundis*) and his discovery and use of unpublished documents; in form, with his invention of a new type of journalistic literary essay. "With the example of Sainte-Beuve," wrote Wallace Fowlie, "the critic became a writer, and literary criticism became an art of writing."[7] More gifted for essays than for works of larger structure (*Port-Royal* is the magnificent exception to this rule), "he accomplished great things within small frameworks" ("Il faisait grand dans de petits cadres"), as one of his contemporaries expressed it (Louis Ulbach, quoted *B* XVI, 375). To borrow a term from musicology, his art was comparable to that "great art in the smaller forms" known as *grosse Kleinkunst*.

A further sign of his creativity was his use of the *article de revue* and the *article de journal* to broaden the range of literary criticism and to make it a vehicle for the expression of nothing less than his own vision of human life. Thus he became a worthy successor of Montaigne, "a Montaigne more concerned with literature than the original, a Montaigne of journalism, one of the last and greatest of French moralists" (Giraud, p. 295). His critical works comprise a human comedy no less absorbing, in some respects even more so, than that of his rival and enemy, Balzac; a collection of human specimens rightly judged by Maurice Barrès to be comparable to the "great menagerie" of Balzac and Shakespeare,[8] who nevertheless far surpass him in creative and imaginative power.

It is doubtful that Sainte-Beuve would have succeeded in elevating criticism to a literary art had he not brought to it his own experience as an artist. Part of the "Sainte-Beuve myth," to be sure, is the notion that his poetry and fiction were no more than aberrant phases of his talent, abortive experiments with no vital connection to the rest of his work. In this book, on the contrary, I have argued that his imaginative writing not only has more merit than it is generally accorded, but that it forms an organic whole with the criticism which is his greatest achievement. To advance this view is not to propose anything startlingly new but merely to confirm the astuteness of certain critics of his own time who perceived that he had succeeded in transplanting, so to speak, his poetic gifts from verse and novel to prose criticism. Charles Labitte, for example, recognized as early as 1839 that Sainte-Beuve had introduced "a personal manner" into criticism, an art which gave his critical essays "a creative value ("une valeur créatrice" [*B* III, 121]); and Edmond Schérer observed in 1862 that his adoption of a full-time career as a critic had not meant a radical break in his evolution, since, on the contrary, "the critic in him began as an artist, the poet and novelist prepared him for another task, and everything that he had been before was put to use in his true and definitive vocation'' (XII, 334).

However, it was left to Sainte-Beuve's young English friend and perhaps his greatest disciple, Matthew Arnold, to express this view most strikingly. In a letter of 1863 to Sainte-Beuve, responding to one of the latter's periodic laments that the critic in him had harmed the cause of the poet, Arnold, after first reassuring him that his poetry had merit and would survive, added this very significant judgment: "But it is above all as a critic that you will live on: is this a cause for complaint? I think not. Great critics (and you are one of them) have always been rarer than great poets; in a great critic there is always, in my opinion, something of the frustrated great poet ("un grand poète un peu supprimé" [XIII, 163]). Shortly after Sainte-Beuve's death, in a published assessment of him consistent with this privately expressed view, Arnold questioned the master's too modest assertion that his critical essays were at best "judicious things in a second-rate genre" (PC I, 517). It would be absurd, he pointed out, to rank Sainte-Beuve with Molière or Milton; it would not be absurd to place him on a level with Lamartine, or even above him, since "first-rate criticism has a permanent value higher than that of any but first-rate poetry and art."[9]

One need not share Arnold's desire to rank authors or agree with his judgments of the poets he mentions in order to accept the point that the phenomenon of Sainte-Beuve led him to formulate: although even the best of critics can never rival in stature the giants of imaginative writing, they *can* achieve greatness and immortality. Sainte-Beuve's strength, after all, lay not in true artistic creation but in what Giraud called "demi-création" (p. 294). This was enough, however, as Arnold recognized in his prophetic remarks, to give his criticism something of that mysteriously suggestive power which enables the greatest literary works to prolong their meaningfulness from one generation of readers to another.

Notes and References

Preface

1. Irving Babbitt, "Sainte-Beuve," in *The Masters of Modern French Criticism* (Boston and New York, 1912; rpt. New York, 1963), p. 160.

Chapter One

1. *Portraits contemporains* (Paris, 1889), II, 495–496. References in the text will hereafter be abbreviated as *PC*. The English translation is quoted from Henry James, "Sainte-Beuve's First Articles," reprinted from *The Nation,* February 18, 1875, in *Literary Reviews and Essays,* ed. Albert Mordell (New York, 1957), p. 80.

2. The edition I have used is Leroy's, *Oeuvres* (Paris, 1956), I (*Premiers Lundis, Portraits littéraires — début*). References in the text will be to volume and page of this edition.

3. "Ma biographie," in *Nouveaux Lundis* (Paris, 1870), XIII, 7. Hereafter abbreviated in text as *NL*.

4. See "Quelques compositions de Sainte-Beuve écolier," in Appendix, *Oeuvres,* I, 591–644.

5. For more on this subject, see R.M. Chadbourne, "Symbolic Landscapes in Sainte-Beuve's Early Criticism," *PMLA,* LXXX (1965): 217–230.

6. See Bibliography under Secondary Sources: Billy, Lehmann, Michaut, Molho.

7. "Notes et remarques," in *Causeries du Lundi* (Paris, n.d.), XVI, 39. Hereafter abbreviated in text as *CL*.

8. *Correspondance générale,* ed. Jean Bonnerot and Alain Bonnerot (Paris and Toulouse, 1935–1975), I, 68. Hereafter abbreviated in text as *B*.

9. See Sainte-Beuve's poem, "A M. Patin, après avoir suivi son Cours de poésie latine," in *Poésies de Sainte-Beuve* (Paris, 1863), II, 253–254.

10. See *Notes inédites de Sainte-Beuve,* ed. Charly Guyot (Neuchâtel, 1931), continued under the same title in *Revue d'histoire littéraire de la France,* XL (1933): 580–594, and XLI (1934): 72–86, 266–284.

11. *Pensées et maximes,* ed. Maurice Chapelan (Paris, 1955), p. 49. Hereafter abbreviated in text as *PM*.

173

12. Maurice Barrès, "Méditation spirituelle sur Sainte-Beuve," in his *Un Homme libre* (Paris, 1905), p. 94.

13. James, p. 80.

14. For comparisons of the different versions, see Gustave Michaut, *Etudes sur Sainte-Beuve* (Paris, 1905), pp. 143–231, and *Tableau de la poésie française au XVIe siècle,* ed. Marcel Françon (Cambridge, Mass., 1963).

15. *Tableau historique et critique de la poésie française et du théâtre français au XVIe siècle,* ed. Jules Troubat (Paris, 1876), II, 1. References in the text will be to volume and page of this edition.

16. Quoted in Marie-Louise Pailleron, *Sainte-Beuve à seize ans* (Paris, 1927), p. 19.

17. James, pp. 81, 83.

18. Raymond Lebègue in *Sainte-Beuve, Lamartine, Colloques, 8 novembre 1969* (Paris, 1970), p. 37; V.-L. Saulnier in his *La Littérature de la Renaissance* (Paris, 1948), p. 91. Sainte-Beuve's estimate of Ronsard remained substantially the same in later essays; see, for example, his 1855 *Lundi* on Ronsard, *CL* XII, 63, 66.

19. See Gustave Charlier, "Ronsard au XIXe siècle avant Sainte-Beuve," in his *De Montaigne à Verlaine* (1946), pp. 129–142.

20. Maurice Bémol, *Variations sur Valéry* (Paris, 1959), II, 25.

Chapter Two

1. Quoted in *Selected Shorter Poems of Thomas Hardy,* ed. John Wain (London, 1966), p. 115.

2. *Poésies de Sainte-Beuve* (Paris, 1863), II, 129. Poems quoted from this edition will be referred to by title, the *Pensées de Joseph Delorme* by number, and other texts (*Vie de Joseph Delorme,* Prefaces, and Appendices) by volume and page number. I have also made use of Gérald Antoine's edition, *Vie, poésies et pensées de Joseph Delorme* (Paris, 1956), especially for its invaluable Introduction and Notes; further reference in the text to "Antoine" will be to this edition.

3. See George Roth, "Kirke White et 'Joseph Delorme,'" *Revue de littérature comparée,* I (1921): 588.

4. Pierre Barbéris, "Signification de 'Joseph Delorme' en 1830," *Revue des sciences humaines* (July-September 1969): 381.

5. Joachim Merlant, *Le Roman personnel de Rousseau à Fromentin* (Paris, 1905), pp. 332–333.

6. *Livre d'amour,* ed. Jules Troubat (Paris, 1906), p. 109. Poems quoted from this edition will be referred to in the text by their numbers (few have titles), and Troubat's Preface, by page number.

7. Gustave Michaut, *Le Livre d'amour de Sainte-Beuve* (Paris, 1905), p. 162. For the prosecution's case, see Gustave Simon, *Le Roman de*

Sainte-Beuve (1906; rpt. Paris, 1926), and for Michaut's reply to Simon, his *Pages de critique et d'histoire littéraire (XIXᵉ siècle)* (Paris, 1910), pp. 156–233.

8. André Maurois, *Olympio ou la Vie de Victor Hugo* (Paris, 1954), p. 229.

9. For a more detailed literary analysis of *Livre d'amour,* see R.M. Chadbourne, "Sainte-Beuve's *Livre d'amour* as Poetry," *Nineteenth-Century French Studies,* III (1974–1975): 80–96. The most objective account of Sainte-Beuve's relations with the Hugos and of his criticism of Hugo the writer is Raphaël Molho's "Critique, amour et poésie: Sainte-Beuve et 'les' Hugo," in Victor Hugo, *Oeuvres complètes,* ed. Jean Massin (Paris, 1967–1969), IV, i–xxvi, and XIII, lxix–lxxxiii.

10. *The Poems of Tibullus,* trans. Constance Carrier (Bloomington and London, 1968), Book I, 1.

11. For further discussion of this question, see Maxwell Smith, *L'Influence des Lakistes sur les romantiques français* (Paris, 1920); Roth; T.G.S. Combe, *Sainte-Beuve et les poètes anglais* (Bordeaux, 1937); and A.G. Lehmann, "Sainte-Beuve critique de la littérature anglaise, une mise au point," *Revue de littérature comparée,* XXVIII (1954): 419–439.

12. Albert Thibaudet, *Histoire de la littérature française de 1789 à nos jours* (Paris, 1936), p. 324. Unless otherwise indicated, references in the text to "Thibaudet" will be to this work. For further on Sainte-Beuve and Baudelaire, see Antoine, pp. cviii–cxxi; Jacques Vier, *Le Joseph Delorme de Sainte-Beuve,* Archives des Lettres Modernes, No. 29, January-February 1960; and Norman Barlow, *Sainte-Beuve to Baudelaire, a Poetic Legacy* (Durham, N.C., 1964). Antoine and Vier also discuss Sainte-Beuve's influence on other poets.

13. See Anatole France, "Sainte-Beuve poète," in his *Le Génie latin* (Paris, 1913); Morice as quoted in Antoine, p. ci; Paul Bourget, "Sainte-Beuve poète," in his *Sociologie et littérature* (Paris, 1906); André Barre, *Le Symbolisme* (Paris, 1911; reprint ed., New York, n.d.); René Lalou, *Vers une alchimie lyrique* (Paris, 1927); John Charpentier, *L'Evolution de la poésie lyrique de Joseph Delorme à Paul Claudel* (Paris, 1930).

14. Ferdinand Brunetière, *L'Evolution de la poésie lyrique en France au 19ᵉ siècle* (Paris, 1894), I, 254; Vier, p. 53; Charles Baudelaire, *Correspondance générale,* ed. Jacques Crépet (Paris, 1949), V, 218; Roland Derche, *Etudes de textes français,* nouvelle série (Paris, 1966), V, 77.

15. T.S. Eliot, *On Poetry and Poets* (New York, n.d.), p. 184.

16. Alfred de Vigny, *Oeuvres complètes* (Paris, 1965), II, 892. In this same passage from his *Journal d'un poète,* Vigny claimed that Hugo appeared to be the master in poetry, but was really the disciple, of Sainte-Beuve.

Chapter Three

1. This remark occurs in a letter of January 25, 1863, to Father Bernard Chocarne which is also quoted in the Appendix added by Sainte-Beuve to the 1869 edition of *Volupté*. The edition used for references in our text is *Volupté*, ed. Raphaël Molho (Paris, 1969), which is also cited for Molho's "Introduction: Regards sur *Volupté*."

2. Appendix, *Port-Royal*, ed. Maxime Leroy (Paris, 1952), I, 959.

3. *Oeuvres complètes de Victor Hugo. Actes et paroles* (Paris, 1937), XXXV, 68. Compare Thibaudet, "The novel is like an autobiography of the possible," in his *Réflexions sur le roman* (Paris, 1938), p. 12.

4. *Volupté*, ed. Pierre Poux (Paris, 1927), I, xxxii. Further references to "Poux" will be to the Introduction and Notes of this edition.

5. "L'Abbé Prévost et les Bénédictins," *Portraits littéraires*, in *Oeuvres*, II, 920.

6. "Madame de Staël," *Portraits de femmes*, in *Oeuvres*, II, 1102.

7. See for example André Bellessort, *Sainte-Beuve et le dix-neuvième siècle* (Paris, 1927), pp. 97–98, and Jean Hytier, "Volupté," in *Les Romans de l'individu* (Paris, 1928), p. 43. Will be referred to as "Bellessort" and "Hytier" in references in the text.

8. For further discussion of the role of place in *Volupté*, see R.M. Chadbourne, "Sentiments et lieux dans *Volupté*," *Cahiers de l'Association Internationale des Etudes Françaises*, no. 26, May 1974, pp. 219–231.

9. Yves Le Hir, *L'Originalité littéraire de Sainte-Beuve dans Volupté*, (Paris, 1953), p. 46.

10. Honoré Balzac, "Lettre sur Sainte-Beuve," *Oeuvres complètes*, ed. Henri Bouteron and Henri Longnon (Paris, 1940), XL, 296.

11. Quoted from a youthful poem, "A Sainte-Beuve"; see Baudelaire, *Oeuvres complètes* (Paris, 1961), p. 199.

12. See, for example, Charles Bruneau, "Une création de Sainte-Beuve: la phrase 'molle' de *Volupté*," in *Mélanges d'histoire littéraire et de bibliographie offerts à Jean Bonnerot* (Paris, 1954), pp. 190–195.

13. Letter of October 14, 1869, to his niece Caroline, written the day after Sainte-Beuve's death. Gustave Flaubert, *Oeuvres complètes, Correspondance, 6e série* (Paris, 1930), VII, 82.

14. See André Vial, "De *Volupté* à l'*Education sentimentale*, vie et avatars de thèmes romanesques," *Revue d'histoire littéraire de la France*, LVII (1957): 45–65, 178–195.

15. For the text of *Arthur*, see Charles Spoelberch de Lovenjoul, *Sainte-Beuve inconnu* (Paris, 1901), pp. 3–140. Sainte-Beuve refers to this work in his review of Guttinguer's own independent version of the story, a second *Arthur* (1836), in *Portraits contemporains*, II, 405–406.

16. See Maurice Regard, *Sainte-Beuve, l'homme et l'oeuvre* (Paris, 1959), pp. 106–107. Further references in the text to "Regard" will be to this work.

17. *Le Clou d'or — La Pendule — Madame de Pontivy — Christel,* ed. Jules Troubat (Paris, 1921).

18. Sainte-Beuve's notes for this novel have been published with commentary by Raphaël Molho, "Un Projet avorté de Sainte-Beuve: le roman de l'ambition," *Revue d'histoire littéraire de la France,* LXI (1961): 203-234. References in the text are to this article. Molho suggests the possibility that Sainte-Beuve may have had in mind still a third novel growing out of this one and developed "dans une direction sentimentale" (pp. 206-207).

19. Le Hir, p. 5.

Chapter Four

1. Bémol, II, 40.

2. Baudelaire, *Correspondance générale,* V, 217.

3. "Charles Labitte," *Portraits littéraires, Oeuvres,* II, 833.

4. Pierre Moreau, "Le Poète dans le critique," in *Sainte-Beuve, Lamartine, Colloques,* p. 7.

5. *L'Ordre et les ténèbres ou La naissance d'un mythe du XVIIe siècle chez Sainte-Beuve* (Paris, 1972), p. 253. Further references in the text to "Molho" will be to this work. See also on this transitional phase in Sainte-Beuve's career Gustave Michaut, *Sainte-Beuve avant les Lundis* (Fribourg and Paris, 1903) and Carl Viggiani, "Sainte-Beuve (1824-1830): Critic and Creator," *Romanic Review,* XLIV (1953): 262-272.

Chapter Five

1. Sainte-Beuve's first book of collected essays was actually the *Critiques et portraits littéraires* (1832, expanded editions 1836, 1839), later divided and regrouped into *Portraits littéraires* and *Portraits de femmes.* For details, see Jean Bonnerot, *Bibliographie de l'oeuvre de Sainte-Beuve,* 4 vols. (Paris, 1937-1952). References in the text to the *Portraits littéraires (PL)* and the *Portraits de femmes (PF)* will be to the Pléiade edition, *Oeuvres,* ed. Maxime Leroy. References to the *Portraits contemporains (PC)* will be to the edition already cited in Chapter 1.

2. Exceptions are essays on Greco-Roman antiquity, the Italian poet Leopardi, and certain authors of French-speaking Switzerland.

3. Lytton Strachey, *Eminent Victorians* (1918; rpt. London, 1973), p. 10.

4. See especially in Volume II, "De la littérature industrielle" and "Dix ans après en littérature"; in Volume III, "Quelques vérités sur la situation en littérature"; and in Volume V, "La Revue [des deux mondes] en 1845."

5. In a variation of this image (in "M. Eugène Sue," *PC* III, 97–98), he suggests that all literary art may be a form of "magic" by which the harsh poisons of life are diluted into agreeable colors.

6. See Bibliography for edition of *Chroniques parisiennes.* The letters on which they are based may be found in Sainte-Beuve's *Correspondance générale,* vols. V and VI.

7. *Cahiers I. Le Cahier vert (1834–1847),* ed. Raphaël Molho (Paris, 1973), p. 226.

8. Michaut, *Sainte-Beuve avant les Lundis,* p. 126. Will be referred to hereafter as "Michaut."

9. Irving Babbitt, "Sainte-Beuve," in *The Masters of Modern French Criticism* (1912; rpt. New York, 1963). p. 150.

10. Compare: "Heureux celui qui est fidèle jusqu'au bout à la haute pensée de sa jeunesse" (*B* III, 25), and this thought of Goethe quoted in Thomas Mann's *Essays,* translated by H.T. Lowe-Porter (New York, 1957), pp. 21–22: "He is the most fortunate man who can bring the end of his life round to its beginning again."

11. Quoted in Bonnerot, *Bibliographie de l'oeuvre de Sainte-Beuve,* I, 28–29. Hereafter abbreviated in text as "Bonnerot."

12. Including his imagery: see Chadbourne, "Symbolic Landscapes in Sainte-Beuve's Early Criticism," esp. pp. 226–230.

13. Mann, p. 56.

Chapter Six

1. Sainte-Beuve returned to Paris with the book "not completed but with its stonework laid (*maçonné*)" (*B* II, 366). The course consisted of eighty-one lessons, only part of which have survived in manuscript form. See *Port-Royal, Le Cours de Lausanne (1837–1838),* ed. Jean Pommier (Paris, 1937); and René Bray, *Sainte-Beuve à l'Académie de Lausanne, Chroniques du cours sur Port-Royal, 1837–1838* (Paris and Lausanne, 1937). My remarks are based for the most part on the book, references to which are to the three volume Pléiade edition, *Port-Royal,* ed. Maxime Leroy (Paris, 1952–1955). A good introduction to Port-Royal and Jansenism is Marc Escholier's *Port-Royal, the Drama of the Jansenists* (New York, 1968), translated from the French: *Port-Royal* (Paris, 1965).

2. Victor Giraud, *Port-Royal de Sainte-Beuve* (Paris, n.d.), p. 17. Hereafter abbreviated in text as "Giraud."

3. Unpublished note on *Port-Royal* quoted in Leroy's edition (I, 1052).

4. Quoted in Charly Guyot, *De Rousseau à Marcel Proust* (Neuchâtel, 1968), p. 148.

5. Vinet's remarks are quoted in part by Sainte-Beuve in an appendix, *Port-Royal* I, 958. The complete text may be found in Vinet's *Etudes sur la*

littérature française au XIXe siècle (Lausanne and Paris, 1908), III, 80–81. Hereafter referred to in text as "Vinet."

6. "Project de Préface," an *inédit* quoted by Molho, *L'Ordre et les ténèbres,* p. 291. Molho argues, as I do, for the work's "unity of composition."

7. Henry de Montherlant, *Théâtre* (Paris, 1968), p. 1137.

8. Quoted from Sainte-Beuve's *Cours de Port-Royal* by Jean Pommier in his *Dialogues sur le passé* (Paris, 1967), p. 137.

9. Balzac, p. 304.

10. Quoted in Arnaldo Momigliano, *Studies in Historiography* (New York, 1966), p. 43.

11. Augustin Gazier, *Histoire générale du mouvement janséniste depuis ses origines jusqu'à nos jours* (Paris, 1923), I, vii.

12. Hippolyte Taine, *Derniers essais de critique et d'histoire* (Paris, 1923), p. 95.

Chapter Seven

1. The first course has been partially published by Françoise Dehousse, *Sainte-Beuve. Ancienne littérature (Partie médiévale). Cours professé à l'Université de Liège (1848–1849)* Paris, 1971). As for the course on Chateaubriand, my remarks in this chapter are based on the book, in the two volume edition, *Chateaubriand et son groupe littéraire sous l'Empire,* ed. Maurice Allem (Paris, 1948). The text of the book is substantially the same as that of the course.

2. Sainte-Beuve admitted as much, without naming names, when he recorded in his notebook: "I find it almost impossible to write about the leading authors of my time, so accustomed have I grown to judging not their works but their personalities, whose mysteries I seek to unravel" (*PM* 264).

3. Jules Barbey d'Aurevilly, *Le XIXe siècle. Des oeuvres et des hommes, Choix de textes établi par Jacques Vier* (Paris, 1964), I, 289. Originally a review of Sainte-Beuve's *Chateaubriand* in *Le Pays,* November 9, 1860.

4. *Physiologie de la critique* (Paris, 1962), p. 212 (original edition, 1930).

5. For a more detailed reassessment of Sainte-Beuve's *Chateaubriand,* see R.M. Chadbourne, "Le Cours de Sainte-Beuve à Liège: un 'Contre Chateaubriand'?," *French Review,* XLIV (1971): 69–78.

Chapter Eight

1. See for example Edith Wharton, *A Backward Glance* (New York,

1933), p. 7: "The compact world of my youth has receded into a past from which it can only be dug up in bits by the assiduous relic-hunter; and its smallest fragments begin to be worth collecting and putting together before the last of those who knew the live structure are swept away with it." The same novelist referred to the *Lundis* as "bracing fare for a young mind" (pp. 66–67).

2. Leon Edel calls it "the best statement I know on behalf of the biographical approach to criticism," in his *Literary Biography* (London, 1957), p. 55. Note, however, that he does not say "the scientific approach."

3. *Sainte-Beuve* (Paris, 1872), p. 256.

4. Roger Fayolle, *Sainte-Beuve et le XVIIIe siècle ou Comment les révolutions arrivent* (Paris, 1972).

5. Regard, comparing Sainte-Beuve to "a kind of Voltaire . . . gone astray in a subservient Senate," provides a good summary of these and other antiestablishment activities on the critic's part (pp. 172–173). The texts of Sainte-Beuve's Senate speeches were published by Troubat in his edition of the *Premiers Lundis* (Paris, 1874), III.

6. George Orwell, *Such, Such Were the Joys* (New York, 1953), p. 72.

7. Gabriel Brunet, "Regard sur Sainte-Beuve," *Mercure de France,* CLXXXIX (1926): 22.

8. Remark reported by Troubat as quoted in Bonnerot, *Bibliographie,* III, 427.

9. Barbey d'Aurevilly I, 32; II, 49.

10. Fayolle, p. 13.

11. "Chaque critique a son gibier favori sur lequel il tombe et qu'il dépèce de préférence [. . . .] —Pour moi, c'est Balzac" — *Cahiers* I, 215.

12. On this last point, see Hytier, p. 77.

13. See B.F. Bart, "Hypercreativity in Stendhal and Balzac," *Nineteenth-Century French Studies,* III, (1974–1975): 18–39. The analogy with Sainte-Beuve is my suggestion, not Bart's.

14. Compare Renan in his *Souvenirs d'enfance et de jeunesse:* "The essence of criticism is the ability to understand states of mind far different from our own" — *Oeuvres complètes,* ed. Henriette Psichari (Paris, 1948), II, 766.

Chapter Nine

1. The edition used in this chapter is: *Etude sur Virgile suivie d'une étude sur Quintus de Smyrne,* 2nd ed. (Paris, 1870).

2. See Pierre Moreau, *La Critique selon Sainte-Beuve* (Paris, 1964), pp. 78–79.

3. In *Virgil,* ed. D.R. Dudley (London, 1969), p. 134. F.M. Combellack calls the essay on Quintus "still the best treatment we have of

this unduly neglected writer" — *Comparative Literature,* VIII (1956): 352.

4. The edition used in this chapter is: *P.-J. Proudhon, sa vie et sa correspondance, 1838–1848* (Paris, 1873).

5. Jules Vallès, "Lettre d'un irrégulier à M. Sainte-Beuve, Sénateur," *Oeuvres complètes,* ed. Lucien Scheler and Marie-Claire Blancquart (Paris, 1970), IV, 737.

6. Maxime Leroy, *Vie de Sainte-Beuve* (Paris, 1947), p. 155.

7. Stewart Edwards, in the Introduction to his edition of *Selected Writings of Pierre-Joseph Proudhon* (Garden City, 1969), p. 13.

8. Bonnerot, *Bibliographie de l'oeuvre,* III, 370–371. For further on the history of the publication of the *Cahiers,* see Molho's Introduction to his edition of *Le Cahier vert,* pp. 9–14.

9. André Billy, *Les plus belles lettres de Sainte-Beuve* (Paris, 1962), p. 14.

Chapter Ten

1. Moreau, *La Critique selon Sainte-Beuve,* p. 9.

2. Babbitt, p. 146.

3. On this last point see Gérald Antoine, "Sainte-Beuve et l'esprit de la critique dite 'universitaire,'" in *Sainte-Beuve et la critique littéraire contemporaine, Actes du colloque tenu à Liège du 6 au 8 octobre 1969* (Paris, 1972), pp. 105–123; and the same author's "Deux idéologies de la 'nouvelle critique': de Sainte-Beuve aux Poéticiens," *L'Esprit créateur,* XIV (1974): 3–16.

4. "He uses all methods and uses them skillfully and deftly, often in a very small space. He is averse only to cloudy speculation and to rigid systematization" — René Wellek, *A History of Modern Criticism: 1750–1950* (New Haven and London, 1965), III, 70.

5. Marcel Proust, *Contre Sainte-Beuve, suivi de Nouveaux mélanges,* ed. Bernard de Fallois (Paris, 1954), p. 137.

6. Henri Peyre, *Observations on Life, Literature, and Learning in America* (Carbondale, 1961), p. 178.

7. Wallace Fowlie, *The French Critic, 1549–1967* (Carbondale, London and Amsterdam, 1968), p. 151.

8. Maurice Barrès, *Mes cahiers, 1896–1923, textes choisis par Guy Dupré* (Paris, 1963), p. 904.

9. "Sainte-Beuve," in *The Complete Works of Matthew Arnold,* ed. R.H. Super (Ann Arbor, 1965), V, 305–306.

Selected Bibliography

Place of publication is Paris unless otherwise stated.

PRIMARY SOURCES

There is no single edition to date of Sainte-Beuve's complete works. Maurice Allem's edition of selected essays from the *Portraits* and *Lundis* arranged according to century and genre and entitled *Les Grands écrivains français* (Garnier: 1926–1932, 23 vols.) is valuable for its notes and cross-references, but is limited to articles on major French writers. The following is a list of the editions referred to in this study. For original dates of publication, where they differ from those indicated here, see Chronology.

Cahiers I. Le Cahier vert (1834–1847). Ed. Raphaël Molho. Gallimard, 1973. First of two projected volumes (the second will contain *Le Cahier brun*) of what promises to be the definitive edition of Sainte-Beuve's notebooks.

Causeries du Lundi. 16 vols. Garnier, n.d. Most of volume 16 consists of a *Table générale et analytique,* or index, of the *Causeries, Portraits de femmes,* and *Portraits littéraires.*

Chateaubriand et son groupe littéraire sous l'Empire. Ed. Maurice Allem. 2 vols. Garnier, 1948. For an index of this work, see C.-A. Sainte-Beuve, *Chateaubriand et son groupe littéraire sous l'Empire.* Index alphabétique et analytique établi par Lorin A. Uffenbeck, Chapel Hill, N.C.: The University of North Carolina Press, 1973.

Chroniques parisiennes (1843–1845). Calmann-Lévy, 1876.

Le Clou d'or — La Pendule — Madame de Pontivy — Christel. Ed. Jules Troubat. Calmann-Lévy, 1921.

Correspondance générale. Ed. Jean Bonnerot and Alain Bonnerot. 17 vols. Paris: Stock and Didier, and Toulouse: Privat 1935–1975. At least two more volumes are projected to complete this magnificent enterprise. Abundant biographical, bibliographical, and historical notes.

Etude sur Virgile suivie d'une étude sur Quintus de Smyrne. 2nd ed. Michel Lévy, 1870.

Livre d'amour. Ed. Jules Troubat. Mercure de France, 1906. Only edition to contain the complete text of this work.

Notes inédites de Sainte-Beuve. Ed. Charly Guyot. Neuchâtel: Secrétariat de l'Université, 1931. Supplemented by Guyot's "Notes inédites de

Sainte-Beuve," *Revue d'histoire littéraire de la France,* XL (1933): 580–594, and XLI (1934): 72–86, 266–284.

Nouveaux Lundis. 13 vols. Michel Lévy, 1864–1870. A *Table alphabétique et analytique,* which also refers to the *Premiers Lundis* and *Portraits contemporains,* was published separately, along with an excellent introductory essay, "Sainte-Beuve et son oeuvre critique," by Victor Giraud. Calmann-Lévy, n.d. (essay dated 1902).

Oeuvres. Ed. Maxime Leroy. 2 vols. Gallimard, 1951–1956. Title misleading: vol. 1 contains *Premiers Lundis* and *Portraits littéraires (début),* vol. 2, *Portraits littéraires (fin)* and *Portraits de femmes.*

Pensées et maximes. Ed. Maurice Chapelan. Grasset, 1955. Title is editor's; handy compendium of those entries from his notebooks that Sainte-Beuve included in works published during his lifetime, plus text (substantially complete) of *Mes poisons, cahiers intimes inédits,* ed. Victor Giraud (Plon-Nourrit, 1926).

P.-J. Proudhon, sa vie et sa correspondance, 1838–1848. Michel Lévy, 1873.

Poésies de Sainte-Beuve. 2 vols. Michel Lévy, 1863. Contains all his published poems including approximately half of those that appeared posthumously in *Livre d'amour* (see above). Also includes *Jugements et témoignages* concerning *Joseph Delorme* and *Les Consolations.*

Port-Royal. Ed. Maxime Leroy. 3 vols. Gallimard, 1952–1955.

Portraits contemporains. 5 vols. Calmann-Lévy, 1889. Extensively enlarged from the original (3 vols., Garnier, 1846) and with the addition of important footnotes.

Sainte-Beuve. Ancienne littérature (Partie médiévale). Cours professé à l'Université de Liège (1848–1849). Ed. Françoise Dehousse. Société d'Edition Les Belles Lettres, 1971.

Tableau historique et critique de la poésie française au XVIe siècle. Ed. Jules Troubat. 2 vols. Alphonse Lemerre, 1876.

Vie, poésies et pensées de Joseph Delorme, Ed. Gérald Antoine. Nouvelles Editions Latines, 1956. Critical edition, invaluable for author's Introduction (over 100 pages) and Notes.

Volupté, Ed. Raphaël Molho. Garnier-Flammarion, 1969. Text is not annotated; editor's "Introduction: regards sur *Volupté*" is excellent.

1. English Translations

Very little of Sainte-Beuve has been translated into English, and good translations of his work are rare. Even the best tend to rob his style of its flavor. The most reliable are: *Literary Criticism of Sainte-Beuve,* trans. and ed. by Emerson R. Marks (Lincoln: University of Nebraska Press, 1971), which also contains a fine Introduction; and *Sainte-Beuve, Selected Essays,* trans. and ed. by Francis Steegmuller and Norbert Guterman (Garden City, N.Y.: Anchor Books, 1963).

SECONDARY SOURCES

Many worthy contributions have had to be omitted from his highly selective list. Some of these are mentioned in the notes and references. For further bibliography, consult: Jean Bonnerot, *Un demi-siècle d'études sur Sainte-Beuve, 1904–1954* (Société d'Edition Les Belles Lettres, 1957); E.M. Phillips, "The Present State of Sainte-Beuve Studies," *French Studies,* V (1951): 101–125; and Maurice Regard, "Esquisse d'un état présent des études sur Sainte-Beuve," *Information littéraire,* XI (1959): 139–148.

ANTOINE, GERALD *and* CLAUDE PICHOIS. "Sainte-Beuve juge de Stendhal et de Baudelaire." *Revue des sciences humaines* (January-March 1957): 7–34. Superb article, with broad implications as to how the personalities of his contemporaries distracted the critic from a juster appreciation of their works.

ARNOLD, MATTHEW. "Sainte-Beuve." In *The Complete Prose Works of Matthew Arnold,* ed. R.H. Super, V, 304–309. Ann Arbor: University of Michigan Press, 1965. Originally published in *The Academy,* November 13, 1869.

_____. "Sainte-Beuve." In *Five Uncollected Essays,* ed. Kenneth Allott, pp. 66–78. Liverpool: Liverpool University Press, 1953. Reprinted from Arnold's famous article in the ninth edition of the *Encyclopedia Britannica.* This and the preceding essay, stressing the poet in the critic and the "naturalist among rhetoricians and politicians," rank among the finest in English.

BABBITT, IRVING. "Sainte-Beuve." In his *The Masters of Modern French Criticism,* pp. 97–188. Boston and New York: Houghton Mifflin, 1912; rpt. New York: Noonday Press, 1963. Emphasizes conflict of "humanism" and "naturalism" in Sainte-Beuve and his finesse in "rendering the living individual." Highly perceptive.

BARLOW, NORMAN. *Sainte-Beuve to Baudelaire, a Poetic Legacy.* Durham, N.C.: Duke University Press, 1964. Focuses on affinities in realm of "moral psychology"; sees both poets as exploring the theological roots of modern *ennui.*

BELLESSORT, ANDRE. *Sainte-Beuve et le dix-neuvième siècle.* Perrin, 1927. One of best overall studies, with many insights into the work; may, however, underestimate the merits of *Volupté.*

BILLY, ANDRÉ. *Sainte-Beuve, sa vie et son temps.* 2 vols. Flammarion, 1952. Most detailed and on the whole best biography. Sympathetic to Sainte-Beuve but recognizes his weaknesses.

BONNEROT, JEAN. *Bibliographie de l'oeuvre de Sainte-Beuve.* 4 vols. Giraud-Badin, 1937–1952. Indispensable guide by the great *Beuvien* who considered himself "le secrétaire posthume de Sainte-Beuve."

BRADFORD, GAMALIEL. *A Naturalist of Souls: Studies in Psychography.* New York: Dodd, Mead, and Co., 1917. Sainte-Beuve as a master of "psychography," or "the condensed, essential, artistic presentation of character."

CHADBOURNE, RICHARD. "La Comédie Humaine de Sainte-Beuve." *Etudes françaises,* IX (1973): 15–26.

————. "Criticism as Creation in Sainte-Beuve." *L'Esprit créateur,* XIV (1974): 44–54. This and preceding article sketch in broad outline the view of Sainte-Beuve developed in more detail in the present book.

FAYOLLE, ROGER. *Sainte-Beuve et le XVIIIe siècle ou Comment les révolutions arrivent.* Colin, 1972. Sainte-Beuve, seen here (primarily in the *Lundis*) as a political reactionary wearing the mask of an impartial literary critic, emerges battered but not crushed from this Marxist interpretation; argument stimulating though not entirely convincing.

HYTIER, JEAN. *"Volupté."* In his *Les Romans de l'individu,* pp. 42–79. Les Arts et le Livre, 1928. Fine analysis of this novel, with penetrating views of the strengths and limitations of Sainte-Beuve's genius as a whole.

JAMES, HENRY. "Sainte-Beuve's Portraits," "Sainte-Beuve's First Articles," "Sainte-Beuve's English Portraits." In *Literary Reviews and Essays.* Ed. Albert Mordell, pp. 74–88. New York: Grove Press, 1957. Astute reviews for *The Nation* (the first, originally published in 1868, the other two in 1875), by a writer who considered Sainte-Beuve, despite his limitations, to be "the acutest critic the world has seen."

LEHMANN, A.G. *Sainte-Beuve, a Portrait of the Critic, 1804–1842.* Oxford: Clarendon Press, 1962. Good study of Sainte-Beuve's "growth to the point where he reaches full maturity."

LEROY, MAXIME. *La Pensée de Sainte-Beuve.* Gallimard, 1940.

————. *La Politique de Sainte-Beuve.* Gallimard, 1941. Valuable contributions from another great *Beuvien* who writes sympathetically of Sainte-Beuve from a socialist point of view.

MACCLINTOCK, LANDER. *Sainte-Beuve's Critical Theory and Practice after 1849.* Chicago: University of Chicago Press, 1920. Generally well-balanced and perceptive view of the *Lundis.*

MICHAUT, GUSTAVE. *Sainte-Beuve avant les Lundis; essai sur la formation de son esprit et de sa méthode de critique.* Fribourg: Librarie de l'Université, and Paris: Fontemoing, 1903. Indispensable "biographie intellectuelle" by great pioneer of Sainte-Beuve scholarship; stresses unity of his inspiration and strong personal presence in his criticism.

MOLHO, RAPHAEL. *L'Ordre et les ténèbres ou La naissance d'un mythe du XVIIe siècle chez Sainte-Beuve.* Colin, 1972. Author, a leader in the recent revitalization of Sainte-Beuve studies, shows how the critic created an image of the French Classical age that allowed him to reconcile his penchant for melancholy and mystery with his need for clarity and order.

MOREAU, PIERRE. *La Critique selon Sainte-Beuve.* Société d'Edition d'Enseignement Supérieur, 1964. Despite occasional wandering from subject and indulgence in biographical details, a perceptive study by the late dean of French *dix-neuvièmistes.*

MOTT, LEWIS FREEMAN. *Sainte-Beuve.* New York: Appleton, 1925. An unjustly neglected pioneer study, long out of print; very complete in its presentation of life and work, rich in insight, and judicious in tone. A new edition would be welcome.

MULHAUSER, RUTH. *Sainte-Beuve and Greco-Roman Antiquity.* Cleveland and London: Case Western Reserve University Press, 1969. A useful survey.

REGARD, MAURICE. *Sainte-Beuve, l'homme et l'oeuvre.* Hatier, 1959. Penetrating study, remarkable for wealth of insight within brief space. Probably best book on Sainte-Beuve to date.

RICHARD, JEAN-PIERRE. "Sainte-Beuve et l'objet littéraire." In his *Etudes sur le romantisme français*, pp. 227–283. Editions du Seuil, 1970. Attempts to show how the critic grasped his subjects by means of a kind of "imagination critique" (through metaphor, etc.). Interesting also as an effort to "rehabilitate" Sainte-Beuve by a leading exponent of the French "new criticism."

THIBAUDET, ALBERT. "Sainte-Beuve." In his *Histoire de la littérature française de 1789 à nos jours,* pp. 280–294. Stock, 1936. Succinct assessment, just in tone and rich in insights, stressing Sainte-Beuve's criticism as a creative form benefiting from his having been a poet.

The following publications devoted entirely or in part to Sainte-Beuve contain a wide variety of interesting papers on him: on the hundredth anniversary of his birth, *Le Livre d'or de Sainte-Beuve* (Journal des Débats and Fontemoing, 1904); on the hundredth anniversary of his death, *Sainte-Beuve, Lamartine, Colloques, 8 novembre 1969* (Publications de la Société d'Histoire Littéraire de la France, Colin, 1970); *Revue des sciences humaines* ("Sainte-Beuve"), July-September 1969; and *Sainte-Beuve et la critique littéraire contemporaine, Actes du colloque tenu à Liège du 6 au 8 octobre 1969* (Société d'Edition Les Belles Lettres, 1972). See also: *Mélanges d'histoire littéraire et de bibliographie offerts à Jean Bonnerot* (Nizet, 1954); and *L'Esprit créateur* ("The Legacy of Sainte-Beuve"), XIV, 1974.

Index

188